G-d, Rationality and Mysticism

G-D, RATIONALITY
AND MYSTICISM

by

IRVING BLOCK

MARQUETTE
UNIVERSITY

PRESS

Marquette Studies in Philosophy
No. 53
Andrew Tallon, Series Editor

LIBRARY OF CONGRESS CATALOGING-IN-PUBLICATION DATA

Block, Irving, 1930-
  God, rationality, and mysticism / by Irving Block.
    p. cm. — (Marquette studies in philosophy ; No. 53)
  Includes index.
  ISBN-13: 978-0-87462-751-0 (pbk. : alk. paper)
  ISBN-10: 0-87462-751-6 (pbk. : alk. paper)
  1. God. 2. Rationalism. 3. Mysticism. 4. Schneersohn, Menahem Mendel,
1902- I. Title.
  BL473.B56 2007
  231'.042—dc22
                                                    2007042940

© 2007 Marquette University Press
Milwaukee, Wisconsin 53201-3141
All rights reserved.
www.marquette.edu/mupress/

Marquette University Press gratefully acknowledges permission from Random House to quote excerpts from *The Light Beyond* by Dr. Raymond A. Moody, Jr., from William Morrow Co. to quote from *After the Light* by Kimberly Clark Sharp, from C.I.S. Publishers & Distributors to quote from *The View from Above* by Rachel Noam, and from Sobel Weber Assoc. for *Saved by the Light* (Harper) by Dannion Brinkley with Paul Perry.

SECOND PRINTING, REVIEWED & CORRECTED, MARCH, 2008.
THIRD PRINTING, REVIEWED & CORRECTED, 2013.

Cover photo by Andrew J. Tallon

❦The paper used in this publication meets the minimum requirements of the American National Standard for Information Sciences— Permanence of Paper for Printed Library Materials, ANSI Z39.48-1992.

Association of American University Presses

MARQUETTE UNIVERSITY PRESS
MILWAUKEE

The Association of Jesuit University Presses

TABLE OF CONTENTS

Dedication 7

Preface.. 9

I. Introduction 11

Part I: G-d and Rationality

1. Rationality.. 17
2. The Validity of Rationality...................................... 27
3. The Teleological Argument 37
4. The Cosmological Argument 51
5. The Argument from Unity...................................... 61

Part II: G-d and Mysticism

6. Creation 73
7. G-d's Goodness.. 85
8. The Moral Sense 101
9. The Meaning of Life 113
10. Near-Death Experiences 131
11. The End.. 191

Index.. 207

For My

Father and Mother,

Chaim Aharon and Sarah Rochel Block

of

Blessed Memory

PREFACE

The first part of this book on rationality and G-d was developed over the twenty-five years that I taught philosophy of religion at The University of Western Ontario in London, Ontario, Canada. I owe a debt of gratitude to the hundreds of students who silently listened to me and on many occasions questioned me. I can apply to them the apt saying from the *Talmud*, Makkoth, 10a "I learned much from my teachers and more from my colleagues, but from my students I learned more than I did from anyone else."

The second part of this book dealing with G-d and mysticism is based on my study of the literature of Chabad Hasidic philosophy and the teachings of the Lubavitcher Rebbe, of blessed memory. Though the two parts of this book could easily be divided into two different books, they really belong together, for it is one of the salient features of Chabad philosophy and the teachings of the Rebbe that everything in heaven and earth are unified and are one with G-d. The recognition of this unity of G-d with all things transcends human understanding but nonetheless can be fathomed by the human mind in some sense. You can somehow know that there is a G-d who cannot be known, paradoxical though this may be. This in essence is the motif of this book.

This book was written for the general public and not just for philosophers. To this end I have tried to avoid the technical jargon of contemporary philosophy. I am of the opinion that if a philosophical argument cannot be understood by intelligent laymen, there is something wrong with the argument. In lieu of this I asked a friend of mine who is not an academic philosopher but a professional psychologist, Dr. Milton Blake, to read the manuscript of the book which he did. He said he understood it and thought it persuasive and made a few worthwhile comments. Another close friend of mine, Mr. Gerson Safran read the page proofs and made numerous corrections that had been overlooked. To both of them I express my thanks and gratitude.

Various chapters and stages of the book have been read at Oxford University, Cambridge University, Princeton University. UCLA, Clairmont Graduate School, University of Buffalo, and The University of Western Ontario.

Finally, I want to thank Dr. Andrew Tallon, the Director of the Marquette University Press for so skillfully overseeing the publishing of the book.

Last, but not least, I thank my wife, Laya, for her constant encouragement and support.

Irving Block
London, Ontario, Canada

INTRODUCTION

The title of this book will raise questions if not eyebrows, for the terms in the title are often considered incompatible. After all, is not rationality often thought incompatible with G-d on the one hand and mysticism on the other? The burden of this book is to argue that this is not so. Rationality is not incompatible with G-d—it is actually more compatible with G-d than it is with atheism. Furthermore, not only is rationality not an enemy of mysticism—it actually supports and nourishes it. These are large and grandiose themes and an unlikely subject for such a small book. However, I believe the points I have to make do not require long expositions. What they do require is clarity and ideally clarity can be attained in short books as well as long ones. The author has tried to make this book both short and clear. The reader will judge if he has succeeded.

Though the book is written from the perspective of contemporary philosophy and in the course of the book I allude to certain contemporary philosophers or schools of philosophy, nonetheless I will be disappointed if it cannot be understood by the intelligent layman. It contains a minimum of jargon and even when I avail myself of its convenience I try to explain it so that a non-philosopher can understand it. The more technical points in philosophy that I discuss are relegated to the footnotes, which can be skipped without interrupting the flow of the argument.

Of the three terms in the title of this book, by far the most difficult to elucidate clearly is rationality. As far as G-d is concerned, no one can elucidate Him, and throughout the book I assume we all know G-d from our common monotheistic background. What I mean by our "common monotheistic background" is not that I am assuming the reader of this book believes in G-d, but that whether one does or does not accept G-d, what one is accepting or rejecting is the monotheistic G-d of Judaism, Christianity and Islam and not some form of paganism, be it ancient or modern. Mysticism, as I will present it, is taken from the writings of Jewish mystical philosophy as this is expounded in the Zohar, Kabbalah and various Hasidic writings. Though the basis of my discussion of G-d in this book is taken from Jewish sources, I believe that what I say is applicable to all three monotheistic religions. There is a common philosophical core that Judaism, Christianity and Islam share with one another and it is this core that is the focus of this book.

Rationality on the other hand is the perennial bug-bear of philosophy and though everyone considers himself an expert on the matter (most people identify it with the way *they* think), it is extremely difficult to pin down or define. In the first two chapters, I try to deal with the question of when a belief is rational and just what is rationality. Chapters 3, 4, and 5 argue for the rationality of G-d through a discussion of the traditional arguments. Chapter 3 argues that it is more rational to suppose there is a mind behind the orderliness of the world than that it came about by chance. Chapter 4 argues that it is more rational to think that the necessary, eternal Being that is the origin of all contingent existence is G-d rather than the world itself. Chapter 5 argues that it is more rational to suppose that there is only one such necessary Being that is absolutely infinite, rather than that there is more than one such being. Though some of these arguments are old, going back at least to Aristotle and have been the subject of intense discussion both in medieval and modern times, I think I have something new to say about them, or in any event a new way of looking at them.

None of these arguments for G-d, however, imply that G-d created the world. Creation is an idea that the ancient Hebrews introduced to the world through the Hebrew Bible. It is not found in any religion or mythology before the Bible spread throughout the world under the influence of Judaism, Christianity and Islam. Plato, Aristotle and almost all ancient philosophers rejected the notion out of hand as irrational. In spite of this, G-d as Creator is the central idea in Judaism as well as in Christianity and Islam and it has been from the notion of G-d as Creator that religion has derived its great power and influence over the minds and hearts of people in every age. Chapter 6 presents what I think is an original argument for Creation.

Creation implies that G-d knowingly created the world for a purpose and that that purpose serves the end of goodness, for G-d Himself is good. None of the previous arguments that G-d is a single, knowing, necessary and absolutely infinite Being imply that G-d is good. Chapter 7 argues that it is more rational to assume that G-d is good rather than that He is evil. Chapter 8 is a further discussion of the nature of morality and the role that G-d plays in the moral life of man. Chapter 9 is a discussion of the meaning of life, as this is implied by G-d's Creation of the world and His goodness. Chapter 10 is a discussion of the phenomenon known as the near-death experience and the role this plays in understanding the oneness of G-d and His unity with the world. Chapter 11 is an elucidation of the unity and oneness of G-d as expounded in Kabbalah and Chabad Hasidic philosophy. The last five chapters bring into focus the existential implications of G-d as the Creator who is good and who is one with the world. The unity of G-d with the world is the essence of what I call the mystical, and this chapter brings together the various facets of G-d's nature discussed in previous chapters. G-d as a knowing Being is the necessary source of the existence of the contingent world and is at the same time one with the world that He created for the sake of goodness, which is realized in the mystical awareness of the oneness of G-d and the world. All this is not a matter of faith or belief in something seen by a few mystics, but is actually a more rational view of the nature of reality than is atheism.

None of these arguments taken individually are rich enough to be an argument for G-d *per se*, but each one argues for a certain characteristic of G-d that monotheism would consider to be a necessary property of G-d, insofar as G-d can have properties. However, taken cumulatively, they are to my mind a powerful argument for G-d. If it can be shown that it is rational to suppose that there is some Being with a mind that is responsible for the orderliness of the world and is a necessary Being which is single and unique, who created the world for some good purpose and who is at the same time one with that world, then I think one has as good an argument for G-d as could be hoped for.

Finally I would like to say a few words about the peculiar spelling of the word "G-d." There is a Jewish tradition that the name of G-d is ineffable. That is, its true pronunciation is unknown, and even its visible form is not to be spelled out, except in the Torah scroll and holy books. But how can one talk about what is ineffable and invisible? This is the paradox about G-d that I grapple with in this book. On the one hand there is something about G-d that one can know and on the other, He is essentially unknowable. His inscrutability, however, is not to be accepted on faith alone. One can *know* that He is inscrutable. That is, rationality can lead one to a Being we call "G-d" whose name is a word that does not signify an object, thing or event in the world, nor even the world as a whole, yet the word is pregnant with meaning and its meaning points to something beyond understanding altogether. To know that one does not know is the essence of all understanding and in this consists our understanding of G-d.

The peculiar spelling of "G-d" calls attention to the fact that this word is different from all other words. His name is not a word whose meaning can be pointed to, elucidated, explained, clarified, verified, etc. His name signifies something mysterious that can never be pointed to or verified.[1] Our rational understanding of the world may entice us to look for G-d where He cannot be found, and when we fail to find Him, we conclude He does not exist. Part of my argument is to explain why it is not reasonable to expect to find Him in those places where people often look, even though it may be easier to look there rather than in more hidden places.

This is reminiscent of a justly famous Chelm story. Chelm was a city of silly people who were always doing silly things with the utmost seriousness. One such story goes that a visitor arrived in Chelm one evening and found a group of men crawling on their hands and knees under a street lamp looking for something. Wishing to be helpful, the visitor asked what they were looking for and was told that one of them had lost a valuable diamond ring. The visitor accommodatingly dropped to his knees and began looking for the ring. After a while of fruitless searching, the visitor asked if they were certain that the ring was lost in this spot. They replied, "No, it was lost on the other side of the street, but there it is dark and no one can see anything!"

Looking for G-d in places where He can be proven or verified may be looking in places where we can see, but they are not the places in which G-d can be found. G-d once gave Elijah the prophet a lesson where He could be found. Elijah, fleeing for his life from Queen Jezebel, had escaped miraculously to a cave on Mount Sinai where G-d had once revealed Himself amidst thunder, lightning, and a loud voice.

---

1 Similarly, the word "Creation" is capitalized throughout, as G-d's Creation of the world is unlike any form of natural or human making.

Elijah went there looking for G-d again. First he heard " ... a great and strong wind rend the mountains, and brake in pieces the rocks, but G-d was not in the wind, and after the wind an earthquake, but G-d was not in the earthquake. And after the earthquake a fire, but G-d was not in the fire, and after the fire a still, small voice" (*Kings* I, 19: 11, 12). This still, small voice is the prompting of the human heart in its search for the mysterious reality of G-d that the mind tells us is there. It may be human rationality that indicates that G-d is there, as I argue in the first part of this book, but it is the human heart that finds in the mystery of G-d's oneness with all things the reality of G-d that transcends the understanding. This vision of the oneness of G-d with all things is the ultimate vision of mysticism, and it is this vision that we pursue in the second Part of this book.

Finally, I would like to add a word about how to read this book. Since, as I have said, the argument is cumulative, I ask the reader to exercise patience in reading it. Many questions or objections one can have might well be dealt with or answered in a later chapter. This certainly applies to the general treatment of rationality in the first two chapters of this book as well as the more specific question of the rationality of belief in G-d. The case for the rationality of belief in G-d is argued for in stages and the full force of this argument does not become clear until one has read the entire first Part.

PART I: G-D AND RATIONALITY

I

RATIONALITY

What is rationality? This is a very broad question that can be approached from different viewpoints. Let us begin with a simple approach to the question and interpret it as asking when it is rational to think or believe something as opposed to when it is irrational to think or believe something.

The first thing that comes to mind is that a rational belief is one that we believe we have good reasons for holding. If I think it is going to rain because I see dark clouds and hear thunder in the sky, that is rational; but if I think it is going to rain because I flipped a coin and it came out tails, that is irrational. We have good reasons for thinking that dark clouds and thunder signify rain for this is what our past experience teaches us about the weather. Furthermore, science has an explanation why rain clouds are dark and are accompanied by thunder whereas we see no connection at all between flipping a coin and the weather. If it should rain when we flip a coin tails, that is just an accident. The flipping of the coin is not the cause of the rain as are dark clouds, and so the flipping of the coin is not evidence for the rain the way dark clouds are.

Causes and evidence are intimately related. The relation of a cause to its effect and of evidence to its conclusion are similar. It's just that the search for causes is backward looking and the thrust of evidence is towards the future, particularly when the evidence is used to make a prediction. To use dark clouds as evidence for rain is rational for the clouds are the cause of the rain, but to take the flip of a coin as evidence for rain is certainly irrational, for no matter how many times the coin falls tails and it rains, we know the flip of the coin is not the cause of the rain.

These examples of rational and irrational belief are extremes. In between these are cases that are not so clear cut. Is it rational to believe in UFOs, or that there is life somewhere else in the universe, or that the green-house effect will ultimately destroy life on earth? There are many situations where people say they can't make up their minds—they need more evidence. There is a certain relationship between the evidence and what the evidence indicates whereby when the evidence (E) is strong, belief in the hypothesis (H) is confirmed, and when the evidence is not so strong, the evidence is only circumstantial. It is difficult to say when the thin line of conviction is crossed, but it is certain that the line is there.

Suppose you are a member of a jury trying a case in which Sam is accused of murdering Joe. The case begins with evidence that Sam knew Joe. No jury would convict Sam on that evidence alone. It has very little to do with the question of whether it was Sam who killed Joe. If it were discovered that Sam disliked Joe then the evidence becomes a bit stronger, though again that does not prove that Sam did it. If, however, we find that Sam's gun is the one that fired the bullets that killed Joe and this gun is found in Sam's possession, the case becomes much stronger. There are juries who have convicted men on less evidence than that. Suppose, however, there is one person on the jury who takes his instructions literally that he should not vote for conviction unless the evidence points to guilt beyond a reasonable doubt. There is a possibility, he argues, that someone else might have borrowed Sam's gun, killed Joe and then replaced the gun. That would explain how the evidence is consistent with Sam not having committed the murder. However, is that cause for a reasonable doubt? Has the thin line of conviction been crossed already so that it is no longer reasonable to suppose that Sam is innocent. How does one determine this? There are no hard and fast rules. One knows, however, when the evidence is overwhelming. Suppose, there is a witness that sees Sam enter the apartment where Joe was murdered. The same witness hears a shot and then sees Sam running out of the apartment with the smoking gun in his hand. Would this be overwhelming evidence? It is almost eyewitness testimony though not quite. One might say that this proves it. Anyone, who now believes that Sam is innocent is just not rational. There is, of course, a slight possibility that Sam still didn't do it. It is possible there was another person in the room who actually shot Joe with Sam's gun and then gave it back to Sam, but in the absence of evidence indicating this, it is too remote to take seriously. However, stranger things have happened!

Rabbinic law specified that no one can be sentenced to death for murder unless there were *two* eye-witnesses to the actual murder itself. Understandably there were very few cases of capital punishment carried out by Rabbinic courts. It was thought that in capital cases it was better to err on the side of leniency. In any event, this is how Rabbinic courts tried to make absolutely certain that no mistakes were made in such cases.[1] The ultimate proof of a fact is that a number of people have actually seen it with their own eyes.

In light of the above let us formulate a definition of rational belief. The definition will not explain what rationality is, and the definition is in fact circular, but I doubt if there is any definition of rationality that is not circular. Nonetheless most people recognize irrationality when they see it, so we define a rational belief as: A belief based on evidence E, such that to accept the truth of E, but to reject the truth of the hypothesis H would be irrational. At what point in the trial of Sam it would be irrational for the jurors to believe Sam's innocence is a matter for conjecture, but surely there is *some* point. Once you cross that point, then to believe that Sam murdered Joe is rational. This notion is identical with the notion of confirmation. To have a rational belief that H, is the same as having evidence that confirms H. E confirms H when the acceptance of E and the rejection of H is irrational. As we said, this definition is circular and really does not explain rationality to anyone who does not already understand it, for it assumes we all know when a belief is irrational which implies that we already know when a belief is rational. What then is the purpose of the definition? It is useful for it sets a recognizable standard on the scale of reasonable belief that determines when we have a 'right' to belief H true. Thus, it might be reasonable or rational to believe that H has a *probability* of being true without believing that H is actually true. On the basis that Sam knew Joe and had a motive for killing him, one might reasonably think there is a probability that Sam might have murdered Joe, but as a juror you could not fulfil your mandate of finding Sam guilty beyond a reasonable doubt on this evidence alone.

---

1 Even so there are cases recorded in the Talmud of miscarriages of justice. See Tractate *Makkoth* 5b.

It would not be rational to convict him, because one could accept the truth of E (in this case, the fact that Sam knew Joe and hated Him) and reject H (that Sam murdered Joe) without being called irrational.

Meteorologists have learned the trick of never committing themselves and therefore they can never be proven wrong. This caution may be due to oversensitivity for always having been the butt of criticism for making false predictions. Contemporary probability theory now enables them to take suitable revenge, by predicating the weather without ever making any false predictions! If there is 80% chance of rain, this prediction remains true whether it rains or not. However, if you have to decide whether to take your umbrella, you have to commit yourself. You have to say "I think it will rain, *therefore* I will take my umbrella." Of course, you might say to yourself, "It might rain, *therefore* I will take my umbrella" in which case you can not be charged with holding a false belief if it should not rain, but you will have taken your umbrella for nothing. As far as practical action goes you might *as well* have thought it was going to rain.

Probability statements are applicable in those grey areas when there is not enough evidence to make up one's mind. However, one can take such an analysis to extremes as when the meteorologist says there is 99% or perhaps 100% probability of rain. Such ways of speaking are misleading. In such cases one actually believes it is going to rain, or one would be foolish not to believe it was going to rain. If it doesn't rain you should be surprised, for you certainly should have thought it was going to rain and you certainly had enough evidence to be justified in thinking it was going to rain. Just look at those black clouds rolling in with the thunder and lightning and listen to the meteorologist 'predict' 99% probability of rain! One would have to be a fool not to think it was going to rain.

Actually the so called 'predictions' of the modern meteorologist are not predictions at all. They are a statement about the nature of the evidence at the moment and not a statement about what the weather is going to be in the future. This is why they can not be proven wrong unless of course they misread the evidence. It's not that the predictions are infallible, it is that they are not predictions in the first place! If you never shoot at the target you can never miss it, but that does not make you a good marksman.

Most of the time we use evidence to form a judgement, and we *do* think it is going to rain, though the meteorologists may still be talking about 80% or 90% probabilities. Most likely they themselves think it is going to rain, because that is what it is rational to think in this situation. When the drops start to fall and it starts raining 'cats and dogs' then we *know* it is raining. There is no more speculation.

There was a time when many philosophers[2] thought that our seeing or feeling the rain and getting wet was 'evidence' that it was raining. This is clearly a mistaken use of the notion of evidence. Evidence is a collection of facts that lead us to conclude that something is going to happen or that something did happen, but this assumes that we can know when the prediction is fulfilled or when we discover the truth about certain facts indicated by the evidence. If we can never know when it rains, how can we have evidence that it is going to rain? If the rain itself is not confirmation of the predication that it is going to rain, then the prediction is neither confirmable nor unconfirmable. Thus the notion of evidence itself presupposes the possibility of confirmation or disconfirmation, for if there is no way to confirm or disconfirm the evidence, we can never know what the evidence is supposed to be evidence for. The sceptical thrust of this argument is obvious and has been drawn to its ultimate conclusion by Saul Kripke[3] who has applied this kind of argument to the area of mathematics where everything is supposed to be cut and dried. If one can never tell whether one has added correctly, there can be no such thing as adding, and similarly for any other mathematical or even logical functions. Every form of knowledge implies the possibility of knowing when you have it right. When the evidence is confirmed, commitment takes over. One says, "It *is* raining" and if it is not raining, one is mistaken. The rain therefore cannot be evidence that it is raining.

---

2 They were called "phenomenalists."

3 See Saul Kripke, *Wittgenstein On Rules and Private Language*, Harvard University Press, 1982, pp. 7-22.

EVIDENCE FOR G-D

The great majority of contemporary philosophers think that belief in G-d is not rational, for there is no evidence that justifies that belief.[4] Though the philosophers do not express it specifically, the way I interpret this is that there is no evidence such that given that evidence it would be irrational not to believe in G-d. Often people try to refute this view by pointing to 'miracles' that have happened to them, or certain spiritual or mystical experiences they have had. However this kind of 'evidence' never reaches the level of confirmation.

A woman once told me that her small child was seriously ill and the doctors told her that there was little chance that her child would live. She and her husband went into the quiet room of the hospital and prayed that G-d should spare the life of their child. They were there praying when a doctor came in and told them that the child had miraculously come through the crises and would most likely survive. The couple felt that their prayers had been answered. Perhaps, but then maybe it was just a coincidence? Does G-d *always* answer prayers? If someone else in their family became ill, would G-d answer their prayers also? If the next time they prayed and their prayers were not answered, would this weaken their faith in G-d? No one would deny that faith in G-d is strengthened by such a miracle, but is this the kind of evidence that would confirm belief in G-d such that in the face of such a 'miracle,' if one still denied G-d, one would be clearly irrational? This seems hardly the case.

Another good example of such 'miracles' are untold numbers of events that intervened in the lives of people who were miraculously saved. Among the most remarkable of these, are stories told by survivors of the Nazi holocaust. Each of these survivors can describe not just one miracle, but numerous miracles whereby their lives were saved. Not all of those survivors, however, came out of the war with their faith in G-d intact. Though their lives were miraculously spared, why were they the only ones in their family to survive? What about their mothers and fathers, sisters and brothers, uncles, aunts and cousins? Out of an entire family why did they alone survive? What kind of G-d is that?

---

4 See particularly, N. R. Hanson, "What I Don't Believe," *Boston Studies in Philosophy of Science*, III ed. Robert S. Cohen and Marx Wartovsky, pp. 467-89.

Perhaps, such 'miracles' are indicative not of a kind, merciful G-d, but a cruel, malicious monster? On the other hand, many Jews survived the holocaust with their faith in G-d as firm as ever and in some cases, even stronger than before. How does one explain this anomaly?

The answer to this question is more complex than the simple relationship of evidence to a conclusion and involves questions that go beyond the scope of the relationship of rationality to faith in G-d.

All we want to say here is that 'miracles' that save the life of someone may play a role in the strength of one's faith in G-d, but that does not imply that such facts are evidence that confirms the *truth* of such beliefs. I do not mean to underestimate the value and importance of such experiences for the people that have them, nor do I in any way want to cast doubt on their truth. I simply question their value as evidence for the existence of the Being we call G-d. One might call such facts circumstantial evidence. Certainly they are *consistent* with a belief in G-d, but it certainly does not seem that such experiences constitute confirmatory evidence as we have defined that concept.[5]

There are some philosophers such as N.R. Hanson who argue that as a matter of fact there is at present no such evidence, but there might be at some point in the future. What would such evidence look like? Hanson describes it for us:

> The heavens open—the clouds pull apart-revealing an unbelievably immense and radiant Zeus-like figure, towering up above us like a hundred Everests. He frowns darkly as lightning plays across the features of his Michaelangeloid face. He then points down—at *me!*—and exclaims, for every man, woman and child to hear: 'I have had quite enough of your too clever logic-chopping and word-watching in matters of theology. Be assured, N.R. Hanson, that I most certainly exist'.[6]

The first question one has to ask here is whether Hanson thinks this is evidence for G-d or is this 'Zeus-like figure' G-d Himself? If this is G-d Himself, then it cannot be evidence for G-d for the reasons given above. However, if it is G-d Himself, this would deny the basic

---

5 In chapter 10, on near-death experiences, I argue that these experiences *do* confirm or tend to confirm the truth of a spiritual realm of existence and are on a different 'logical' level from 'miracles' that save our lives.

6 op. cit., p. 472.

thesis of monotheism that G-d is not a finite figure that has a visible form. This is nothing else than idolatry! Let us suppose then that the 'Zeus-like figure' is not G-d Himself but only evidence for G-d. The question is, how does one know that this is evidence for G-d? Keep in mind that you cannot know that E is evidence for H unless you know what it is like for E to confirm H and you can not know this unless you recognize the truth of H when you see it. Thus you cannot know that dark clouds is evidence for rain unless you now know what it is like for it to rain and you can't know what it is like for it to rain if you can not recognize rain when it falls. However, who can recognize G-d? Does He manifest Himself in the form of a 'Zeus like figure'? The Hebrew Bible expressly warns against looking for images or physical forms whereby G-d might manifest Himself.

> ...a voice of words did you hear, but you did not see a form other than voices...And you shall guard yourselves scrupulously, for you saw no form on the day G-d spoke to you on Horev from the midst of fire. Lest you become corrupt and make for yourself an idol in the form of any image male or female. The form of any animal on earth, the form of any winged bird that flies in the heavens. The form of any creeping thing on the ground, the form of any fish which is in the waters under the earth. (Deuteronomy 4:12-18).

No one raised in this tradition would ever suppose that a 'Zeus-like figure' could be a manifestation of G-d, much less G-d Himself. An ancient Greek might, but Hanson was not addressing himself to an audience of ancient Greeks. He was speaking to modern man, and this man, be he theist or atheist, if he looked up in the sky and saw Hanson's 'Zeus-like figure' would first of all be frightened out of his wits. Secondly, he might think earth was being invaded by outer-space creatures. If this figure proclaimed that he was G-d, only an imbecile would believe it. If this 'Zeus-like figure' started throwing its weight around and zapping houses, trees or even people, then we could be sure earth was being invaded, and it would be no Orson Welles hoax. Or maybe it *is* a great big hoax being played on us by some evil galactic scientist. Perhaps it is some fantastic Hollywood production or some gigantic hologram. Who knows what miracles modern technology can produce? Any of these scenarios would be consistent with the 'Zeus-like figure'. Probably the *last* thing one would think is that this is a manifestation of G-d. Why in the world would G-d appear in such an outlandish fashion? Then again, how should G-d manifest Himself? How is anyone supposed to recognize Him if He should want to manifest Himself in some fashion? Let us not talk about prophesy, for we are suppose to be establishing a criterion for a *rational* belief or acceptance of G-d and prophesy is not relevant here. Prophetic visions may indeed be genuine manifestations of G-d and I would not want to deny the truth of prophecy. However, prophetic visions are not evidence for G-d for the simple reason that they are *revelations* of G-d and only the true prophet can know that his prophecy is genuine. However, no prophet ever takes his prophetic vision as *evidence* for G-d. That would be as absurd as taking rain drops as evidence for rain. As for as a rational belief in G-d consisting of evidence that somehow *confirms* G-d's existence, we are arguing that there is no such thing. I would ask anyone who supposes that he can produce such evidence to ask himself how he can know that any event or fact about the world that he takes as evidence for G-d is just that, since he has never confronted G-d or seen G-d 'face to face'. This is similar to a person claiming he has evidence for the existence of UFO's when neither he nor anyone else, so far as we know, has ever seen one or been inside of one, to say nothing of having flown one. Again I am not trying to deny the existence of certain phenomena, photographs etc., that people *claim* is evidence for UFO's. I am saying that one cannot justifiably take these phenomena as evidence for UFO's, using the notion of 'evidence' as this is commonly used in science or in weather reports and common sense knowledge of the world. The only thing that could rationally convince one of the existence of UFO's would be the capture of one that might be put on display. Once we know what one looks like or how it works etc., one might then have evidence for having sighted one, the way one can have evidence for an airplane overhead from the sound that the airplane makes in the sky. However, before the existence of airplanes, such a sound in the sky could never have been evidence for the existence of an airplane. Who knows what someone in the 19th century would have thought if he heard a sound like that in the sky? Even if some imaginative person then would have claimed that he had heard a gigantic bird or perhaps even a machine flying in the air, no one would be justified in thinking that the sound he had heard was evidence for the truth of such a belief, unless he had seen or heard an airplane before, and even then who knows what he might have seen? In other words, the only person who can properly claim to have evidence for G-d is someone who knows G-d when he sees Him. Furthermore, people who claim that G-d talks to them or that they have visions of Him, must first be able to know that it is G-d speaking or appearing to them and not the Devil.

True prophets are a different story. They *know* that it is G-d, but it is another, very complicated problem how anyone *else* can tell whether they are true or false, particularly in an age when people no longer believe in prophets. One needs to fill in a lot more about who or what we take G-d to be before we can begin to approach the question of what kind of person is likely to be a true prophet. Does this mean that belief in G-d is irrational? I do not think so but to make this point clearer, we must go a bit deeper into the notion of rationality. So far we have been talking about when it is rational to say that you know some fact about the world to be true. This is what many philosophers say rationality consists in and to claim to know something that does not meet this standard of rationality is to misuse the notion of rationality. Empirical knowledge and rationality are synonymous for these philosophers and the only kind of knowledge that is worthy of the name is empirical knowledge of the world of which natural science is the model *par excellence*. I believe the notion of rationality is much broader than the empirical philosophers take it to be. Certainly empirical confirmation is part of what we mean by rationality, but it is not the whole story. In the next chapter we take up the 'rest of the story.'

2

THE VALIDITY OF RATIONALITY

In the previous chapter we addressed the question of when it is rational to hold a certain belief. The kinds of beliefs we used as examples were weather reports, questions of who-done-it murder mysteries and possible sightings of UFO's. These are all facts or events that are part of the world or thought to be part of the world. It is no wonder then that G-d does not fit into the 'logic' of facts and events that compose the world, for G-d is not a fact or even a thing in the world as is the force of gravity for instance. G-d cannot be observed, and therefore he is not subject to empirical investigation or confirmation by evidence, as we argued in the previous chapter. This does not mean, however, that belief in G-d is irrational as many philosophers have argued. Not everything rational is subject to such investigation or confirmation. There are certain principles or rules of thought or beliefs about the nature of reality that are fundamental in the sense that all knowledge presupposes them, though these principles themselves are neither demonstrable nor confirmable. They are beliefs that are called *a priori* in philosophical terminology. That is, they are accepted as true or taken for granted and it is not possible or even rational to question them. There have been attempts to question them but such attempts inevitably lead to skepticism of *all* knowledge which is certainly not rational.

The best example of this in the history of philosophy is David Hume's attempt to question the principle of induction. Hume argued, correctly, that our knowledge of the world is garnered from our past experience, meaning by this not just one's own personal experience, but the experience of mankind generally. Science is essentially the sum total of past human experience. No individual or age starts from the very beginning. We have always inherited the results and achievements of former generations unless some cataclysmic event wipes out a culture, as perhaps happened in the dark ages. In any event what we know about the world is the collective experience of humankind and no one really starts from scratch.

Furthermore, a great deal of our knowledge of the world is expressed in terms of our expectations and predictions about the future. Infants quickly discover that things fall and that if you don't watch yourself you can get hurt. We learn to depend on gravity. No one is seriously worried that one might suddenly fly off into outer space together with everything else on earth that's not tied down. People had no such fears long before gravity was 'discovered' by Newton or long before scientists were able to accurately describe this mysterious force. This did not prevent people from dealing with this force successfully. That is, they built stair cases in two-storey houses to go up and down, knowing that they could not fly like birds. Generally speaking, people got along quite well from a practical point of view.

Hume's question was, given that past experience teaches us that gravity is a fact about the world, to which all past human history testifies, how do we know that what we call gravity will continue to be a fact about the world ten minutes from now, or at any time in the future? Hume generalized this into the question of how *anything* that we say we know about the world, will hold true in the future. Since the future is something *no one* has experienced, we are not entitled to claim that we have any knowledge of it whatsoever for all knowledge is derived from our past experience. Some have tried to argue that our future expectations are generally confirmed, not only in our own lives, but in the lives of all people who have lived in the past of which we have any record. Why isn't that evidence for the future? Hume answers, again correctly, that even though the world may have run along certain lines in the past and no one has yet been 'let down' by gravity, the fact remains that we have no guarantee that the world might not radically change at any moment. Our minds have grown accustomed to expect the future to be like the past much as Pavlov's unfortunate dog was trained to think it was going to be fed when it heard a bell ring. The dog had no rational justification for believing this, but expected it nonetheless, and salivated when it heard the bell even though it wasn't fed. Expectations then are not the same thing as rational justification. Hume not only admitted that we do expect the future to be like the past, but that we could not live in the world without that expectation and no one should even try to get along without it. If one tried to do so, the different ways that one might quickly come to one's end are innumerable, from jumping out the window to get to the ground floor, to eating the fork instead of the egg. Nature has implanted in us the instinct to expect the future to be like the past as it has in all animals, but there is no proof that the belief is true, nor could it possibly be confirmed by any evidence from past experience. Man is no more rational than Pavlov's dog in his expectations.

If one consistently follows Hume's argument to its inevitable conclusion, ludicrous paradoxes result. Let's say you sit down to breakfast, having read Hume the night before. You are determined that you will not be seduced by Mother Nature and that you will do your best not to believe anything about the future. Most likely you will have already given in to this 'un-get-overable' temptation, in order to have walked from your bed to the breakfast table. For instance, you somehow got out of bed, brushed your teeth and performed the complicated tasks of taking a shower and getting dressed to say nothing of walking down the stairs to the kitchen (and why have you gone into the kitchen to satisfy your hunger rather than the basement or the attic?). Forget this for the moment. Let us concentrate on eating breakfast rationally without giving in to the instinctive, non-rational belief that the future will be like the past. You have before you a place-setting with a couple of your favorite fried eggs on the plate with toast and butter just as you like it. Your mouth begins to water as you catch yourself acting just as Pavlov's dog would have. You try to hold back your mouth from salivating—this time you are determined to eat 'rationally'. (There might be a problem of how you know that eating is what is going to assuage your hunger pains, if you can allow yourself the luxury of being able to judge that pains in your stomach *are* hunger pains which you know from experience are relieved by eating wholesome food—but let's ignore this also.) Now you sit down to the plate with the eggs and you are determined to try and put into practice a rational act which is not motivated by the belief that the future will be like the past. The question arises, what shall you eat? From your past experience you know you like eggs and that they are wholesome food, but you cannot count on past experience. Perhaps this time, the eggs will turn into poison. Maybe you should try the fork? Remember now, you have nothing to go on. Your past experience is not evidence to guide your *rational* expectations of the future. Since you have no idea what to eat and barring past experience, *anything* might as well be wholesome food as anything else. One might as well flip a coin as to whether one should eat the eggs or the fork. This is the conclusion of Hume's argument! The paradox of this conclusion needs no comment. Any normal person would consider such a conclusion to be the epitome of irrationality. Hume must have gone wrong somewhere, but the question is where?

Given Hume's premise, that *all* empirical knowledge is derived from experience and must therefore be confirmed by evidence, it is difficult to see that he has gone wrong at all, for the inductive principle that the future will be like the past cannot be confirmed as Hume has argued. Furthermore, since the principle is not logically necessary, it cannot be admitted as a valid part of human knowledge, as Hume argues at the beginning of Section IV of the *Enquiry Concerning Human Understanding* that all human knowledge must belong to either logic and mathematics which he calls 'relations of ideas' or to our empirical knowledge of the world which he calls 'matters of fact'. Propositions belonging to the former are necessary truths whose denials are contradictions. Thus $2+2 = 4$ is necessary and its denial is a contradiction as is the logical inference of *modus ponens* which is that, 1) if p then q, and 2) p, therefore 3) q. However such knowledge gives us no information about the world. It cannot tell us how many marbles are in a bag or when something is going to happen. Knowledge of the world is what Hume calls 'matters of fact' and propositions of this kind are never necessarily true and their denials are never contradictions. Any proposition which claims to be part of human knowledge must fall into one of these two categories. Either it is necessarily true in which case it gives us no knowledge of the world and belongs to the realm of mathematics or logic, or it is an empirical statement about the world whose truth must be able to be confirmed or disconfirmed by empirical evidence. If a proposition belongs to the first category of relations of ideas it is said to be true *a priori*. That is, its truth can be seen independently or prior to any empirical knowledge of the world. If a proposition belongs to the second category of matters of fact, its truth can be ascertained only by or posterior to some observation of the world and it is therefore said to be a proposition whose truth is known *a posteriori*. The principle of induction that the future will be like the past is not a necessary truth whose denial is a contradiction. Indeed it is conceivable that the world might change any moment in some radical way. Its truth therefore cannot be known *a priori*, according to Hume. In order to be a part of rational knowledge of the world it must be known *a posteriori*, that is, there must be some observation or evidence that the future will be like the past.

However, Hume in Section IV of the *Enquiry*, argues with eloquence and power that there is no such observation or evidence and therefore according to Hume's analysis of human knowledge, the principle of induction should not be admitted into the category of propositions that constitute valid human knowledge. Thus when we sit down to the breakfast table we cannot *know* that it is rational to eat the egg rather than the fork. Of course we *will* as a matter of fact eat the egg rather than the fork, but this is because we are creatures of habit, not because we are rational. Man is definitely not a *rational* animal as Aristotle had supposed. He is simply an animal like other animals who acts and lives by instinct rather than rationality.

It is easy to see that belief in the existence of G-d is equivalent with the principle of induction. Since the existence of G-d is not a necessary truth, it cannot be said to be true *a priori*. That is, one can imagine a G-dless world no matter how frightful or awful one might consider this. On the other hand, as we have argued in Chapter One, and as Hume, Hanson and many philosophers since Hume have argued, there does not seem to be any way of confirming the truth of G-d's existence by observation or by evidence in the ordinary sense. Therefore it would seem that there is no way of empirically determining the truth of His existence and thus a proposition affirming G-d's existence cannot be known to be true either *a priori* or *a posteriori*. Thus G-d and the principle of induction seem to be equally barred from being admitted into the realm of human knowledge.

Members of the philosophical group known as the 'Vienna Circle' and other positivists in the first half of the 20th century utilized a similar argument to ban all 'metaphysical' propositions from being a topic of discussion by scientists, philosophers or anyone concerned with the pursuit of human knowledge, i.e., any serious intellectual. A 'metaphysical' proposition was defined as a proposition that was neither logically necessary (its negation was not a contradiction) nor empirically verifiable. Under this characterization the principle of induction and statements about G-d could equally be classified as 'metaphysical' propositions.

This modern development of the conception of human knowledge which had its origins in David Hume has been challenged by Ludwig Wittgenstein.[1] He and others made the point that basic principles upon which rational thinking and knowledge of the world depend are presupposed in our thinking and what is rational is not their rejection but their acceptance. As to the question of how one can demonstrate them or prove them, Wittgenstein's position is that they need no proof. What we call rationality or rational thought is tied to them much as the idea of being unmarried is involved in the meaning of the word 'bachelor'. It would be absurd to ask why the word 'bachelor' means 'unmarried man'. The answer is simply, that's what the word means. If someone wanted proof for this, one would point to examples of how this word is used in the English language. The 'proof is in the pudding'.

Similarly, if one wants to act or think rationally in the world, one has to assume the future is going to be like the past. If one wants proof for this, the answer has to be, the 'proof is in the pudding'. That is, if one rejected this principle, what we call rational action would cease. The skeptic demands that everything be doubted until proven true, but as Wittgenstein argued, doubt is only possible in a context where something can be known.[2] If nothing can be known, nothing can be doubted. Certain assumptions or beliefs we have about the nature of reality must be taken as true *before* anything can be known and these beliefs are accepted as true *a priori*. This is a rejection of the fundamental position of Hume and the empirical tradition in philosophy that has developed from him, that all *a priori* propositions must be logically necessary and give us no real knowledge of the world. That the future will resemble the past is not a logical truth whose denial is a contradiction, but it is something we all do take as true *a priori*. Hume called this belief custom or habit and denied that it was rational because it could not be proven or had no 'rational ground'. Those following Wittgenstein would say that the principle of induction is one of the 'rules' guiding rational action. This is how we go about acting

---

1 See his *On Certainty*, Basil Blackwell, 1969.

2 Ibid., see paragraphs 193-255.

2 ? THE VALIDITY OF RATIONALITY

rationally. It is what everyone calls acting rationally. The question of whether the world might not radically change at any moment is irrelevant. If the world should radically change so that eggs suddenly became poison to the human digestive system and metal suddenly became digestible, it would still be rational to eat the eggs and not the fork until one discovered the change. If everyone began contracting food poisoning from eating fresh eggs and suddenly found metal to be digestible and wholesome for the body, it would no longer be rational to eat the eggs and not the fork. However this would be the new rational course of action, assuming that our past experience is a guide for our future expectations. If things began changing in a sudden and unpredictable fashion, so that our past experience would no longer be a reliable guide for the future, then there would be no such thing as acting rationally. The whole concept of rationality would fall by the boards. Whatever we decided to do, we would just simply have to pray and hope it would turn out, for there would be no criterion of rational choice. Today the egg may nourish, but tomorrow it may suddenly be poison, and the day after tomorrow it may again be wholesome food. The only thing to do when you sit down to breakfast is to pray not for the food, but that whatever you choose to eat will turn out to be food and not poison. It is therefore not possible to doubt the principle of induction and remain rational. One is rational by simply taking for granted the principle of induction *a priori*.

There are other such principles that lie at the very foundation of rational thought and knowledge which cannot be doubted without pain of irrationality and which are neither logically necessary nor empirically confirmable. For example, the principle of sufficient reason proclaims that every event has a cause, or that there are no uncaused events. This principle is not logically necessary as one can imagine uncaused events and the business of the magician is to make it appear as if he were producing them, but neither he nor you think that he is really doing so, for no rational, thinking person believes that something can come from nothing. On the other hand this principle can not be proven by empirical observation for to demonstrate its proof one would have to have observed all events and be able to ascertain that each of them had a cause. It goes without saying that this is impossible, for to have observed all events one would have to know that one had accounted for *all* events and this is logically impossible for by definition one cannot empirically know that one has observed all events. Nonetheless, if anyone ever entertained the possibility of uncaused events he would be deemed irrational.[3]

The principle of sufficient reason constitutes part of what we mean by rationality and all thinking people accept it *a priori* without question. One could mention numerous other *a priori* beliefs that are accepted because the human mind finds such beliefs irresistible as the continuity of space and time and the validity of human memory generally. In all these examples, we accept without question their truth and they as a matter of fact define or determine what one means by rational thought about the world.[4]

Some philosophers have recently argued that belief in G-d should similarly be treated as an *a priori* belief that needs no proof or empirical verification.[5] The theist need not consider that the onus of proof for G-d lies on him. It is with this belief that he begins and this determines how he thinks about the world. The argument is that the theist has as much justification for his belief in G-d as the scientist does in his acceptance of the principle of induction or the principle of sufficient reason. There is, however, an important distinction between belief in G-d and the kinds of fundamental beliefs about the nature of reality

---

3 I am told that in particle physics today some physicists entertain this very possibility due to their inability to explain certain quantum phenomena. This really proves the point. That is, because certain phenomena appear *inexplicable*, the physicist says they appear to be uncaused. As long as the physicist fails to find a cause for such phenomena, they will remain inexplicable. However, any way of explaining these phenomena will immediately be seized upon by these very physicists, for the mind abhors uncaused events as much as nature abhors a vacuum.

4 I really believe that David Hume thought this way, though it does not come through clearly in his *Enquiry*. He is reported to have written to John Stewart in 1754 the following, "But allow me to tell you that I never asserted so absurd a Proposition as *that anything might arise without a cause.* I only maintained, that our Certainty of the Falsehood of that Proposition proceeded neither from Intuition nor Demonstration, but from another source." What this other source might have been I have no idea. This, however, is what I would call a 'rational intuition'.

5 See Norman Malcolm, "The Groundlessness of Belief," *Reason and Religion*, ed. Stuart C. Brown, Cornell University Press, 1977.

that all rational people hold. That is, while it is in some fundamental sense irrational to reject the principle of induction or the principle of sufficient reason, it is not irrational to reject a belief in G-d. Many highly intelligent people claim they do not believe in G-d. These people may be misguided, in error, or perhaps evil, but one cannot say that an atheist is irrational the way one could be said to be irrational if, upon reading Hume, he decided to reject the principle of induction.

The question then becomes: granted that one cannot be said to be irrational if one believes in G-d, for one may choose to accept G-d *a priori* for whatever reason; nonetheless there seems to be no need to accept such a belief in order to *avoid* irrationality as is the case with certain fundamental principles that we have discussed. Why then should one believe in the existence of G-d rather than not? So far as I can see, neither Norman Malcolm whose views I have alluded to in the previous footnote, nor any other philosopher who follows the views of Wittgenstein, have presented any reason for accepting G-d rather than rejecting Him. Though I think Wittgenstein correct in rejecting the Human or empirical conception of human knowledge, it seems to me that no one has stated a convincing case for believing in G-d such that it could be said that belief in G-d is more rational than atheism, though atheism cannot be said to be irrational.[6] I do think that such a case can be made out, and in the next three chapters I will try to state that case.

In these chapers, I discuss respectively the teleological argument, the cosmological argument and another argument which I shall call the argument from unity. These arguments are ordinarily presented by their proponents as proofs for G-d and the criticisms made of these arguments are that they do not constitute proofs for what we ordinarily mean by G-d. I am inclined to think that these criticisms

---

6 This is not inconsistent with what we said in Chapter 1, pp.17-21, where belief in an empirical fact about the world is rational when the evidence for that fact is such that acceptance of the evidence would render denial of the fact irrational. There we are talking about the confirmation of facts. Here we are talking about what is involved in accepting certain basic principles of reasoning. I am suggesting that while some of these principles cannot be rejected without appearing to be irrational, there are, however, others that might be rejected without that appearance. What we mean by this will be explained in somewhat more detail in Chapters 3, 4 and 5.

are basically correct but they do not neutralize the force that these arguments really do have which is quite substantial. Taken together, these arguments—while not constituting a proof for G-d—seem to me overwhelming. If you wonder how something could be 'overwhelming' without constituting a proof, the answer is that by 'proof' philosophers have usually meant that one could show that the existence of G-d is either: 1) logically necessary as a theorem in mathematics or logic, or 2) an empirical fact about the world that is verified by empirical evidence. G-d is neither of these and therefore it is not surprising that there are no 'proofs' for Him. However, there are forceful reasons for believing in G-d, such that the rationality of the belief is inescapable. In the next three chapters I try to show why I think it is inescapable.

3
THE TELEOLOGICAL ARGUMENT

It is very easy to misrepresent the teleological argument and the history of this argument has been a history of misunderstanding. I will present my own version of this argument and in passing will remark on how I think the argument in the past has been mishandled by protagonists and antagonists alike. It may well be that my version of this argument is so different from the usual one that it doesn't merit to be called 'teleological'. However, this is the version of the argument that I think is forceful. Furthermore, it is very much like a view that Aristotle held.

Suppose you are shipwrecked and are walking along the beach of what appears to be a deserted island. You look down in the sand and see the following design: #. What you would naturally think is that someone has been here and drawn this design. The island obviously is not as deserted as you originally thought. You might or might not like the prospect of meeting someone else on the island, but you would be convinced that there was someone else on the island, for it is not possible that a design of this sort could have been produced in the sand by accident. Only another person could have drawn it. The inference from orderliness or design to mind is inescapable. To avoid it one has to go to all kinds of outlandish lengths to try to 'explain' how this design might have come about by accident. It is logically possible it was made by four coconuts that just happened to fall off a nearby coconut tree and rolled in such a way as to form these lines. Let's not worry about what happened to the coconuts or the lines that should extend from the tree to the design. We can say that some monkeys carried off the coconuts and the wind obliterated part of the lines. It is possible that all this might have happened but it is not the explanation that would naturally occur to anyone unless he were so obsessed with the fear of meeting someone else on the island that he would go to any length to convince himself that the design came about by accident. All things being equal, it is not the best, or most rational explanation. Orderliness implies mind. This is what one might call a natural intuition of the human mind, and this essentially is all that the teleological argument is saying. Given the orderliness of the world it is more believable to suppose that it was due to the planning of some mind than that it came about by accident. It is not quite correct to say that this is an argument at all. It does nothing more than point to the fact that our minds find it difficult to believe that the orderliness of anything is the result of an accident. Aristotle had argued against Empedocles that it is absurd to suppose that the orderliness and regularity of nature is an accident. In fact, an 'accident' is defined by Aristotle as an exception to the regularity of nature. Regularity and orderliness imply mind and any other view of the matter is just not rational.

It is important to notice that by looking at the design in the sand one could not tell the purpose for which this design was drawn. It might have been to serve as coordinates for drawing a map. It might have been for the purpose of playing tic-tac-toe, or it may have been drawn for no reason at all. Perhaps the one who drew it was just doodling with nothing particular in mind. The point is that orderliness *per se* does not reveal what purpose this orderliness is supposed to serve unless the orderliness fulfils some obvious function as the eye serves the function of sight. As I expound it, the teleological argument says nothing about the purpose or the reason for the orderliness—just that there had to be some mind behind it. Likewise, if one is talking about a world that consisted of one hydrogen atom, one might not know what purpose such a world might serve, but everything being equal, it is not reasonable to believe that this atom came about by accident. We may of course believe that it came by accident from some previously existing atom or some kind of initial conditions that could give rise to a hydrogen atom in some predictable fashion. That is not what we mean here by 'coming to be by accident'. What the teleological argument means to deny is that something orderly could come from something lacking order altogether. That orderliness could come from chaos by accident is simply not believable. Furthermore I do not believe that there could be any probability calculation that could project that something orderly might possibly come from chaos, for there would be no initial conditions that could serve as a basis for the calculations. For example, what might be the probability that a potted plant will fall on your head while you are walking in an open

3 ᠅ THE TELEOLOGICAL ARGUMENT

field with no airplanes flying overhead? Now there is a probability calculation that can project the probability that a monkey walking over the keys of a typewriter could type out a meaningful English sentence to say nothing of *War and Peace*. The probability is no doubt very low, and G-d knows what the probability of typing *War and Peace* might be! However, there is some probability of that happening, because there are certain conditions present, namely a typewriter and a monkey who obeys the command to walk over the typewriter for billions or trillions of years! However, suppose there is no typewriter. Under those conditions, what is the probability that a monkey walking on a typewriter will produce an intelligible English sentence? The wrong answer would be zero. For that implies that you can make a calculation of *some sort*, but in the absence of any typewriter, there could be *no* calculation that could say what is the probability of a monkey producing an English sentence by walking over a typewriter. One might as well ask what is the probability of an English sentence appearing miraculously on a wall. Another way of asking the same question is, 'What is the probability of a miracle happening?'. Again the wrong answer is zero, unless you mean by 'zero' that there is no way of making any calculation whatever. What is certainly wrong is that if you wait an eternity there is some probability that a potted plant will fall on your head in an open field with no airplanes flying overhead, or that a monkey will type an English sentence without a typewriter or that sooner or later you will be able to walk on water if you try an infinite number of times. Similarly, anyone who argues that given an eternity there is *some* probability that order will come from chaos is simply mistaken. Chaos provides no basis at all for any kind of probability statement about what might happen. If a hydrogen atom would come from chaos it would be as much of a miracle as if it came from nothing. One might as well ask, 'What is the probability that a hydrogen atom could come from nothing?'.

One might claim that orderliness is eternal, but that would not explain why the world is orderly rather than chaotic, or why it has the order it does rather than some other. The only thing that can explain orderliness is mind. Without mind, one is inclined to say that chaos is what one should expect. That orderliness could exist at all without mind would indeed be the biggest miracle that one could imagine.

However, it is not rational to believe in miracles, nor is it rational to think that the orderliness of the world just happened.

David Hume's famous critique of the teleological argument[1] is ineffectual against the form of the argument I have presented above. His critique in the *Dialogues* is aimed at the formulation given this argument by William Paley, the Archdeacon of Carlisle. Interestingly enough, though Paley did not publish his book, *Natural Theology, or Evidence of the Existence and Attributes of the Deity* until 1802, six years after Hume's death, and Hume never mentions Paley by name. Most philosophers today regard Hume's critique of this argument as definitive and indeed it does demolish the argument as it was presented by Paley. However, the way Paley presented this argument is fallacious, or rather it does not present the crux of the argument with clarity.

He argued that if you were walking across a field and stubbed your foot on a rock, you would not wonder how the stone came to be in the field. Where else does one find stones? However, if you found a watch you would wonder what a watch was doing there even if you had never seen a watch in your life! The reason we would wonder about the metal object and not about the stone is that while the stone does not appear to serve any purpose, the watch does, and by inspecting the parts of the watch we can discover what that purpose is, i.e. to tell time. We would not think that such an object has come from the ground the way we see that a rock does. It must have been manufactured by someone and dropped in the field, but no one in his right mind would suppose the watch had been there from time immemorial as the rock! Paley argues that we would think this way about the watch even though we had never before seen a watch being made. The world is like the watch except that the world is much more cleverly contrived than the watch and therefore our conviction that the world was similarly contrived by some mind is much stronger. What else is this mind other than G-d?

One question immediately strikes us and that is, if we have never seen a watch, as Paley grants, how would one know that the purpose of this object with a dial is to tell time? Even more, if one had never seen a dial before, how would one know the purpose of these numbers formed in a circle, and how does one know that these funny looking

---

1 See parts 2 and 5 of his *Dialogue Concerning Natural Religion*, 1779.

marks are numbers? What renders the argument convincing is that
we know what a watch is and that watches are made by men. Hume
argues in his critique that no one has ever observed a world being
made, so we have no conception what was required for the making of
it. The analogy of the world to the watch is so remote that it is weak
to argue from one to the other. Secondly, Hume argues, the world
appears to contain many imperfections in spite of its awesomeness, so
that the mind that created the world, though impressive, might not be
perfect or even infinite. Indeed, following the analogy of the watch,
just as many men might have been involved in the manufacture of
the watch, so many deities might have been in on the creation of the
world and none of these deities would necessarily have to be infinite
or perfect to create the orderliness of the world. Thus, this argument
might convince one that mind is behind the world but does not show
that that mind was infinite or that there was only one mind behind
it. It doesn't even show that the mind behind the world was good. It
might have been evil! The goodness, infinity, and unity of G-d, however,
are necessary attributes of G-d as we conceive Him. Thus, while this
argument might support the view that *some* kind of mind is behind
the universe, it does not argue for G-d as we ordinarily think of Him.

It seems to me that these arguments of Hume have force. Indeed,
I think that the teleological argument does not demonstrate that the
mind behind the world is either infinite, good, or even one, but it
does argue forcibly that *some kind* of mind is behind it. Nonetheless,
such a mind *per se* is not what we ordinarily mean by G-d, so that
Hume may be correct in his claim that the argument cannot be said
to argue for G-d as we know Him. This, however, does not blunt
the real force of this argument as we have been presenting it. This is
simply that the teleological argument points to what might be called
a rational inclination of the human mind to attribute the orderliness,
or the intelligibility of the world to *some* mind. Hume's *Dialogue* is a
critique of Paley's argument from the analogy of man-made objects
which is irrelevant to the way we have been presenting this argument.

There is, however, one passage in Hume that does suggest a rejection
of the formulation of this argument, though it is not very clear. In Part
II, Philo says to Demea that the existence of final causes *per se* does
not entail mind except in so far we have perceived that such causes

proceed from some kind of mentality, for we all know that watches are made by men. This is why we do not think the watch came from the ground when we find one in the field as Paley suggests. However, no one has ever seen a world being made and therefore "For ought we can know *a priori*, matter may contain the source or spring of order originally within itself, as well as mind does; and there is no more difficulty in conceiving that the several elements, from an internal unknown cause, may fall into the most exquisite arrangement, than to conceive that their ideas, in the great universal mind, from a like internal unknown cause, fall into that arrangement."[2]

Hume seems to be saying here that the orderliness in the world might be due to certain 'unknown causes' inside matter and not to a Divine Mind. This, however, just pushes the question one step back, for these unknown causes do not bring about the orderliness of the world 'by accident'. There is a regularity to it all. The teleological question is, 'Why this regularity rather than no regularity?'. Why should the world be intelligible? Hume appears to think that this 'unknown cause' itself requires no explanation. It just is there. It might even be eternal. The thrust of the teleological argument is to object and ask why this regularity rather than no regularity or chaos. If one wishes to cut the matter short and say that one should not ask questions for which there is no way of determining whether the answers are true or false, we simply reply that we feel impelled to ask the question nonetheless and that the only possible answer is that it is the brainchild of some mind. The question may be transcendental as is the answer, but then the human mind may have 'ungetoverable,' transcendental inclinations which no amount of philosophy is going to repress. "Why is the world orderly or why does it have this order?" is a natural question that most people find difficult not to ask, even though they may have never taken a course in philosophy. If you do not want to ask it, you have to train yourself not to ask it.

When in physics we run up against one of those mysterious constants and ask, 'Why does light travel 186,000 miles per second?,' or, 'Why is gravity a force that attracts rather than repulses?,' and the scientist answers that that is just the way it is, take it or leave it; we mutter

---

2 David Hume, *Dialogues Concerning Natural Religion*, ed. Stanley Tweyman, Routledge, 1991, pp. 111-12.

under our breath something like, 'There has *got* to be an explanation whether the scientist will ever find it or not'. At that point, we have left science behind and are expressing the transcendental nature of our understanding. When Hume suggests that the 'internal, unknown cause' of the intelligibility of the world itself needs no explanation, he is mistaken. It does need an explanation and the only possible explanation is mind. If Hume wants to avoid the answer, he is pursuing the right tactic, for the only way of avoiding this answer is not to ask the question. It is as if the question and answer were made for one another like a hand and a glove. Mind and orderliness are inseparable. If the world can be understood it is orderly. If it is unintelligible, that is just what we mean be chaos. Orderliness and intelligibility are two sides of the same coin. To say that something is orderly but unintelligible is a contradiction. There may be some forms of orderliness that are unintelligible to your mind or my mind or perhaps to the human mind, but there can be no forms of orderliness that are unintelligible to any mind. The notion of an unintelligible orderliness is a contradiction as much as is a round square. That the world is orderly implies that there is some mind that can understand it. It is a short step from that to positing a mind as the origin of the orderliness of the world. As far as the origin of that mind itself, that is a question we take up in the next chapter in our discussion of the cosmological argument. It really doesn't belong in a discussion of the teleological argument per se. As far as the teleological argument is concerned, that mind *may* have come from some other mind, etc. What this argument excludes is that the orderliness of the world or the mind that planned the world came from chaos or from nothing. This is not logically impossible, but it is certainly not reasonable, just as it is not logically impossible that an intricate design may have come about in the sand by chance, but it is not reasonable to think that it did. It is not 'the simplest' explanation.[3]

It may be that one could deny this without being irrational as would be the case in denying the principle of sufficient reason or the validity of memory generally. There is perhaps a degree of the rational force a belief might have, such that in some cases, rejection of that belief is irrational, and in others, it is merely 'unreasonable'. In saying that ac-

---

3 For a discussion of the 'simplest' explanation as this is meant in the philosophy of science, see Chapter 5, pp. 62-64.

ceptance of mind as the source of the orderliness of the world is more
'reasonable' than believing that it came about by chance or accident,
we mean that it is the explanation to which we are most naturally
inclined. Our fellow stranded on an island would most naturally be
inclined to think that the design was drawn by someone for whatever
reason, than to suppose it was formed randomly by rolling coconuts.
It might have been so formed, but it would not be reasonable to suppose so, and the only reason one might want to think so, is that his
fear of meeting someone on the island has overcome what he himself
knows is the most reasonable explanation. Such people we describe
as 'hiding their heads in the sand'. These 'head-hiders' are aptly so-
called, for what they are doing is denying what any reasonable 'head'
(mind) would naturally think.

There is a corollary to this argument which, so far as I know, was
first propounded by Charles Sanders Peirce[4] and later promulgated in

---

4 The first paragraph of Peirce's "Neglected Argument for the Reality of
G-d" says that G-d is the "… creator of all three Universes of Experience"
(6.452). The most important of these is the world of 'thirdness' which is
the realm of knowledge and meaning, i.e. the human mind is capable of
knowing the truth of the world of 'secondness' which is the forces that
move the objects of reality according to the laws of nature. That the thinking pattern of human thought should conform to the pattern of nature so
that it is possible for the mind to have knowledge of some reality outside
itself can be due to no accident. When one thinks or 'muses' about this,
one is led irresistibly to G-d as the origin of all orderliness, whether it be
in reality or in the mind. I think that Peirce would say with me that this
is eminently rational. Nonetheless, this is not the conclusion of some
argument, or as Peirce said, an 'argumentation' (6.456). It is a conclusion
drawn from 'direct experience.' "Would you make it a result of some kind
of reasoning, good or bad? Why, reasoning can supply the mind with
nothing in the world except an estimate of the value of a statistical ratio,
that is, how often certain kinds of things are found in certain combina-
tions in the ordinary course of experience" (6.493). One does not come
to G-d as a result of any such statistical investigation any more than one
comes to an explanation of *anything* through statistics. All you have to do
is to "… open your eyes" and your heart, which is also a perceptive organ
"and you see Him" (6.493). This opening of the eyes is what Peirce calls
'musing' (6.452—6.465) which is simply meditation on the 'hypothesis'
of G-d as the origin of the finite world and its orderliness as one finds it in
Peirce's Three Universes. In writing to Lady Welby, Peirce said that "… to

our own day by Richard Taylor.[5] This argument goes something like this: There is an orderliness in the world and there is an orderliness of the human mind we call intelligence. These two systems of orderliness might not have interfaced with one another but in fact they do. This is what makes science possible. It is not reasonable to suppose that this fit between the mind and the world is an accident. The fact that the mind is 'tuned in' to the world must have been planned or perhaps is a reflection of the fact that the orderliness of the world and the human mind are different aspects of the one universal mind we call the mind of G-d.

The real force behind this argument is, however, that our rational intuition dictates that orderliness of whatever kind is inseparable from mind or understanding, and it is this intuition that is the basis of the teleological argument for a mind as the origin of the orderliness of the world. This argument, therefore, has nothing to do with purpose *per se*, or that the world is 'fine-tuned' to support human life or anything else. The wealth of discussion that has centered around whether the

believe in reasoning about phenomena is to believe that they are governed by reason, that is, by G-d." See *Semiotic and Significs: The Correspondence Between Charles S. Peirce and Lady Victoria Welby*, ed. C.S. Hardwick, Indiana University Press, 1977, p. 75. All other citations in this footnote are from the collected works of Charles Sanders Peirce, *Collected Papers*, ed. C. Hartshorne, P. Weiss, and A. Burks, 8 vols., Cambridge: Harvard University Press, 1931-58. Reference is by volume and paragraph number: read 6.467 as volume 6, paragraph 467.

I do believe that Peirce's notion here of 'musing' is close to if not identical with my notion of 'rational intuition' (which I took from Hume—cf. p. 34, footnote 4) when I say that if one thinks about the orderliness of the world it is a rational intuition that this orderliness is the result of some mind and not due to an accident. A remarkable comment by Peirce in which he elaborates this idea occurs in 6.501 as follows:

Let a man drink in such thoughts as come to him in contemplating the physico-psychical universe [the worlds of secondness and thirdness] without any special purpose of his own; especially the universe of mind which coincides with the universe of matter. The idea of there being a G-d over it all of course will be often suggested; and the more he considers it, the more he will be enwrapt with Love of this idea. (The words in brackets are mine.)

5 Richard Taylor, *Metaphysics*, 4th ed., Prentice Hall, 1963, pp. 112-15.

so-called 'anthropic principle'[6] can explain this fine-tunedness without G-d is not relevant. One might even side with the supporters of the anthropic principle and admit that the fact that the world does ever so delicately provide a friendly environment for human existence, does not in itself argue for a mind behind the world. Nevertheless, it would still be true that what does argue for a mind behind the world is that we cannot rationally entertain the prospect of *any* kind of orderly universe, with or without humans, coming about by chance. It is equally as great a miracle that the world supports cockroaches as much as it is that it supports sentient observers.[7] What the teleological argument says is that it is not reasonable to suppose that the existence of a world that is orderly *in any sense* could come about by chance or accident. I do not find anything in the anthropic principle that gainsays this.

It would, of course, be arrogant to end a discussion of the teleological argument without discussing what is taken by many philosophers and scientists alike as the ultimate refutation of the argument, namely the theory of evolution. I myself am inclined to think that the theory of evolution is a red herring in the discussion. In so far as it is a straightforward scientific or empirical thesis about the growth and development of the world as we know it, it has nothing to say that is relevant to the discussion. It is simply describing, correctly or incorrectly, how the world came about from the first hydrogen atom, if indeed that is how the world began, down to and including the origin of man and the rise of human civilization. So far as I can see it has nothing to do with answering the question, 'Why is the world orderly?'.

There is one facet of the theory of evolution that does appear to be in conflict with the teleological argument and that is the claim that the orderly development of the world came about randomly, by accident, and is not the result of the planning or orderliness of some mind. However, this aspect of the theory is not an empirical claim that could be proven or confirmed by science or any empirical evidence.

6 See Brandon Carter, "Large Number Coincidences and the Anthropic Principle in Cosmology," in Longair, M.S. (ed.) *Confrontation of Cosmological Theories with Observational Data*, Didrect: Reidel, pp. 291-98.

7 A friend of mine who is writing a Ph.D. dissertation on the immune system of the cockroach tells me that cockroaches are unbelievably complicated and their immune system is, relatively speaking, even more 'fine tuned' than that of humans.

It is what I would call a 'metaphysical' thesis and since I am going to use this term 'metaphysical' in a specific sense, I might as well say now how I mean it should be taken. I mean by a 'metaphysical' thesis, a belief, statement, or claim about the nature of reality as a whole with nothing left out. Thus, if one says that only matter exists or that there is no G-d, this is a metaphysical statement. This is what I call 'metaphysical materialism'. This claim could never be confirmed or proven by science or any empirical evidence. It may well be that many people, including scientists, believe this, but it cannot be that science led them to this conclusion unless they are confused about science. The reason science or empirical knowledge can say nothing about the nature of reality as a whole is that it can never be empirically verified that whatever one may know about the world is all there is to know. Therefore, statements about the world as a whole cannot constitute empirical knowledge but simply bear testimony to the fact that the human mind does ask metaphysical or transcendental questions for which there can only be metaphysical or transcendental answers.

If one desired to stay away from metaphysics, what one should say about the evolutionary development of the world is that science itself cannot explain how or why it developed the way that it did any more than science can explain why there is a force of gravity. That is the way the 'cookie crumbled,' or that is just the way things happened. If, for whatever reason, one does not believe in G-d or some mind behind the universe, one will be inclined to say it came about by chance or randomly for that is the only metaphysical view one *can* take about the matter, if one rejects mind. The rejection of mind is the result of opting not for science but for another competing metaphysical thesis, namely what I have called 'metaphysical materialism'. The reason why someone might espouse metaphysical materialism has little or nothing to do with science but with metaphysics, which is why many good scientists believe in G-d and many people who know nothing about science are atheists. Knowledge of science is no more relevant to be-lieving or not believing in G-d than playing baseball. One might say that delving into the wonders of the universe should bring a person closer to G-d, if the teleological argument is valid, though we do not see this actually happening. Quite the contrary; the proportion of baseball players who believe in G-d may well be higher than the proportion of astrophysicists. This may be due to the unpredictability of the game. Baseball players, as is well-known, are very superstitious and grasp at anything for good luck.[8] This does not mean that the study of science should lead you to atheism or that playing baseball should lead you to G-d. Why people do or do not believe in G-d is more complicated or subtle than philosophers or theologians make out. I think it rare that anyone believes or does not believe in G-d because of any philosophical argument. We will go into this question in a later chapter. For the present, we simply say that the claim of the proponents of evolution that the world developed the way it did randomly or by chance and therefore was not guided by any kind of mind is a metaphysical statement and not something that can be demonstrated by the theory or by any other empirical or scientific data. If you want to avoid metaphysics, you should admit that you have nothing to say about the origin of the universe and just describe the evolutionary process that science traces in the world without commenting on whether it took place randomly or otherwise. Whether the process takes place randomly or is guided by some mind is irrelevant to the description of the process *per se*, though it is an interesting question in itself as are most metaphysical questions.

The current debate whether science can show that the world came about by chance or whether the 'creationists' can show that it was created by G-d represents a confusion on both sides of the question. Furthermore, the decision of the court to rule in favor of one side or the other as being more consistent with science simply compounds the confusion. The question is not a scientific question and therefore cannot be answered by science. If a school board or a teacher wants to teach pure science and not get involved in metaphysics, they should say that they know nothing about the origin of the world and get on with describing the world as we see it.

There is a story that illustrates this point. Once during the period of the Spanish Inquisition, a close friend of the king was charged with heresy and condemned to be burnt at the stake. The king interceded on behalf of his friend and the Inquisition—in deference to the king—

---

8 There is the story told about Yogi Berra, the great Yankee catcher, that in a tense World Series game, when the batter crossed himself as he stepped up the plate, Yogi said to him, "How about letting G-d watch this one!"

stayed the execution for a year. The year ended and the king interceded once more, and again the condemned man was given another reprieve for one more year. Finally, the day for the execution arrived and the man was taken out to be burnt at the stake. As they were about to light the faggots, an earthquake occurred. Everyone fled in terror, and the man escaped with his life. He now wants to know whether it was G-d who saved his life by making this 'miracle' happen, or is he just a very lucky man. Let us say the man is genuinely puzzled by the question and is earnestly seeking an answer. How could we help him? Let us suppose for argument's sake that the science of seismology was highly developed in the 16th century to the point that this earthquake could have been predicted. Would that answer the question? That does not explain how it came about that his execution after two delays was scheduled for the precise time and place of the earthquake. Was that an 'accident' or was the hand of G-d behind it?

The answer to the man's question is apparent. If he believes in G-d, he will certainly think this 'miracle' was His handiwork. If he does not believe in G-d, he will simply consider himself lucky. If he is undecided whether there is a G-d, he will *never* be able to come to any conclusion on the matter on the basis of this 'miracle'. If he takes this 'miracle' as evidence that confirms the existence of G-d, he is simply mistaken for the reasons we discussed in the previous chapter. In any event, the *only* explanation of this miracle is that G-d was behind it. To say that it was an accident or a coincidence is to say there is no explanation. It just happened and there is no way that one could have predicted in advance that this 'accident' would happen even if one could have predicted the earthquake. What if the man had been taken out for execution five minutes earlier or a day later?

Similarly, if one believes in G-d one will see in the wonders of nature the incomparable wisdom of G-d. If one does not believe in G-d, one will say the world just happened by accident to turn out the way it did. If, however, one believes that the world came about by chance or accident, that is tantamount to saying that there is *no* explanation for the orderliness and intelligibility of the world. This flies in the face of our rational intuition that there *has* to be an explanation, for our natural inclination is to assume that orderliness *per se* is inseparable from mind and intelligibility as we have argued. This mind, however, need not be the mind of G-d. It could have been some finite, evil, or doodling mind. There might even have been a committee of minds behind the world, which would more than explain its imperfections. That the mind behind the world is that of G-d requires more argumentation than the teleological argument on its own can provide. For this we have to turn to the arguments in the succeeding chapters which attempt to bring out the force of the claims that G-d is a necessary being, that there can be only one G-d, that He created the world from nothing, and that He is good and not evil.

In our next chapter we take up the cosmological argument that G-d is a necessary being. In succeeding chapters we discuss the further questions of His unity, His Creation of the world and His goodness.

4
THE COSMOLOGICAL ARGUMENT

As the teleological argument revolves around the question of the orderliness of the world, so the cosmological argument also revolves around a question, but one that is significantly different. The question this argument poses is, What is the origin or the cause of the existence of the world regardless of its orderliness? It is difficult to state the sense of this question, but one way of putting it is, Why should anything exist? The presupposition of this question is that existence calls for an explanation. There has to be some reason why whatever exists does exist, but we do not feel inclined to ask why something does not exist unless there is some good reason for thinking that it should exist. Thus if UFOs exist there has to be some explanation how they came to exist, for they could not have popped into existence from nothing. However, if UFOs don't exist, no reason is required to explain their non-existence unless there is some good reason for thinking that they should exist. All things being equal non-existence requires no explanation, but existence does. The question then is, what is the explanation of the existence of the world? It is important to note that as in the case of the teleological argument, the question that is posed is a metaphysical one. It is not about the existence of any particular thing like a UFO or even this universe. If some astrophysicist should come up with an explanation for the 'big bang,' assuming that our universe began with a big bang, this would not answer our question, for we could still ask what was the cause of the big bang and so on ad infinitum.[1] The same problem

---

1 Stephen Hawking in his book, *A Brief History of Time*, Bantam Books, 1988, seems to think that if he could describe how our universe came into existence he could explain how G-d created the world. Perhaps, but not necessarily. Maybe there existed a world previous to ours the collapse of which gave rise to this universe and would therefore not explain how G-d created our universe. One would have to know that it was G-d who was the immediate cause of the 'big bang' and not something else. I would like to know how Stephen Hawking knows this.

is posed in the Greek myth that the world rests on the shoulders of
Atlas and Atlas is standing on a giant tortoise. Somewhere along the
line the buck has to stop, but it can only stop at something that is
the cause of itself as Spinoza said and is therefore eternal. What one
means by a 'cause of itself' is not that it brought itself into existence,
which is a contradiction, but that it is dependent on nothing else for
its existence. This has been called 'necessary existence' in philosophical literature and it is eternal.[2] Its eternality, however, is a result of its
necessary existence and this is to be distinguished from the possibility
of something being eternal but not necessary, as in the case of something whose existence *is* dependent on something else even though
it be eternal. Thus if a light emanating from an electric bulb should

---

2 Many philosophers including Russell have found a 'necessary being' to be
   incomprehensible or nonsense. It is indeed incomprehensible in that we do
   not know *how* something could be necessary, but *what* a necessary being
   is seems simple enough. It is simply a being that depends on nothing else
   for its existence. It is absolutely independent of the existence of any other
   thing. It is what satisfies in the highest degree Aristotle's criterion for a
   'substance,' i.e. independent existence or what he called 'separability.' The
   closest Aristotle ever got to this was his *Nous* which he called god. However,
   neither Aristotle's *Nous* nor even G-d are logically necessary for the denial
   of anything's existence, even G-d's, is not a contradiction. Although Anselm
   (1033-1109) tried to argue that G-d's existence *was* logically necessary, I
   believe that his ontological argument that tried to prove this, is mistaken.
   It does not follow from the fact that one can conceive of G-d as the most
   perfect being or as a being greater than which cannot be conceived of, that
   such a being does in fact exist. Although I know of no refutation of this
   argument that is conclusive, I do not, in any event, think the argument
   valid, primarily because if it were, it should follow that the denial of G-d
   should be a contradiction.
       However, this does not appear to me to be a contradiction. Quite the
   contrary, it is possible to imagine nothing existing which is why the existence of anything is an occasion for wonder. This wonder is the origin of
   the cosmological argument. The allaying of this wonder is G-d, not because
   G-d's non-existence is a contradiction, but because, as we shall argue
   subsequently G-d's existence is the most rational answer to the question
   why anything exists.
       (This footnote was inspired by a discussion I had with Rogers Albritton,
   however, it should not be assumed that he would agree with anything I
   have written here.)

be eternal, that would not entail that this light is not dependent on anything else for its existence. It could be eternally dependent upon the electric current passing through the bulb assuming the current and the bulb are eternal. Eternality does not entail necessary existence but necessary existence entails eternality.

Once one sees that necessary existence is the only possible answer to the question where the world came from, the next step is to identify this necessary being. The cosmological argument claims that the only thing this fits is G-d. In fact G-d by definition is a necessary being. The question is, What is a necessary being? What one ordinarily means by G-d in monotheism is primarily a Being that is dependent on nothing else for His existence but everything else depends on Him.[3] This is the definition that Maimonides gave of G-d, and G-d as a necessary Being is contrasted with everything else that is said to exist contingently.[4] The atheist replies that one is not required to answer in this manner, but that one could just as well say that the world itself is a necessary being. The dispute reduces to the question whether G-d is a better choice as the necessary being that explains the world or whether the world itself is a necessary being and thus requires no explanation. There is one thing, however, upon which both the theist and atheist must agree, and that is that only a necessary being can answer the question of the origin of the world. If the cosmological argument achieved nothing else, it would be significant for that alone. In fact I am inclined to think that the *most* significant achievement of this argument is simply that it forces anyone who asks this question to admit the existence of some necessary being. The simple question of the origin of the world, which anyone can understand, contains within itself metaphysical implications such that it requires as an answer a concept or notion that clearly transcends human understanding. No one really knows what a necessary being is except that whatever it is,

3 See Maimonides, *Mishneh Torah*, Book I, chap. 1, para. 1.

4 The father of this argument was probably Aristotle, but he used it with regard to motion. Aristotle did not ask for the cause of the existence of the world, but the cause of its motion. The answer had to be an unmoved mover. Similarly, the cause of the existence of the world has to be an un-caused cause or, as Spinoza said, a cause of itself (*causa sui*). I am indebted to Sir Anthony Kenny for pointing out to me that Spinoza was the first to use this term.

it requires nothing else for its existence. If a hydrogen atom were a necessary being, it would simply be a hydrogen atom that requires nothing else in the world for its existence. Of course, all the hydrogen atoms with which we are conversant are not like this—they all came from other elements and require all kinds of conditions, forces, etc. to remain in existence. Our notion of a necessary being is essentially a negative one. We recognize something as necessary by the fact that it does *not* depend on anything else. We can, therefore, recognize what renders something not necessary, or contingent, by its dependence on something other than itself, but no one can say in virtue of what something *is* necessary.

Given this, some people have argued that it doesn't make very much difference what one says is necessary, G-d or the world. In either case one has only a negative notion what that means. In any event, one has no real understanding of the matter. Indeed to say that the world itself is necessary and therefore eternal is to transform the world into some kind of deity. In any event, the argument does not demonstrate the existence of G-d, unless one means by "G-d," some form of pantheism that identifies G-d with the world. Indeed many Eastern religions seem to be saying something very close to this. However, the notion of G-d as a transcendent being that is familiar to Judaism, Christianity and Islam is not necessarily implied by the cosmological argument, though of course G-d as a transcendent being certainly fits the requirement of being a necessary being. What should be noticed however is that the necessary being required as an explanation of the existence of the world does not entail that this necessary being *created* the world in the sense in which the Hebrew Bible proclaims that "In the beginning, G-d created the heavens and the earth." What it entails is that the world is dependent on G-d for its existence, but this dependency itself, for all we know, might be eternal.

Aristotle had a cosmological view very much like this. His Prime Mover was a necessary being that is the eternal source of all the various 'forms' we find in the world but these forms are co-eternal with the Prime Mover. The forms themselves can be neither created nor destroyed.[5] This is the reason Aristotle says that the species are eternal

---

5 See *Metaphysics* Book VII, ch. 11.

and did not 'evolve' from one another as Empedocles had said.[6] This view of Aristotle is a perfectly valid answer to the cosmological question of the origin of the world, or rather that part of the world that Aristotle called 'forms'. There is, however, another aspect of Aristotle's world that is eternal but *not* dependent on the Prime Mover and that is matter. Thus in the case of Aristotle's famous bronze sphere, both sphericity (the form) and bronze (the matter) are eternal. The form has its origin in the Prime Mover in some way that Aristotle never clearly explains. The matter, however, though eternal, is not dependent on the Prime Mover for its existence and must be said to be a necessary being in its own right. Of course what is eternal in the case of the bronze sphere is not the sphericity of this piece of bronze, but rather sphericity and bronze. At no point was the world ever devoid of spherical-shaped things or bronze. Here we see that Aristotle thought there were two necessary things in the world—what he called Nous or god and something he called matter.

Another ancient example of a metaphysical theory involving more than one necessary existent being is that of atomism. Democritus and, after him, Lucretius, posited an infinite number of indivisible, eternal atoms that 'rain down' from some source and by their 'swerving' they combine with one another to form all the varied things and phenomena of the world. Thus the existence of everything is contingent upon the atoms, but the atoms themselves depend on nothing for their existence. Thus atoms qualify as entities whose existence is necessary and there are an infinite number of them. It would thus seem that the notion of a necessary being is compatible with there being more than one of them—in this case an infinite number.

Aristotle and Democritus are interesting examples of how the cosmological question can be answered without a commitment to creation or even to the existence of only one necessary being, for in Aristotle's cosmology there are two necessary beings, namely, the Prime Mover and matter,[7] while atomism is committed to an infinite number of

6 Aristotle thought the theory of evolution propounded by Empedocles was patently absurd. See *Parts of Animals*, Book I, ch. 1, 640a, 10ff.

7 It is a moot point in Aristotle whether there is any such thing as pure Matter that exists apart from all forms. Regardless of this question, the matter that composes the world taken in its entirety has necessary existence and can never be created or destroyed.

such entities. Therefore, if one means by "G-d" a single unique Being, Creator of the world and everything in it, such that *everything* that exists is dependent on G-d, the cosmological argument alone, does not demonstrate the truth of this notion. That G-d is the one and only necessary being and that nothing else that exists is necessary, requires more than what the cosmological argument, as I am describing it, can deliver. All that we are arguing here is that the only way one can give an explanation of why anything exists is to admit the existence of *something* that exists necessarily.

This is not the same thing as saying that the existence of this thing is *logically* necessary. If I am not mistaken this was the point Anselm was making with his ontological argument. Being *logically* necessary means that the denial of it is a contradiction. Anselm's ontological argument was meant to show that the denial of the existence of G-d involves a contradiction. This is not the place to describe Anselm's ontological argument. I myself cannot say what precisely is wrong with it. I think that most attempts to refute it, including Kant's, fail. Nonetheless I think it false, simply because I think its conclusion that the denial of G-d's existence is a contradiction, is false. Hume was correct in claiming that the existence of nothing is logically necessary. Anything that does exist might conceivably not exist, including G-d. To see this one doesn't have to find out what is wrong with Anselm's argument. One just has to see the conclusion is false. What is to the point is that while one may not be able to prove the existence of G-d, there are a number of good philosophical reasons which renders belief in G-d reasonable and rational.

We argued in chapter three that it is more reasonable to think that there is some mind behind the orderliness of the universe than to suppose that it came about by accident or chance. The point of this chapter is to argue that while everyone must grant that the origin of the universe lies in something whose existence is necessary and eternal, it is more reasonable to suppose that this necessary being is G-d, rather than the universe itself.

If one looks at the vast literature on this question it might appear that there is no clear winner. The discussion as it exists is inconclusive. People take sides in this argument according to some predilection they have about the matter that appears unrelated to the force of the argument. I believe, however, that there is an argument that favours G-d over the world and the remainder of this chapter will be taken up with presenting this argument.

In the first place, what one means by the world or the universe, and I am using these terms synonymously in this context, is not that it is a necessary being. If one should 'discover' that the universe is not necessary, it would not cease to be our universe nonetheless. The necessity of the universe being necessary is not like a that of a bachelor being unmarried. A married bachelor is a contradiction, but a contingent universe is not a contradiction. That is, it is not part of what one means by the universe that its existence be necessary.

On the other hand, being necessary is not something anyone could demonstrate empirically. It is not a fact about the world that science could discover or reveal. The only reason, then, to proclaim that the universe is necessary is that it answers the question, or rather forestalls the question, How did the world come into existence? In other words, it is a purely *ad hoc* answer. It does not relate to anything we know about the world or could know about the world empirically, nor, as we have said, is it what one means by the world. The only thing it does is to answer the question, but the answer doesn't tie up with anything else that we know about the world. It's like someone answering the question, where a person came from by saying that he just dropped from the sky. It is an answer, but it is really not an answer. It doesn't give any information that fits in with anything else one knows about the person, as would the answer, that he just came from playing squash fits in with that person being an avid squash player.

G-d on the other hand is precisely what one means by a necessary being. Anything that is not necessary could not be G-d, and a contingent G-d is as much a contradiction as a married bachelor. It is as if the question of the origin of the world and G-d were tailor-made for one another. Indeed, to proclaim that the world itself is necessary is a way of avoiding the question. This response to the question is perfectly legitimate. It is certainly possible that one can believe that the world itself is necessary. Almost all the ancient philosophers including Plato and Aristotle accepted this view in one form or another. The point we are trying to make here is that this is an odd and unnatural way of dealing with the question. One might sympathize with the Greeks who had no conception of G-d as a necessary being except perhaps Aristotle's Prime Mover, and even that is not clear. Certainly Zeus did not fit this bill. However in our religious tradition, G-d is the necessary being upon whom all other things depend for their existence. It certainly seems as if G-d is a more natural and intuitive answer to the question than to assume that the world itself is necessary. As we said before, it is as if the question itself is rhetorical. Once the question is asked, the answer is evident. The first task is to get yourself into the position of asking the question. This is not easy, for one first has to feel the *wonder* of the existence of anything. We ordinarily take existence for granted. The question, Why should anything exist? sounds silly. What could be more natural than existence? However, upon reflection, one can see that what is most natural is that nothing should exist. This is the reason that existence requires an explanation but non-existence does not. If you can manage to enter the mind-set whereby the existence of anything becomes a wonder and not something to be taken for granted, you are in the position from which the cosmological argument appears forceful. If the existence of the world is something to wonder at, one is not going to be satisfied with the answer that the world itself is a necessary being, for if it were in any way apparent, by definition or by empirical observation, that the world were necessary, one would not wonder at its existence. One can only wonder at the existence of something that might not exist. This is the reason one cannot wonder at the existence of G-d, for G-d by definition is a necessary being. However, this does not entail, as we said earlier, that G-d's existence is logically necessary.

One cannot wonder about the possibility of a necessary being. One knows that *something* necessary must exist because something contingent exists. The question is whether this something is G-d or the world itself. G-d is a more intuitive and rational answer than the world, for it was our wonder about the world itself that led us to the necessity of a necessary being. If it be true that the world itself is necessary, then this aspect of the world is certainly not that aspect of the world that led us to ask the question, Where did the world come from? One might as well call that 'aspect' of the world whereby the world is necessary, 'G-d'. It may be that at this point the dispute becomes one of semantics. What is certain is that our scientific or ordinary conception of the world is not one of a necessary being so that if it is necessary, this necessity is not anything that science or empirical observation could discover. If one insists that the world is a necessary being, one is committing oneself to a property or aspect of the world that is mysterious and lies beyond the ken of human knowledge and it may well be that this is what some people mean by 'G-d'. If so, the two possible answers to the question of the origin of the world, G-d or the world, turn out to be different ways of expressing one answer —namely, a necessary being, whatever that is.

It is clear from this, however, that the necessary being indicated by the cosmological argument is not necessarily unique or one, and furthermore, there is nothing in the cosmological argument *per se* that entails that this necessary being upon which everything else depends, created the world. It is possible, as we mentioned before, that G-d and the world are co-eternal, the world being eternally dependent on G-d. These two points, the uniqueness and oneness of G-d, and G-d as Creator of the world require separate treatments or discussions. In Chapter 5, we take up the question of the uniqueness or oneness of G-d and in Chapter 6, we turn to one of the most difficult topics of this book, namely G-d as Creator. It will be seen that the discussion of G-d as Creator is pivotal to the subsequent discussion of the goodness of G-d and the mystical side of G-d's relation to man and the world.

5
THE ARGUMENT FROM UNITY

In the previous chapter, we argued that one is forced to admit the existence of a necessary being once the question is posed as to the origin of contingent existence. Furthermore, it is more rational to suppose that this necessary being is to be identified with G-d rather than with the world itself. However, it remains to be argued that this necessary being we call G-d is one and not more than one, to say nothing of an infinite number of such beings. To do this, we must pursue our discussion of rationality further than we have done so far.

As we mentioned in Chapter 1, the notion of empirical confirmation is an important element in our concept of rationality. We discussed in Chapter 2 the need for accepting certain *a priori* principles or beliefs about the nature of reality that might be termed 'rational intuitions'. In this chapter, I would like to try and point out that there is something more fundamental to the notion of rationality than either empirical confirmation or *a priori* beliefs about the world and this has to do with the concept of understanding *per se*. What makes anything intelligible is that it displays, expresses or evidences some kind of unity. Let me give some examples.

Take a typical case of a Sherlock Holmes mystery. Holmes is able to identify the murderer because he has a remarkable ability to put things together that would escape the notice of most people. The tell-tale clues are woven together to form a consistent story. It all 'hangs together'. In other words, a unity is found to hold between a lot of facts that appear disconnected. This explains how Holmes is able to solve the crime. The criminal, of course, confesses but Holmes knew for certain who was guilty simply on the basis of the power or unity of the explanation he had found connecting all the clues together. At least this is how a Sherlock Holmes story goes and we find them pretty convincing.

Even in science, unity or explanatory power sometimes counts as a sufficient condition of rational acceptance. When Einstein was informed in 1919 of the observations made during the eclipse of the sun confirming his general theory of relativity, he said nonchalantly that he didn't expect anything else. He knew his theory had to be true independent of any observations solely on the basis of its scope, power, beauty, and above all, the unity that it brought to bear on the physical phenomena of his day. Of course empirical confirmation through successful prediction is necessary, but this is not why Einstein was convinced that his theory was true.

What these examples from Sherlock Holmes and Einstein have in common is that while empirical confirmation is necessary to establish truth, it played little or no role in convincing either of these 'men' that they had hold of the truth and that it was not only rational for them to believe that they had the truth but they were absolutely certain that they were right. They might have been proven wrong but they thought they were entitled to believe they were right and the reason for this had nothing to do with verification but with the nature of the explanation itself. That is, it brought all the relevant facts together in a way that gave them unity. In the philosophy of science they call this element of explanation 'simplicity'. The best explanation or the one that is most rational to believe is the one that is the 'simplest'. This does not mean it is the easiest to understand or the most obvious explanation. Quite the contrary, often the simplest explanation is the most difficult to discover and requires a sophistication of understanding that goes beyond the superficial. Thus Sherlock Holmes' solution to the crime was not obvious to the police, Dr. Watson, or anyone else who knew about the case. Holmes' revelation of the guilty party came as a surprise to everyone, but once Holmes explained the reasoning that led him to his conclusion, it became obvious who was really guilty and the only thing remaining was the man's confession or attempt to escape but this is incidental to the story. The story is virtually over when Holmes presents the reasoning whereby he was led to the true criminal. It is obvious and brings all the facts together in a way that leaves no doubt about the matter. The reason Holmes' explanation is so convincing is that it is the simplest possible one. That is, it is the only explanation that combines the relevant facts into a single, unitary explanation. It has power for it can explain more facts in the case than any other theory and it has beauty because it moulds a number of diverse elements into a single explanatory scheme. The more diverse and apparently incompatible the elements, the greater the beauty of an explanation that can in some surprising way mould these elements together to form a whole. Beauty in the arts is very close to this notion of beauty in a scientific or mathematical theory, for an important element in this beauty is the unity of a work of art and the more diverse elements the work can wield together in some surprising way, the greater the beauty. This notion of unity and beauty thus described are the main ingredients that compose what is called 'simplicity' in theory construction.

So far as I know there is no argument that can demonstrate or prove that it is more rational to accept the simplest explanation of a number of diverse phenomena, all other things being equal, but it certainly has a strong intuitive appeal. It may be that part of what we mean by a rational explanation, is that it is the simplest in the sense that it displays the greatest unity and beauty as we have described this.

There is no doubt that this was behind Einstein's conviction that his general theory of relativity was true before he had any empirical confirmation. If it weren't true, then G-d simply must have made a mistake in forming the world. This is not arrogance but the conviction of a man who has seen the connection or unity of physical phenomena more deeply and more profoundly than anyone had ever seen before. If Newtonian mechanics were the last word in physics, then G-d would have missed an opportunity of making the world more profound, sublime and beautiful than He might have made it.

The seeing of unity in the midst of complexity is the key to under-standing generally. This is the dawning of the 'light,' the feeling of 'eureka,' the flood of understanding that comes when we are wrestling with the solution of some problem. We suddenly see a connection between things—an idea brings them together. We speak in the sin-gular here. We say 'Now I see *it*,' 'I have *the* solution,' 'I understand *it*'. We don't say 'Now I see *them*,' 'I have the solution*s*,' 'I understand *them*.' This is not just a matter of grammar. It expresses the idea that when one understands something, it is a unity—a connection—that one understands and though the elements connected be multifarious and diverse, the idea that connects them is single. One gets *the idea* for a novel, a painting, a play, a song or melody. In all these cases it is the unity that makes it what it is. The book can contain thousands of words, many plots, sub plots, characters, etc., but there must be a unity. All these elements must fit together to form a *single* whole or harmony. Otherwise the novel is a bad one or not a novel at all, but disconnected events. The same applies in all instances of art and communication. It is the unity of an idea, a story, a symphony that gives it its power and beauty. In science and conceptual understanding generally, this unity plays a crucial and central role in drawing the mind to assent. This 'drawing' or attraction of mind we call rationality and the fact that the mind is drawn towards unity and beauty as we have described it, simply expresses the idea that rationality and unity of understanding are internally related. That is, the pursuit of unity is part of the what we mean by rationality.

That this is so, is indicated by the fact that not everything that attracts assent is called rational. Our minds can be moved to accept as true, explanations or theories that are popular or which cater to our needs in some way. One might want to believe the truth of a theory because one has been awarded a large grant to do research on it. Not every inclination of the mind to accept as true some explanation or theory is rational. We mean to restrict rationality to the assent of the mind as it pursues understanding for its own sake or truth, apart from 'ulterior' considerations. I am suggesting that this pursuit of understanding is nothing else than the pursuit of unity in the midst of diversity and that this is part of the meaning of rationality. It is only part of rationality, for not every explanation that displays unity or beauty is true. However, it is certainly rational to believe that of competing theories, the simplest will prove true.

The thesis I would now like to argue for is that G-d is the simplest explanation of the world. This does not mean that one understands how G-d made the world. One would have to be G-d to understand this. It means that of the various possible explanations of the world or why anything exists rather than nothing, G-d is the simplest. Keep in mind that 'simplest' here does not mean easiest to understand or something superficial. On the contrary, as we have said earlier, the simplest explanation is one that has the greatest unity and which weaves the most diverse and apparently incompatible elements into a single harmony.

What G-d brings to the world is a unity and a harmony that all other explanations lack. This in itself does not prove that G-d exists but that of competing, metaphysical views about the origin and existence of the world G-d is the most rational because He is the 'simplest' explanation. It really makes no difference what alternative metaphysical view one might have about the nature of reality. Any view other than G-d will lack the simplicity of G-d. The reason for this is that any other metaphysical view leaves open the possibility that there are worlds other than the one described by the particular metaphysical view in question. For example, in the case of metaphysical materialism, which was mentioned previously as an alternative explanation of the world, there is nothing that precludes the possibility that there might be some other world in existence separate and distinct from the one we inhabit. It might even be another material world of which we have no knowledge. The point is that metaphysical materialism entails only that the world which is continuous and one with our world contains only material matter and forces. In other words, metaphysical materialism entails that the world in which we live and do science contains only material matter and forces, but this in no way excludes the possibility of worlds of which we are completely ignorant that may contain whatever you please. Of course there is no evidence for the existence of such worlds, but that is not the point. The point is that metaphysical materialism in itself does not exclude their possible existence. If one wonders why we call such a view 'metaphysical,' the answer is that the claim that everything in our world is material and that there are no non-material things or powers is not one that could be confirmed or proven by empirical evidence and so is taken as true *a priori*. If one is not prone to metaphysical materialism, one might adopt some other metaphysical view about the nature of our world such as Aristotle's, for example. However, as long as it is not centered in the notion of G-d, there is nothing in that view that excludes the possibility of other separate and distinct worlds. What I mean by 'separate and distinct' worlds, is not that there may be other systems of existence which we know nothing of now but which we might some day come to know, but that there are systems of existence about which it will never be possible for us to know anything. For the only way we could know something about some other world would be if that other world shares something in common with ours. However, if it shares something in common with ours it is not entirely separate and distinct and our rational intuition would continually seek a way of merging these apparently distinct worlds into one.

A good example of this is the attempt of contemporary physicists to find a unified field theory that would unite relativity theory and quantum theory. We have here two distinct systems of explaining physical phenomena that belong to one world, for everyone believes that the 'world' of sub-atomic particles and the 'world' of large size objects are really one world and not two. There may be no evidence for any connection, but this is irrelevant to the thrust of our natural inclination to seek unity. It would certainly become a more rational world if we could find such a connection. If one cannot be found, we will just have to reconcile ourselves to a world that is not as rational as we would like to see it. As Einstein is reported to have said, there is no reason for thinking G-d made a messy world if He could have made a neat one. This drive towards unity is directed not only at the unity of the world we live in, but at all of reality. That is, that there really is only one world and though we may never understand it completely and its unity may constantly elude us, we nevertheless are committed to pursuing it. If we were to be told by some angel that there was a unified field theory but that we would have to work very hard to achieve it, it would be irrational for us to be content with what we have, even though there might not be any profitable or important technical uses of this new-found knowledge. It was no doubt this rational urge for unity that moved Einstein to seek a unified field theory in the 1930's even though there was no evidence for such a theory and many of his colleagues ridiculed his attempt to find one.

For the same reason that it is rational to pursue unity or simplicity in our understanding of this world, it is rational to pursue unity period. That is, not only is it rational to suppose that the world we live in is unified but the world we live in is the *only* world there is, i.e. there are no unknown worlds that are separate and distinct. If there were, reality would not be one and simple. It would be messy and complex. The only metaphysical view of reality that ensures this simplicity is G-d. Any other view is subject to the possibility of messiness and complexity. This is why G-d is the simplest explanation of the world.

One might ask why G-d ensures this simplicity. Perhaps there are worlds apart from G-d? The answer is that G-d includes everything there is, for G-d by definition being absolutely infinite includes everything that exists, so that nothing can exist outside G-d. If there were any such thing, G-d's existence would be limited which is a contradiction. G-d is the only notion that unifies all of reality so that by definition there could not exist worlds apart from G-d. The meaning of the term 'G-d' entails the unification of all being. There is no other notion that does this other than G-d. The term 'reality' or 'being' used in philosophical contexts does not imply that all reality or all being constitutes a single unified world.

The fact is that every philosopher that has ever promulgated a metaphysical view about the nature of reality has maintained that his view constituted the whole of reality. This is a reflection of our rational pursuit of unity but it is ordinarily not justified by the metaphysical view held by that philosopher.

A good example of this is Aristotle. The world or 'heaven' as Aristotle calls it consists of finite space that contains a finite amount of the five basic elements that move in a natural motion. Some move up, others down, and still others in a circle (*De Caelo I*, chapter two). Aristotle argues that this 'heaven' or world is one, unique and complete (*De Caelo* 279a 12), and that there is no body outside of the heaven (278b 25). His argument for this in *De Caelo I*, chapters eight and nine is not very persuasive. It is based on the assumption that the elements of any other world would be composed of the same basic elements as this world, i.e. air, fire, earth, and water plus aether as the fifth element. The natural motions of air and fire are straight up, that of water and earth are straight down and the natural motion of the aether is circular (See *De Caelo I*, chapters two and three). What moves in a circle cannot change its position, so the aether of this world which moves in a circle cannot shift to encircle some other world and since the natural motion of the four elements are straight up or straight down in this world, they could not so move naturally in some other world since their natural motion is straight up or down in this world. One might ask, however, why is it necessary that the elements of some other world be the same as this world? The truth is that Aristotle has no persuasive argument for his view that there is only one world. The only reason

Aristotle is so insistent upon the oneness and uniqueness of the world is that the rationality of the human mind finds the idea irresistible.

The same question can be raised about the oneness and uniqueness of the Prime Mover which is what Aristotle means by god. The Prime Mover is the source of the eternal motion of the world though it itself is unmoved and not part of the world. It is a wholly immaterial being which Aristotle calls *Nous* or Intellect. (See *Metaphysics* Book 12, chapter seven). Aristotle insists there can only be one such *Nous* and his argument here is a bit more persuasive than his argument for the oneness and uniqueness of the world, but even here it is not entirely convincing.

It goes as follows: A single definition of man is one definition though it may apply to many different men. What makes men different, however, is not their definition but the matter that composes them. The Prime Mover, however, contains no matter and so there can be only one Prime Mover per definition much as there can be only one class of all men (*Metaphysics* Book XII, 1074a 30-35).

I do not find this argument convincing as the Prime Mover is a particular and not a class or universal, so the argument is not valid. True, there is only one definition of a Prime Mover, but if we think of the Prime Mover as a particular non-material living being whose only function is pure intellect (*Nous*), the question arises why there cannot be a number of such Intellects? If one asks how would one distinguish such Intellects from one another, the answer would be whatever determines the Prime Mover to be a particular in the first place. In other words, if there is no matter in the Prime Mover, there must be *something* that renders the Prime Mover a particular other than matter and this is what renders the Prime Mover a "living being, eternal and most good" (*Metaphysics* 1072b 27). The connection of the Prime Mover with the world is simply that it is the source of all motion in the world. Thus the Prime Mover and the world form a 'closed' system that defines the reality of all being. Aristotle is insistent that there can be only one such system, but I do not find anywhere in his writings a convincing argument for this. There is nothing in Aristotle's account, so far as I can see, that precludes the possibility of a number of Prime Movers each being the source of the eternal motion of a different, finite world. Nonetheless, Aristotle denies this possibility as well as the possibility that our world itself might be governed by principles or substances that have no connection with one another (*Metaphysics* 1076a 1-5). The desire for unity permeates the whole structure of Aristotle's entire philosophy and it is certainly fitting for Aristotle to quote Homer at the end of *Metaphysics XII* as a concluding line to his philosophy, "the rule of many is not good: let there be one ruler" (*Metaphysics* 1076a 5).

My point is that this pursuit of unity is the central thrust of the rational mind, and one can well sympathize with such a goal. However, G-d is the only concept or idea that mandates this goal. G-d by definition is the only ground for the unity of all being, by right of the fact that G-d is the only Being whose existence precludes the possibility of anything existing independently of Him.

What has been said here regarding Aristotle can be applied to almost all other metaphysical systems. Philosophers throughout history have supposed that their metaphysical system constituted the whole realm of existence and that the main purpose of the system was to show how everything that exists forms a unity. These systems attain this unity with varying degrees of success. I am inclined to think Aristotle's system achieves this better than most. However, without exception, all these philosophers take for granted that their system constitutes the totality of all being. This assumption is generated by what I have called the rational pursuit of unity but in most cases it is unwarranted.

Spinoza is the only philosopher who seems to have been clearly aware that the unity of all being depends on the notion of G-d. There certainly have been many theological views of reality—be they Jewish, Christian, or Moslem—that are centered in G-d, and these views certainly assume that their metaphysical view encompasses all of reality, but they do not seem to realize that G-d alone justifies such a position. To my knowledge, Spinoza is the first philosopher to have enunciated such a view in clear, unmistakable language. The notion of independent and eternal existence is conveyed by the notion of substance in Spinoza. This is the necessary existent being of Chapter 4 that is required by the cosmological argument as the explanation of contingent existence. Most propounders of this argument have identified this substance with G-d, but for Spinoza this is a mistake, for the notion of substance itself does not entail that there can be only one substance. There might be many necessary beings distinct from one another constituting different worlds that have nothing in common. Spinoza argued in *The Ethics* (Part I, Proposition 5) that two substances can have nothing in common and entertains (temporarily) the possibility of two substances that have nothing in common (Part I, Proposition 2). Of course, if there could be two substances having nothing in common, there is nothing to prevent the existence of an infinite number of substances having nothing in common. Spinoza, however, rejects this possibility by introducing G-d in Proposition 11, who by definition contains all of reality, or in the technical vocabulary of *The Ethics*, G-d consists "… of infinite attributes, each of which expresses eternal and infinite essence." This is what Spinoza means by calling G-d an "*absolutely* infinite being" which distinguishes G-d from something that is merely infinite like the infinite series of finite modes of extension or the infinite series of integers. In other words, nothing can exist outside of G-d, so G-d by definition unifies all reality into a single substance, and is thus absolutely infinite. If one examines Spinoza's arguments for this in the three proofs and the scholium of Proposition 11, one will, I think, not be impressed by them. They appear singularly circular, and indeed they are, for Spinoza's definition of G-d is nothing more nor less than a being that unifies in itself all of reality. Spinoza is simply articulating the notion of G-d as the unity of all things and he is perceptive enough to see that the notion of substance as a necessary being does not achieve this by itself. Thus, the cosmological argument discussed in the previous chapter may demonstrate the requirement that *something* be necessary before anything can be contingent, but it does not limit the number of necessary beings that might exist. Only G-d can do this by limiting everything to one thing, namely Himself. Thus, the desire of the rational mind for ultimate unity is satisfied only by G-d, and therefore G-d is the simplest explanation for everything. G-d is not just one, He is everything that is or could be, for nothing can exist outside of Him. He is, in other words, absolutely infinite.

If we go back now and collect the various attributes of G-d as we have scattered them about over the last three chapters, we conclude that G-d is a knowing being that exists of necessity and is eternal and that He unifies within Himself all being, so that it is a contradiction to suppose that anything could exist independently of Him. Though we have not 'proved' these attributes true of G-d, we think that good reasons have been given why one should accept them.

Remember, however, that though we argued that the teleological argument does not argue for the existence of a single, infinite mind but rather, some mind even though finite; and the cosmological argument per se does not argue for a single, infinite necessary being, just something whose existence is necessary. It follows, nonetheless, from our argument from simplicity and unity, that just as it is rational to assume that G-d is single and absolutely infinite whose existence encompasses everything that exists, then His other attributes must be similarly single and infinite in their own right. That is, G-d's knowledge must also be complete and infinite. There cannot be something His mind does not know. Similarly, just as we argued in our discussion of the cosmological argument that there must be *something* that exists necessarily in order for anything to exist contingently, so the argument from unity demands that there can be only one such necessary Being whose existence encompasses all of existence.

Thus as we stand at the end of our deliberations of what rationally can be said about G-d, we conclude that He should be absolutely infinite. That is, there can be only one necessary Being whose existence includes the existence of all other things for nothing can exist apart from Him.[1] Furthermore His knowledge must also be complete and there can be nothing He does not know. He is thus omnipotent and omniscient. This description of His attributes does not follow from any single argument from three different ones, namely the ones contained in chapters 3, 4, and 5 of this Book. Given this argument, we conclude that the existence of G-d in traditional monotheism is the most rational conception of G-d that one can have.

However, this is not the end of G-d. In fact, one might say that we have hardly begun to describe what is most important and fundamental as far as the role that G-d plays in the life of man. For in our description of G-d so far, G-d is not yet the benevolent and good Creator of the world who brought the world and man into being for some

---

1 This is precisely the point Spinoza is making in his *Ethics*, Book I, when he argues that there can exist only one substance which is nothing other than G-d, a substance that is constituted from an infinite number of attributes. See particularly Propositions 7-9.

Divine purpose. It is this notion of G-d that renders G-d existentially important for man, and is the power and staying force of G-d in the life of man. The central idea in this conception of G-d is the notion of G-d as Creator, which has not yet been discussed and is a most difficult aspect of G-d to come to grips with. It was precisely this aspect of G-d that Spinoza rejected and for which he was excommunicated by the Jewish community of Amsterdam.

It is interesting to note that Maimonides in his *Guide for the Perplexed* thought he could demonstrate the necessary existence of G-d, but did not think he could demonstrate that G-d Created the world.[2] Nonetheless, G-d's Creation of the world is a fundamental belief in Judaism, as well as in Christianity and Islam. Furthermore it is the conception of G-d as Creator which is the origin of what Judaism takes to be the mystical side of G-d's relationship with man. We turn then to Part II of this book in which we discuss Creation and mysticism as this is conceived of in Judaism. In particular, our attention will focus on ideas and doctrines found in the literature of Jewish mysticism generally and particularly in the writings of Chabad Hasidic literature. We therefore begin the second part of this book with a discussion of Creation.

---

2 See his *Guide for the Perplexed*, Part II, chapter XIII—XXV, particularly chapter XXV.

PART II: G-D AND MYSTICISM

6

CREATION

Creation is a Jewish idea. Before the Hebrew Bible, the notion of Creation was unknown to human civilization. If one reads the myths of ancient cultures be they Chinese, Indian, Egyptian, Babylonian, Assyrian or Greek, one will not find the notion of a purely spiritual power that created the world from nothing. In these myths, the world evolved from night, darkness, mother earth, the infinite or some other vague source. However the notion that the world was created from absolutely nothing is not to be found in any of these so-called 'creation myths.' As a matter of fact, there is no word in the Greek language that can properly be translated as "creation."[1]

Furthermore, the idea is foreign to all the ancient philosophers. Plato's Demiurge and Aristotle's Prime Mover did not create the world but simply fashioned the disorderly motions into the regularity of the world as we know it (Plato) or was the source of the forms that compose the substances of the world (Aristotle). All the Pre-Socratic philosophers thought of the world as eternal and coming from atoms or other elements that were eternal. It is safe to say that before the advent of Judaism, Creation was unheard of.[2] Furthermore, the familiarity of

---

1 In the *Septuagint*, the Greek translation of the Hebrew Bible, the first sentence reads, "*En arxei epoisen ho Theos ton houranon kai tain gain.*" The English translation of the *Septuagint*, published in England in 1794, translates this sentence correctly as "In the beginning G-d *made* the heaven and the earth." The Greek verb *epoisen* generally means to produce something. It in no way carries the meaning of Creation as this is understood in the Hebrew Bible, nor does any other Greek word in classical Greek literature that was written before the influence of the Hebrew Bible.

2 This is true as far as we know from the written records of the times. In Jewish tradition, however, this idea was disseminated by Abraham after the notion had been forgotten by the descendants of Adam. According to *The Bible*, Adam certainly knew that G-d created the world and presumably

the Western world with the idea that G-d created the world does not exist in any of the Eastern religions. The origin of this idea among Jews, Christians and Moslems is of course the first sentence of *The Hebrew Bible*, "In the beginning G-d created the heaven and the earth." The question I would like to address is, what arguments can be brought to support Creation other than belief in the Divine revelation of *The Hebrew Bible*? This is a tall order, for it is acknowledged that Creation transcends human comprehension, so it seems almost contradictory to propose an argument to support a notion that defies understanding.

In particular, the notion of the Creation of a finite world is inconsistent with that of G-d as an absolutely infinite Being as follows: Either the created world is part of an absolutely infinite Being or it is not. If it is part of such a Being, then something has been added to it which is impossible for nothing can be added to an absolutely infinite Being. On the other hand, if the created world is not part of the absolutely infinite Being, then such a Being is limited in that there is something it does not contain, which is also impossible. Therefore, the creation of anything is inconsistent with the existence of an absolutely infinite Being.

In spite of all this, there is an argument that has some force in supporting the fact of Creation if not its intelligibility. This argument is like arguments for the fact of free will, in that while everyone believes they have free will and is prepared to argue for this, no one, so far as I know, has ever explained how free will is possible. There are numerous facts about the world that are inexplicable, the most significant being the origin of the world itself. The argument I present here does not attempt to explain Creation, but rather to argue that the fact of Creation does have rational support.

It is important to note that this argument does not purport to argue for the *existence* of G-d *per se*, as do most arguments for Creation. Rather the argument builds on arguments we have presented in ear-

---

passed this information on to his children, which explained the absence of grandparents on either his or Eve's side. Maimonides in his *Mishneh Torah*, explains that in the days of Enosh, Adam's grandson, people began to worship the heavenly bodies and other powers as aids of G-d that were involved in the workings of the world. After a while G-d as Creator of heaven and earth dropped out of the picture altogether. (See the "Laws of Idol Worship," chapter 1.)

lier chapters. In Chapter 3 we argued for the existence of a knowing
Being and in Chapter 4 we argued for the existence of a necessary
Being, but neither of these arguments implies that this Being Created the world.[3] The argument presented here claims to be different
from all other arguments for Creation in that it discusses the notion
of Creation *apart from* arguments purporting to demonstrate the
existence of G-d. Assuming that it is rational to suppose that there
is some necessary, knowing Being who is one and absolutely infinite
on the basis of our arguments in Chapters 3, 4, and 5, the argument
we propose here is that it is also rational to suppose that this Being

---

3 See the Guide for the Perplexed, Part II, Chapters 21-25, in which Maimonides argues that G-d's necessary existence can be demonstrated, but
not His Creation of the world. In this Maimonides disagrees with Saadiah
Gaon who argues in *The Book of Beliefs and Opinions*, Treatise I, Chapters
1 and 2, that one can demonstrate beyond a shadow of doubt that G-d
created the world. I do not find the arguments of Saadiah Gaon convincing
and side with Maimonides on this issue. I think it would be out of place
to go into this matter at length here. In short, however, my own reasons
for thinking that neither the cosmological argument nor the teleological
argument can be used to demonstrate that G-d created the world are as
follows:

The cosmological argument, as Maimonides presents it (correctly in my
opinion), simply demonstrates that the contingent existence of the world
could not exist unless there were some Being whose existence is necessary
upon which the existence of the world depends. This dependency is not
the same thing as Creation. That the world depends upon G-d constantly
for its existence does not entail that there was a 'time' when the world
did not exist. Perhaps the necessary Being of G-d and the dependent,
contingent world are co-eternal? Saadiah, in his argument, does not even
discuss the necessary Being of G-d. Furthermore his arguments based on
the impossibility of the world being infinite are questionable. As far as
the teleological argument is concerned, the fact that the orderliness of the
world implies the existence of a mind behind that orderliness again does
not entail that that mind created that orderliness. It could be, as Aristotle
said, that the orderliness of the world is an eternal spin-off of G-d's mind
and though the mind of G-d is the source of that orderliness there was
never a time when that orderliness did not exist. Furthermore, the existence of orderliness in the world does not entail that there was only one
mind behind the world. Perhaps there was a 'committee,' which would
explain some of the world's imperfections. These points have already been
elaborated on in Chapters 3 and 4.

created the world. So far as I know, this argument does not yet have a name, so for purposes of convenience I hereby dub this argument, "The Argument from Finitude." The remainder of this chapter will attempt to expound this argument.

THE ARGUMENT FROM FINITUDE

It is a *sina quo non* of monotheism that G-d is absolutely infinite. That is, there are no limitations to His Being or power or any other characteristics whereby G-d is described. I simply take it as a given that G-d is a Being with no limitations.[4] The creation of a finite world by an infinite Being appears to involve a contradiction called in formal logic a "destructive dilemma" in which either horn of the dilemma involves a contradiction. Namely, if the finite world is part of G-d, something has been added to an absolutely infinite Being which is impossible, and if the finite created world is not part of G-d, then such a Being is limited, which again is impossible. Given this dilemma, the question is, how can the fact of Creation be rendered not only intelligible but also rational?

This question is different from the one that was the origin of the cosmological argument. There the question was: Given the possibility that nothing might exist, Why should anything exist? Here the question is: Given the fact that an absolutely infinite Being exists, how could anything finite exist? Even though the world as we know it might be eternal, as indeed the Greeks thought, this does not gainsay the indisputable fact that it contains finite individual things such as the reader and the author of this book, to name two. How did these finite things come to be? If an infinite Being composes all of reality it would seem inconsistent with His existence that anything finite could exist. The Greeks were not faced with this problem as their idea of

---

4 The most persuasive argument for this is the ontological argument. Though it is questionable whether this argument demonstrates the existence of an absolutely infinite Being we call G-d, as it claims to do, nonetheless what the argument does succeed in doing is to get us to see that in the monotheistic tradition what we mean by G-d is a Being greater than which cannot be conceived of. Anything less than that is not what we mean by 'G-d.' Such a Being by definition would have to be absolutely infinite, otherwise a Being greater than it *could* be conceived of, namely one that was absolutely infinite.

the origin of the world included neither the notion of an *absolutely infinite Being* nor that of a Creator.[5] Most philosophers when they speak of G-d do not think of Him as an absolutely infinite Being, but limited in some form or other. Almost all philosophers think of G-d as being limited at least by what is logically possible. That is, G-d could not have made a logically impossible world. Since what is logically possible is determined by human intellect, G-d is limited to what the human mind can understand.[6] Spinoza is the only philosopher to conceive of G-d as an absolutely infinite Being. Spinoza, however, rejected the notion of Creation and therefore had no way of 'explaining' the existence of the finite world, which in the terminology of his philosophy translates into his inability of explaining the existence of 'finite modes.' This is the greatest weakness of Spinoza's philosophy.

This brings us to the crux of our argument. If one accepts the notion of G-d as an absolutely infinite Being, the existence of a finite world becomes inexplicable. However, there are forceful arguments that lead us to accept G-d as a knowing, necessary Being who is absolutely infinite. On the other hand, it is undeniable that finite things exist. The only way of reconciling these two inconsistent facts is to ascribe the existence of the finite world to an act of G-d's inscrutable will that transcends human understanding. This is exactly what Creation is. That is, G-d brought into existence, in a manner we know not how, the finite world in which we live. The only way of avoiding this conclusion is to maintain that G-d is not absolutely infinite or that finite objects and things do not exist. It is possible to reject either horn of

---

5 For example, in the *Timaeus*, Plato's Demiurge in the formation of the world of Becoming was limited by the 'disorderly motions' or the materiality of the Receptacle which exists independently of the Demiurge. Aristotle's Nous was also limited by matter which co-existed eternally with Nous as the source of the materiality of all finite substances.

6 Thus Leibnitz argued that when G-d created the world, the type of world he created was limited to the number of logically possible worlds. Even if the *number* of logically possible worlds be infinite, G-d is still limited to what the human mind can comprehend. Spinoza, to my knowledge, is the only major figure in the history of philosophy to argue that G-d in His essence transcends human understanding, for G-d consists of an infinite number of attributes of which only two can be grasped by human reason, i.e., extension and thought.

this dilemma, but the argument from finitude is that: 1) it is more rational to accept G-d as a Being that is absolutely infinite than not, and 2) it is obvious that finite things exist, 3) therefore, it is rational to accept G-d's Creation of the world as an inscrutable act of His will. This implies that Creation was a conscious act of G-d and not a natural emanation or effect of His of which He may have been unaware, as Aristotle's *Nous* is unaware of the world of sub-lunar substances that have been formed as a natural consequence of *Nous* upon matter. Thus the world was intentionally created by G-d implying that there was a reason for the Creation and that the world is not some unconscious 'doodle.' Given the fact of Creation as we have expounded it here, namely that it was an inscrutable act of G-d's will, it follows that it is rational to assume that G-d created the world for a purpose, just as it is perfectly rational to assume that if a person is working hard at something, there is some reason or purpose why he is working so hard, in contrast with someone taking a leisurely stroll down the street. Why G-d would have wanted to create the world is another question. All that we are arguing here is that G-d had to go 'out of his way,' so to speak, in order to do so. In other words, the world of finite events and things cannot be part of G-d's essence, since G-d's essence is absolutely infinite and nothing can be part of this essence without itself being infinite. There is no room in G-d's infinite Being for anything finite. How then can our understanding come to grips with the existence of a finite world? The only possible answer is Creation and this act of Creation requires that G-d had to remove in some way his infinite essence or constrict it to make room for finitude. This 'constriction' is referred to in the language of Kabbalah as *tzimtzum*. This idea had its origin in the teachings of Isaac Luria, (1534-1572) a 16th century mystic who is the father of what we call today 'Kabbalah.' There are various interpretations of the notion of *tzimtzum*, but the one we follow here is the one expounded in the literature of *Chabad* philosophy.[7]

---

7 An outline of the various ways of interpreting the 'tzimtzum' notion of
   Isaac Luria is traced in a letter written by the Lubavitcher Rebbe Mena-
   cham Mendel, of blessed memory, written in 1939 from Paris to Rabbi
   Yerachmiel Benjaminson in America. The basic bone of contention among
   students of Kabbalah after Isaac Luria was whether the notion of constriction (*tzimtzum*) was to be taken literally as applying to G-d's very Being
   or only to the light emanating from G-d. Generally the view of Chabad

This literature goes into the matter at great length, but I shall present only some of the salient features of this view.

There are two ways of understanding the relationship between G-d and the world. One way is called 'The Higher Understanding' and the other way is called 'The Lower Understanding.'[8] This is roughly equivalent to the way G-d understands His relationship with the world and the way man understands the relationship of the world with G-d. In the Higher Understanding, G-d is reality and the world is unreality. In the Lower Understanding, the world is reality and G-d is unreality.[9] 'Reality' and 'unreality' here are epistemological terms that are an index of a kind of understanding. That is, in the Higher Understanding, G-d does not see the world as really existing for the finite world cannot exist side-by-side with G-d. In order to create the world G-d had to bring forth a situation that would give the appearance to man of a finite world that exists independently of G-d. In truth, however, such a world is unreal as far as G-d Himself is concerned. Let us try to give an analogy that might help to explain this idea.

Imagine that by dreaming one could create entities that have an existence in their own right. This, of course, is unlike real dreams where the so-called 'dream entities' have no reality of their own. Let us imagine for the moment that our dreams *do* have genuine creative power that can bring into existence entities that have a reality of their own that could include real people and things, and that these entities cease to exist when we wake up. As far as *we* know such dream worlds might indeed be created by our dreams and destroyed by our wakings in a manner such that we have no awareness of them, other than the fact that we dreamt them. Thus if you dream about a snake pit writhing with snakes, the snake pit would have a reality of its own that is dependent for its existence upon your dreaming them. You

on this matter is that 'constriction' is not to be taken literally, and that G-d's infinite Being by definition cannot be constricted or removed to make room for the world. In other words, the essence of G-d's infinite Being permeates every particle of the finite world. This is the essence of mysticism in Judaism.

8 In the Hebrew terminology of Chabad philosophy, this is called *daath elyon* and *daath tachton*.

9 There is some resemblance here with Parmenides 'Way of Truth' and 'Way of Appearance.'

never meet these snakes in real life. You know when you wake up that the snakes do not really exist, and whatever existence the dream snakes had, ceases when you wake up. Nonetheless, let us suppose that your dreaming brings into existence, temporarily, dream snakes that have a life and reality of their own which as far as the snakes are concerned is totally unconnected with your dreaming. In other words, the snakes writhing in this pit are unaware that their existence depends on your dreaming them and that they will cease to exist when you wake up from your sleep. How could one possibly explain to the snakes their true situation in a way that they could understand? Even if the snakes had a human intelligence as the original snake that led Adam and Eve astray is purported to have had, how could they understand that they will cease to exist when you wake up from your sleep. Wouldn't the snakes say that this is utterly preposterous and that there is absolutely no empirical evidence for this wild idea? That is, there is no evidence that there is some mysterious sleeper whose nightmare is keeping the snakes in existence. Imagine now that the snakes created by your dream are just ordinary snakes with a snake's understanding, whatever that is. Think how far removed that snake's understanding is from the truth, i.e., that its very existence depends upon a human being having a nightmare. Multiply this 'distance' by infinity and you will get an idea how far we are from understanding G-d's Creation of the world! The difference is that the snakes have a conception neither of a human being nor of a dream, whereas we do have some conception of G-d and what it means for G-d to have created the world. We do not mean to imply that G-d's Creation of the world is to be compared with someone having a dream in every respect. For one thing, G-d's Creation of the world, as we argued before, had to have been an act of His free will as it could not be part of His Essence, nor could it have emanated from his Essence. Dreams however are not acts of will. They generally are understood as having causes rooted in the psyche that is not subject to free will. If you understand what a human being is, you can understand what having a dream is and that dreams are not volitional. You cannot say this about G-d. That is, you cannot say that if you could understand the nature or essence of G-d, you would then understand that G-d created the world. An understanding of G-d *per se* could in no way enable one to understand that G-d should have created the world. Our argument from finitude is required to reconcile G-d's absolutely infinite Being with the existence of a finite world that is not part of His essence insofar as we can understand His essence. However, there are some aspects of the dream metaphor that can fruitfully be utilized to explain the notion of what we call 'The Higher Understanding.' Let us try to draw out the relevant points of this analogy.

The dream is G-d's Creation of the world. If you ask me whether my nightmare about the snake pit really exists I will tell you 'it's just a dream.' So for G-d, the world that He created has no real existence and therefore its finitude is not a contradiction to His absolute infinity. It is, so to speak, just a dream.

As far as the snakes are concerned, they really exist as do you and I. They do not consider themselves a figment of anyone's dreams any more than you and I do. What the snakes have no knowledge of and which they have no reason whatsoever to think is true, is that their existence depends upon the dreams of some creature they know not what! Human beings, however, are not snakes and they have the capacity to conceive that their existence and that of the entire world depends upon the creative act of an omniscient, omnipotent absolutely infinite Being they call 'G-d.' Furthermore, they have rational grounds for believing that such a Being exists and that therefore the existence of the finite world is the result of a creative act of G-d that defies human comprehension, as we have argued. Though we have a glimpse of this truth with our minds, it is only a glimpse of something about which we have no real understanding. The logic of the human mind, displayed by science, common sense and courses in logic recognizes the reality of the world but not that of G-d. As far as our understanding goes, though we may have some glimpse or intuition of some higher Being we call G-d, nevertheless we have little or no understanding of this Being. The world has tangible reality and G-d is something very abstruse and ephemeral. This is what is called 'The Lower Understanding.' We can, through certain acts of meditation or through sudden intuitions, have some insight into the Higher Understanding in which the unity of G-d with the world is revealed to our understanding or awareness. However, these unusual acts of human awareness are uncommon and attained only by select individuals at rare moments. It is not the ordinary human awareness of the world.

There is another aspect of the unity of G-d and the world that is well illustrated in this analogy and that is the manner of the dependency of the world on G-d and how that dependency is a relationship of knowing. Just as the dream snakes are dependent for their existence on my dreams, so the world and everything in it down to the last quark is dependent for its existence on an act of G-d's knowing which is identical with the act of G-d's Creation. Just as the continued existence of the dream snakes over time is identical with my dreaming them, so the continued existence of the world and everything in it down to the last sub-atomic particle is identical with G-d's knowing it. In fact G-d's knowing it is identical with its existence which completes the unity of G-d's knowledge with the world, as Maimonides writes: "He (G-d) is the Knower, He is the Thing Known and He is the Knowledge itself. All is one. This matter is beyond the ability of our mouths to relate, or our ears to hear, nor is there the capacity within the heart of man to grasp it in its entirety."[10]

The world and G-d are really one but this unity defies understanding and as Maimonides goes on to say in the same passage quoted above, G-d knows the world by knowing Himself and this knowledge is the source of the very being of the world. The creative act of G-d whereby He maintains the existence of the world is identical with that whereby He knows the world, but this knowledge is not something external to G-d as our knowledge is external to us. G-d's knowledge can not change, increase or decrease as our knowledge does as we mature and later become enfeebled, for a *sina quo non* of G-d is that He does not change. The Creation cannot have made any difference to G-d. He must be the very same G-d after Creation as before Creation. This, of course, defies human understanding, but this should come as no surprise, for G-d indeed surpasses human understanding. What we *can* understand, however, is that such a G-d must exist in order that we should be able to come to grips with 'understanding' Creation insofar as we can understand it. Our conclusion is that Creation must be the origin of the world, though this fact transcends our understanding. Thus, even though Creation is an act of G-d that in some sense ex-

---

10   See *Mishneh Torah*, "Laws of the Foundation of the Torah" 2:10.

tends beyond His essence as this is understood by the human mind, nonetheless, it is compatible with the absolute unity of G-d and the world, though this unity as well as the creative act itself defy human understanding.

It is interesting to note that for Maimonides and the philosophy of Chabad, faith in G-d is not described as a belief that G-d exists. Both Maimonides and the literature of Chabad claim that reasonable or rational support for this belief can be found though they may not amount to a demonstration or proof. However, the absolute unity of G-d with the world defies human comprehension altogether and about this nothing can be said. This is what must be accepted on faith alone and this is the meaning of the pronouncement, "Hear O' Israel, G-d our G-d, G-d is One." This is interpreted to mean not just that there is only one G-d and not two or more, but that G-d and the world are one and unified. It is this mysterious and baffling unity of G-d and the world that is the motif of Jewish mysticism found in the Kabbalah and in Hasidic literature generally. Furthermore it is the notion of Creation that has the most important existential implications for man. It is G-d as a loving and compassionate Creator in whom we find comfort and to whom we pray. No one ever prays to the G-d of the philosophers, i.e., an omniscient, necessary Being. G-d's Creation of the world furthermore implies a purpose to the world and everything in it. This lends meaning to life in a way that cannot be attained by pursuing one's self-interest. The whole power of the idea of G-d in the life and actions of human beings flows from this notion of G-d as Creator and the unique role that G-d plays in our lives is inseparable from this idea that was introduced to the world for the first time in the first sentence of the Hebrew Bible.

In all this, we assume that G-d is good and His creation of the world is also good and serves some good purpose which is connected with the purpose of human life generally. This assumption, however, does not follow from anything we have said so far. G-d's goodness, as we shall see, requires a separate argument in itself. Our next chapter addresses this argument.

7
G-D'S GOODNESS

A teacher of mine[1] once shocked me and the rest of the class by saying that it was perfectly possible for G-d to be the omnipotent, omniscient master of the world, etc., and at the same time be an absolute stinker. This is a colorful way of saying that none of the attributes that go to compose the traditional description of G-d entail that G-d is good. He might be the epitome of evil. My former teacher was correct. G-d's goodness does not follow from any other attributes. The goodness of G-d requires a separate argument. The purpose of this chapter is to provide such an argument.

It is important to note that we do no take this argument for G-d's goodness as an argument for the *existence* of G-d. Rather, as we said previously in our chapter on Creation, we are assuming that Chapters 1 through 5 are a persuasive argument for the rationality of the belief in the existence of a Being we call "G-d." Assuming this argument, we now ask, is it more rational to accept that this Being is good rather than evil, or perhaps indifferent to human good and evil?

There can be do doubt that G-d's goodness is a necessary attribute without which G-d would not be G-d. If G-d were indeed evil, we would not call Him G-d but something else. Descartes entertained the possibility that the Creator of the world might be evil, but he called such a Being, not G-d, but an evil Demon.[2] In spite of all his feigned skepticism, Descartes could not bring himself to believe that G-d was really evil, for that would have been the end of Descartes' search for infallibility in human knowledge. This argument today strikes a weak chord, for we are not hung up on the infallibility of human knowledge the way Descartes was. It could be that human knowledge is an illusion and man is a creature that the fashioner of the world made for the purpose of tormenting. Certainly, survivors of Auschwitz had good reason to doubt G-d's goodness and many of them did. The question

---

1 Henry David Aiken who taught ethics at Harvard in the fifties and early sixties.

2 See his *Meditations*, meditation 1.

is, what argument, if any, can be brought to show that it is rational to think that G-d is good and not evil or indifferent.

The first step in this argument is to show that it is rational for one to want to be good oneself, and after that we will argue that it is rational for one to think that G-d is good. The first question we must address, then, is why is it rational to desire goodness?

Let us begin by repeating something we said earlier: What is rational is not what can be proven, but certain intuitions we have about how everyone thinks. For example, the logical inference *modus ponens* is a rational inference not because it can be proven, but because it expresses something about how the human mind thinks. Everyone accepts its validity because we realize that without it we would be unable to think or reason at all.

Similarly, the reason we accept the rationality of the belief in induction is not because it can be proven, for Hume's main claim to fame is that he showed that it could not be proven either logically or empirically. The reason we say it is a rational belief is that without it there could be no knowledge of the world, and it is certainly rational to believe that knowledge of the world is possible. Similarly I will argue that it is rational to want to be good because everyone in fact desires this, not because of some utilitarian argument that purports to show that goodness leads to happiness, but simply because everyone wants to be good whether or not it makes them happy. Indeed, the good man can be happy *only* in the pursuit of goodness. We are not good because we pursue happiness; we are happy because we pursue goodness. Some suppose that they can be happy in pursuing not goodness but pleasure. That way lies perdition. Plato called it 'moral ignorance' and spent a good deal of his philosophy arguing against it. The good man wants to be good for the sake of goodness. The question is, why is this rational? Another way of putting the question is, why is it irrational to want to be evil?

The first thing to notice is that what is rational is not the actual *achieving* of goodness, but the desire to achieve it. If one fails to attain goodness, we have simply made a mistake and the realization of this is a bitter pill to swallow. What we are arguing is that no one *wants* to be evil, in much the same way as no one doubts the principle of induction or the principle of sufficient reason. In other words it is a fact about the way people think.

Not even those whom many people think of as evil, thought of themselves as evil. Hitler, for example, did not think of himself as evil.[3] He thought of himself as the savior of mankind who was out to rid the world of evil.[4] He may have been mistaken, though there is no reason to think that he or any of his devoted followers ever thought so. What some of his followers did think is that Hitler made certain tactical errors, such as not invading England in 1940 or attacking Russia in 1941, which led to his losing the war. If in some rare moment of self-revelation a person recognizes himself as truly evil, this does not mean that this person desires it and pursues it intentionally. Quite the contrary. If and when that moment of truth arrives, it normally brings feelings of remorse. One cannot realize that one is evil without feeling remorse. This 'cannot' is a logical 'cannot.' That is, there is something normative in desiring the good, so that if one really desired evil that person would be thought of as a madman, much in the same way as we would consider 'mad,' someone who did not believe that the future was going to be like the past or that there might be uncaused events.[5] That is, such thinking runs counter to the way people actually do think. This is a fact about human nature, such that it sounds inconsistent (though it is not a formal contradiction) to say "I know I am evil but I do not regret it"; just as it sounds inconsistent (though it is not a formal contradiction) to say "I do not believe the future will be like the past," all the while smoking a pipe in a calm and deliberate manner. If one really believed this, how could one be so calm? How does one know that the pipe will not explode in one's face? There is no formal contradiction here, but the actions belie the words.[6] Similarly, if a person declares that he pursues evil with his whole heart, he is either lying or he is truly a madman.

3 Nor did the millions of Germans who enthusiastically followed him to what they believed was the greater glory of Germany.

4 At least this is what he said in his speeches and in his book *Mein Kampf*, and there is no reason to think he was not serious about this.

5 There were some who considered Hitler a madman, because they thought he actually desired evil, but they were mistaken.

6 This is just one example of the truth that formal consistency is only a necessary condition of rationality, not a sufficient condition. Another example is

It is a normative fact about human nature that we are inclined to pursue goodness and believe that the future will be like the past. By a 'normative fact,' I mean that anyone about whom these facts are not true, will be judged completely mad by the rest of us. If you want to be rational this is how you must think. This sounds tyrannical but what this really means is that if you are rational this is how you *will* think. You really have no choice. The point of this is that there is a perfectly good sense in which a person can be called 'rational' for pursuing what one takes to be good and avoiding what one thinks is evil.[7]

Given that one seeks moral goodness, how should one come to grips with a world that was created by a Being who is evil? If the fashioner or maker of the world is evil, it follows that the world itself is evil or that it serves some evil purpose or design. Man belonging to such a world becomes unavoidably part and parcel of that evil. This is an intolerable position for any human being. The only rational alternative is to commit suicide and cease to be part of that world. It may be that this will not remove one from evil but simply effect a transfer of one's soul to some more evil world. The best thing for one to do in this situation would be to do away with oneself altogether, if one could. The only thing a rational person can do in this case is to play the odds. Remaining in this world would be evil and suicide would

---

Wittgenstein's promulgation of what he called 'Moore's Paradox' in which it is pointed out that the statement "It is raining, but I don't believe it" is not a formal contradiction, but it would certainly be irrational for someone to say this. Though Wittgenstein never says so, what I believe is behind this paradox is the assumption we all make that when anyone says anything, we assume that the speaker believes that what he is saying is true. This is a perfectly rational belief, for otherwise language and communication would be impossible. This is an argument for the irrationality of lying that goes deeper than the one given by Kant in his ethical philosophy. Kant argues that it is inconsistent for someone to lie for if everyone lied, no one would believe what anyone ever said, so there would be no point in lying. Here the argument is that unless one could assume that when people speak they tell the truth, discourse would cease altogether. A language in which one lies as a rule could not exist.

7   Thus Anna Frank in her diary was being perfectly rational when she said, in spite of all the evil around her, "… I still believe that people are really good at heart. I … can't build up my hopes on a foundation consisting of confusions, misery and death," *The Diary of Anna Frank*.

certainly remove you from this evil. Whether it will land you in a world more evil than this is questionable. Perhaps the 'heavenly' world designed by our Evil Demon is not quite as bad as this one. In any event, an uncertain evil is better than a certain one, so suicide would be a rational option in such a situation. However, all other conditions being equal, self- destruction is not a rational choice, for the instinct of survival and self-preservation is implanted in every living thing.

The phrase 'all other conditions being equal' requires some comment. We mean that under normal circumstances it is irrational for a person to commit suicide. However, there are certain situations in which an argument can be made supporting it. If someone is suffering from a painful, terminal illness a case for suicide might be made. Given the choice of death or participating in evil, the moral heroes of all ages have chosen death. One might agree that in certain regrettable situations, suicide might be a rational choice, but the point here is that these are *regrettable* situations. It would be better if there were no disease or illness in the world, and it would certainly be better if there were no evil. An ideal world would be one in which no one would wish to commit suicide, for everyone would be happy. In such a world suicide would be irrational. 'To be or not to be,' under ideal circumstances can never be a question. However, if the Creator of the world were truly an Evil Demon, the 'normal' circumstances of life would call on all decent people to commit suicide. Suicide, however, runs contrary to human instinct and will always be deemed rational to avoid at all costs. Thus if one is painfully ill to the extent that one wishes to take one's own life and modern medicine offers hope of return to normal health, it would be irrational to choose suicide because you can't afford the treatment. You should beg, borrow or even steal to regain your health and this would be the rational thing to do. A rational rule of thumb is, avoid at all costs situations that render suicide rational.

If now we return to our original question whether the Creator of the world be good or evil, the only rational reply which allows one to go on living is that He is good. As far as reconciling this with the fact of the existence of evil, we say that some way must be found of resolving this apparent inconsistency. This would certainly be more rational than assuming that the Creator of the world is an Evil Demon.

There is, however, another alternative to assuming that the Creator of the world is either good or evil and that is to assume that there is no Creator of the world and the world itself is neither good nor evil. Moral values of good and evil would then be purely human values that man brings to the world. This is the predominant view in moral philosophy today which began in modern times with David Hume and has had an impact not only on moral philosophy but on the thinking of society in general as this is expressed in politics, law, and social practices of the day. What, I think, is not sufficiently noted is that moral value in a secular world is significantly different from that of a world created by a good, beneficent Divine Being. In particular, the nature of moral judgement is transformed in such a way that one can begin to question whether there is any justification of what traditionally has been called 'moral judgements.' There have been attempts by some philosophers to maintain the integrity of moral judgements in the face of a world without G-d. Kant attempted to do it in one way and Nietzsche in another, but, I believe, they both failed. The remainder of this chapter will attempt to expound more clearly the idea that the essential force of a moral judgement disappears without G-d, and moral judgements become in such a context quite different from how we ordinarily think of them even in a secular society.[8]

The particular aspect of traditional moral judgements that cannot be sustained without G-d can be called the 'categorical element.' What I mean by the categorical element in moral judgements is the fact that for any act that one considers morally good or bad, one will feel a categorical responsibility to do or avoid the act. In other words, our judgement that x is good contains in it the command, "Thou shalt do x." It may not contain it logically in the sense that my judgement that x is good does not entail that I will feel an obligation to do x. I might be weak-willed or have the moral defect of not feeling a strong desire or obligation to do x, though I know full well that x is the right and good thing to do. However a virtuous person or a person of moral integrity will feel an obligation to do what one thinks is morally right. This obligation is, as Kant said, categorical and not hypothetical. This

8 Again I emphasize that this dissolution of moral judgement in a secular society is not an argument for the *existence* of G-d, but is meant to call attention to a consequence of rejecting G-d. Some philosophers such as Nietzsche pursued this consequence with gusto.

means there are no excuses. "Thou shalt not lie" means there is no excuse for lying. This is contrasted with playing the piano. It sounds a bit absurd to say "Thou shalt practice playing the piano" as if there were no excuse for not playing the piano. There are circumstances under which it might be appropriate to say such a thing, as in the case where someone has committed oneself to becoming a concert pianist or is simply taking piano lessons voluntarily. We all know that some people do not take such lessons voluntarily and that sometimes it is forced upon them by well-meaning parents. In such cases, that person may have a good excuse for not practising the piano. The injunction to practise the piano is dependent upon a certain kind of commitment. That is, it is hypothetical. However, the command not to lie is not hypothetical. It is categorical, meaning that it is not up to anyone to *decide* whether they want to be bound by this injunction. They *are* bound by it by the mere fact that they are human beings living in the world. This is what is meant by the command, "Thou shalt not lie." Kant's point about a moral judgement being categorical and not hypothetical is incontrovertible. I think Kant has here captured the essence of a moral judgment. The question is, how can one explain or justify this unique quality whereby moral judgments are seen as categorical?

Kant tries to explain this as a result of reason. He thought that we can see that certain moral judgements are dictated by reason and we can will that all people in the name of consistency follow this kind of reasoning and act as we are acting. However, if one examines how Kant argues this in specific instances, it is rarely convincing. Quite the contrary. If one reads closely his arguments given in the four examples of how one can solve particular moral problems, they appear singularly arbitrary and unconvincing.[9] Furthermore, even if one could make out a case that human reason *per se* can resolve moral disagreements and/or moral dilemmas, this would not instil into moral judgements what we have called the categorical element. The normative element in reason simply says that this is the correct way of reasoning. It is correct to use *modus ponens*, the principle of induction and the prin-

---

9 See his *Grounding for the Metaphysics of Morals*, 3rd edition, trans. James Ellington, Hackett Pub. Co., 1993, pp. 30-32 (*Academy* original pagination, pp. 422-23).

ciple of sufficient reason. If you reason any other way, you are simply mistaken. However, it is absurd to demand "Thou shalt reason with *modus ponens.*"

In the first place, such a demand is absurd because one has no choice. One cannot reason any other way. To take a different example, to demand that one shall use induction in one's reasoning is like demanding that one breathe oxygen. In either case, you have no choice. You cannot survive without induction or oxygen. One can, of course, commit suicide but under normal circumstances this is certainly not a rational or viable option, as we have tried to argue. We all realize, however, that we can act immorally if we so choose, and often the temptation is great. "Thou shalt not lie," however, rings in our ears as a clarion call and touches our conscience if we are decent.

Secondly, if one misuses reason or makes a mistake in one's reasoning, this is no cause for condemnation. One simply corrects the mistake and moves on. If the mistake is uncorrectable we have compassion for the unfortunate person and consign him to an institution. "It's a pity," we say, "The man thinks he's Napoleon." We have no such compassion for a liar. We say, "Let's not have anything to do with him. He is evil!." If he claims to have an excuse, we say, "Sorry, no excuses."[10] It is this categorical element that cannot be justified or explained by reason as Kant supposed. The question is, how can it be justified? The answer is that only G-d can justify it. That is, we think of immoral acts as going contrary not just to our will, but to G-d's will. All that we can say with our human reason is, "You know, you really shouldn't lie, it's not nice. Besides, just think what the world would be like if everyone lied. It would be intolerable! Even you wouldn't want to live in such a world. Why do you feel you can make yourself an exception? Don't you see that you are being inconsistent?" The liar might be impressed by this reasoning, or he might not if the stakes were high enough. He might say, "Who cares about consistency, if I can make a buck!" Furthermore, who's to say the liar doesn't have a valid excuse, if the bucks are big enough! So goes human reasoning. Only G-d can say, "Thou shalt not lie."

---

10   We are not talking about 'white' lies. The 'white lie' is a justified lie. It's the exception that proves the rule. For real lies there are no excuses. One simply should not lie.

Nietzsche tried to preserve this categorical force in his notion of the 'ubermensch'—the superman who by force of some inner will becomes the source of categorical value. Nietzsche thought, correctly, that the alternative to categorical value was utilitarianism or what today is called 'consequentialism.' He condescendingly called it the pursuit of 'miserable ease.'[11] He knew full well that the pursuit of pleasure and happiness as the ultimate goal of moral action cannot sustain the earnestness of the categorical imperative. "Thou shalt not x," becomes "x is unwise (imprudent, counter-productive, injudicious, ill-advised, foolish, rash)" or any other host of words that signify that it would be better if it were not done. However, none of these terms carry the force of a duty or a responsibility. In other words, in utilitarian ethics the notion of categorical responsibility disappears and along with it the "Thou shalt..." and all that this implies. Nietzsche deplored this. A moral value had to be something that was inviolate for which one should be prepared to give one's life.[12] Nietzsche thought the true source of this categorical value was the human will. In Nietzsche this becomes a very subtle matter and it is probable that he did not mean by this what Hitler thought he meant by it when Hitler crowned him the prophet and philosopher of the Nazi party. This is not the place for a lengthy exposition of the thought of Nietzsche, but no matter how one understands the ego or the will or whatever Nietzsche meant by the 'will to' it is a mistake if not a disaster to attribute to human will, the categorical force and earnestness of moral judgements. No human will is that large or powerful. Nietzsche, however, was certainly correct in sensing in utilitarianism an enemy of the categorical force of moral judgement which he thought so important to preserve. The reason for this is that the notion of a moral judgement undergoes a radical change in utilitarianism. From being a judgement about moral right and wrong, the judgement becomes one of prudence. Some might prefer the term 'wisdom,' but the effect is the same. When utilitarians say x is wrong, what they mean is that x is unwise, or imprudent or injudicious, etc. because the consequences are unwanted. There is no sense of "Thou shalt not..." here. One simply has to take a close look

---

11   See his *Thus Spake Zarathustra*, Part I, Zarathustra's Prologue, Section 3.

12   See his *Thus Spake Zarathustra*, Part I, in the section entitled "A Thousand and One Goals."

at the consequences and you will see that you wouldn't want to do it. "Thou shalt not x" means that under no circumstances should you do x. Forget about the consequences—they are not relevant. The only thing that is relevant is that x itself is wrong and that is why you should not do it.[13] The criterion of a moral act in contrast to a prudential one is

---

13   What is often overlooked is that consequences are often part of the act itself. Thus what makes a 'white lie,' 'white,' is not something different from the lie but is part of the lie. Thus if I tell someone a lie in order to save a person's life, the motivation and the consequences become part of the lie itself and nullify its evil. One cannot separate lies either from their motivations or their consequences any more than one can separate an explosion from the motivation behind it or its consequences. In one case, an explosion is a necessary step in the construction of a building; in another, it is a dastardly act of terrorism that kills innocent people. To talk about an 'explosion' here that is morally neutral and which is said to be good or evil depending on its consequences is an abstraction from a fact which in reality is inseparable from its motivation and consequences. Similarly, the squeezing of the trigger of a revolver is an abstraction from an act of murder or from innocent target practice. When we judge human actions, we judge the *entire act* which here includes both motivation and consequences. It's not that the murder is a 'consequence' of pulling the trigger. Pulling the trigger, in the case of someone pointing a revolver at another person with the intention of killing that person is itself an act of murder. Just how distant the consequence has to be before we consider it a 'consequence' and not part of the act itself is relative, but judges and jurors seldom have difficulty in making this distinction. It would be absurd for a defense lawyer to argue that his client was not guilty of murder because the act of pulling the trigger of the gun, which is the immediate cause of the death, is itself not an act of murder but some morally neutral act, distinct from both its consequences and the motivations behind it. The case of a motorist who accidentally killed a pedestrian while running a red light is different. In this case it would be correct to argue that the driver was not guilty of murder for the act of running the red light was not an act of murder and the death of the pedestrian was simply an unwanted consequence of this act. The deciding factor in both cases is the motivation behind the act which is itself an integral *part* of the act and determines that the act of pulling the trigger is an act of murder, while the act of running the red light is not. Of course, running a red light might be an act of murder in addition to being a traffic violation, if one ran the light with the express intention of murdering someone.

that in the former, one feels that consequences are irrelevant. Let us illustrate this with an example.

Some argue that abortion is morally wrong because it is really murder or something akin to murder. As such, the consequences of an abortion are irrelevant. It might be that the abortion will make the woman very happy and relieve a lot of social pressure and future responsibility. All that is irrelevant simply because, according to this view, abortion per se is a *moral* evil. Could a 'hit man' argue that murdering people is justified because he can make a good living from it and enjoy the kind of life style that makes him happy? The fact that one could be happy and sleep at night after murdering someone for money shows how evil that person really is. His conscience no longer bothers him the way it would if he were decent. Similarly, one who thinks that abortion is a moral evil would say that a woman who has an abortion and who can sleep at night, knowing that she has murdered her unborn child, has taken a step down the slippery slope of moral evil. It is irrelevant that the woman is happy with the result, and feels relieved from the responsibility of raising an unwanted child, as well as the stigma of being an unwed mother, etc. The fact that the woman feels no remorse about the matter simply shows how low she has sunk.

Perhaps the moral evil into which she has fallen is not as blatant as that of our 'hit man,' for abortion is not really first degree murder in any view or under any law that I know of. Nonetheless, it is still considered a moral evil today by many and any woman who has an abortion and the doctor who performs it are both guilty of moral evil and the fact that both are happy with the outcome makes it even worse. Furthermore, any society that permits abortion is an evil society as much as any society that practices racial discrimination. This is a fair representation of the view that abortion is a moral evil.

On the other hand, many people today do not feel that abortion *per se* is morally evil. It is or should be a straightforward prudential matter and should be decided in each situation by the specific consequences. In some situations an abortion would be bad and would lead to unwanted consequences. In others, it might be good and everyone concerned would be happy with the result. There is no *a priori* yes or no to the question whether abortion is good or bad. It all depends on the consequences and each case must be judged on its own 'merits,' so to speak.

The point we are arguing here is that however one might decide the issue in any given situation, the decision would not be a *moral decision* but a prudential one. For this reason, in the event one could reasonably surmise that an abortion would have 'injudicious' or 'ill-advised' consequences, one should judge the abortion to be bad, but it would be inappropriate to say "Thou shalt not have an abortion," for abortions are not categorically evil. There are many 'excuses' that justify abortions.

The debate between 'pro-life' and 'pro-choice' now going on in our society reveals a much deeper rift in the thinking of people than do straightforward cases of moral disagreements. In ordinary cases of moral disagreements the parties square off against one another and it is clear to all what is at issue. The United Nations declares apartheid to be immoral while most white South Africans considered it to be morally good. The Nuremberg tribunal that tried Nazi war criminal declared the genocide of the Jews to be immoral while Hitler and many of his followers declared it to be morally good. These are straightfor-ward cases of moral disagreements that arouse high feelings on both sides. However the debate about abortion is not such a clear-cut issue. Though it is true that the 'pro-life' side declares abortion to be a moral evil, and the 'pro-choice' side deny this, they do not go so far as to say that abortion is morally good. What the 'pro-choice' people seem to deny is that the question is a moral issue in the first place. They seem to be arguing as if it were a strictly prudential one that should be decided on the basis of projected consequences.

I say that this is how the 'pro-choicers' *seem* to argue, but the fact is that many 'pro-choicers' would say that their dispute with the 'pro-lifers' is a moral disagreement similar to other moral disagree-ments. I think this is a confusion that masks the real issue which is simply that the 'pro-lifers' are maintaining the traditional view of moral judgements as categorical imperatives in which consequences are irrelevant, while the 'pro-choicers' reject this notion of morality in favor of a utilitarian or consequentalist notion that defines moral value in terms of consequences, and as such rejects the notion of the categorical element in moral judgements.

What utilitarians and consequentialists are really doing is substituting the notion of prudence for morality, thinking that they are one and the same thing. This is nothing else than a matter of mistaking one thing for another[14] Prudence is prudence and morality is morality and they are not the same, any more than a prudent man is *eo ipso* morally virtuous. The two are different as everyone knows. The reduction of morality to prudence is another one of those false reductions with which the history of philosophy is replete.[15]

I doubt if human society as we know it can exist devoid of morality in the sense in which Kant understood it. I do not think human society can avoid the categorical imperative, and I do not think the 'pro-choicers' can avoid it either. For at some point they will inevitably proclaim some categorical moral value that is not grounded in the consequences of actions and which they take to be valid *a priori*. For example, implicit in the pro-choice view is the notion that respect for human rights is a categorical, moral value. That is, they would be hard pressed to deal with a society in which the repression of human rights had beneficial circumstances. They would argue that there can be no such society and no one would really want to live in such a society. How can one be so certain about this?[16] It appears as if they are treating respect for human rights as a categorical value that is taken to be valid *a priori*.[17] Morality, as even the 'pro-choicers'

14   One can easily understand why G.E. Moore chose for the motto of his critique of utilitarianism, *Principia Ethica*, Alice in Wonderland's justly famous remark that "Everything is what is and not another thing."

15   Other examples of similar such falsities have been the attempted reduction of knowledge to sense-perception, metaphysics to semantics and mathematics to logic.

16   I have heard some recent emigres from Russia say they prefer the repression of the K.G.B. to the lawlessness of present Russian society. There can be no doubt that there was greater repression of human rights under the K.G.B.

17   Wittgenstein is reported to have said that the hedonist principle that people desire nothing but pleasure is not an empirical sentiment but functions as an *a priori* principle. See O. K. Bouwsma, *Wittgenstein Conversations 1949-51*, ed. J. L. Craft and Ronald E. Hustwit, Hackett Publishers Co., 1986, pp. 58-9. The idea behind this statement of Wittgenstein's is that any system of morality, that purports to be a system of *morality*, will be grounded in some categorical *a priori* value.

understand it, would disappear, for even they say "Thou shalt respect human rights." That is, for repression of human rights, there are no excuses. If so, the question for the utilitarian 'pro-choicer' is, what could be the ground or justification of this categorical judgement? The most common answer is in terms of consequences, namely that a society that respects human rights will be one in which the people are happy and content and, one in which any rational person would want to live. This may be true but this cannot be the ground of the categorical judgement "Thou shalt respect human rights," for if the moral value of this judgement is dependent upon consequences, it cannot be an *a priori* judgement as all categorical judgements must be. It must be determined by the empirical facts of the particular case in question, and therefore can never be judged *a priori*. The confusion of utilitarianism and consequentialism is that it takes some values as *a priori* while insisting on empirical facts to justify the moral value assigned. One cannot have it both ways. Consistent utilitarians must make peace with the implication of their theory that when morality is reduced to prudence, categorical, moral value disappears.

As far as human rights are concerned, there is no reason why the utilitarian should not seek a society that represses human rights but which has more beneficial consequences than a free society. There is no *a priori* reason to exclude such a possibility. It may be that contemporary Russian society is such an example. If one listens to how 'liberal' people talk, be they 'pro-choicers,' gays, lesbians or advocates of assisted suicide, they talk as if they have the right to live the kind of life-style they choose or the right to end living altogether if they so choose and this right is categorical and *a priori*. The fact that a recent consequence of homosexuality has been the contraction and spread of the HIV virus has not led to questioning the *moral right* that homosexuals have to live the kind of life style they prefer. It may have led some people to avoid homosexuality as a matter of prudence, but it need not have changed their view that they have a moral, categorical right to live that way if they so choose. In fact, it could be that if someone were prepared to continue living a life-style that endangered his life, because he wanted to exercise his inviolable right to live as he saw fit, he would surely be considered a martyr who died for the cause by the homosexual community. The unwanted consequences of homosexuality need not undermine the view of such people that they have a right to practice homosexuality *no matter what the consequences.* It may not be wise or prudent but that does not gainsay their right to practice it. Sometimes they may be inclined to quote the United States Declaration of Independence guaranteeing their right to "life, liberty and the pursuit of happiness" as long as they do not intrude on the rights of others.

The question I would now like to pose is how they or anyone can argue for or justify such categorical rights without G-d? The United States Declaration of Independence loudly proclaims G-d as the source of these rights: "We hold these truths to be self-evident. That all men were created equal: That they were *endowed by their Creator* with certain inalienable rights; that among these are life, liberty and pursuit of happiness."

Though this appears to espouse a consequentialist theory of morality, the point that justifies rebellion is that everyone has G-d given rights that not even the King of England can abrogate. How the modern-day moral 'liberal' would rewrite the Declaration of Independence without G-d, I do not know. One of the points of this chapter is that it cannot be done. Without G-d, categorical morality as we know it, must disappear to be replaced by prudence. I think that even utilitarians would balk at this idea when its full consequences are drawn.

The above remarks say nothing as to *how* G-d is to be the ground of categorical, moral value. This is a very difficult question which has no simple or easy answer. It seems to me the answer is certainly not as straightforward as some people make it. For instance, many who argue that G-d is necessary for morality say that the reason why "Thou shalt not steal" is a moral imperative is because G-d commanded it, or that it somehow expresses G-d's will.

It seems to me that the matter is more complex than this, for not everything that G-d commanded in the Bible is understood as morally good. G-d commanded Abraham to slaughter his son as a sacrifice but we do not view this command as a *moral* imperative, nor did Abraham. If he had, this command would not have been the test that G-d meant it to be. It would not have been much of a test if G-d had simply commanded Abraham not to steal or murder. These are the kinds of things one might expect from G-d. The command to sacrifice his son was the supreme test for the very reason that it was, as Kierkegaard described it, a "teleological suspension of the ethical."[18] It went counter to Abraham's moral intuitions and feelings. It was obeyed by Abraham simply because G-d commanded it. What G-d commands is no doubt an imperative and a categorical one at that, but it is not necessarily a *moral* imperative. That is, just because G-d commands it we do not *therefore* understand it as morally good. Being commanded by G-d is not a necessary and sufficient condition for understanding that something is morally good. There are many examples in the Bible of G-d commanding something that to all intents have nothing to do with morality *per se*, as for example the command to Israelites that they should not wear garments made of wool and linen.[19]

Whether or not one believes in the Bible, one is still faced with the question, of what else is required to transform G-d's command into a *moral* imperative other than the fact that G-d commanded it. When G-d says "Thou shalt not steal," we say "Of course!" but when He says "Thou shalt not wear garments of wool and linen," we say "O.K., if You say so!" The Rabbinical commentaries on the Bible make the interesting point that the true test of faith and commitment to G-d is more clearly expressed in obedience to the commandments for which there is *no* reason, other than the fact that G-d commanded them.[20] If one obeys the command not to steal, it may simply be for the reason that one *understands* stealing to be morally wrong whether or not G-d commands it. It is clear that our perception that stealing is morally wrong is not dependent on G-d's commanding it. There are other factors that enter into our perception of this. A difficult question in moral philosophy is, what are these factors? What is the origin of our conception of moral good and evil? I have indicated earlier that I do not think reason can provide an answer to this, nor can man's will, and certainly not utilitarianism or prudential consequences. The answer to this can be found, I believe, in something I call the 'moral sense.' In the next chapter we take a closer look at this 'moral sense.'

---

18   See his *Fear and Trembling*.

19   Deuteronomy, 22:11.

20   See Rashi's commentary on the Bible, *Numbers*, 19:2.

8

THE MORAL SENSE

What I mean by the moral sense is well-illustrated in one of Plato's earlier Dialogues.[1] Plato recounts how the gods gave to each species of animal the precise kind of abilities and instincts to survive. To the weak they gave speed, to those with strength they gave slowness of movement so the weaker could escape. To the smallest of all animals, the birds, they gave flight. To the animals living in cold countries they provided thick hair for warmth, and to each species they gave just those kinds of bodily mechanisms and instincts to survive in its environment. After they had taken care of all the animals, they finally came to man and to their consternation discovered that all the natural protections and instincts had already been apportioned out and there was nothing left for man. Man was about to come naked into the world without any means of survival. The situation was saved by Zeus. He imparted to humans respect for one another and a 'sense of justice' (*aido to kai dikein*—322 c), and this enabled man to form societies and live together in friendship and unity and thus survive.

I know of no other ground of morality or the moral sense than this. I do not mean that it was Zeus that implanted this sense of justice in human beings, but however it got there, the point I want to argue here is that it needs no ground or justification any more than *modus ponens* needs a proof of its validity.[2] As we said earlier, no proof could be more persuasive than *modus ponens* itself, and no argument supporting justice could be more compelling than justice itself. It is to the credit of John Rawls to have pointed out that justice as fairness cannot be reduced to some utilitarian value.[3] It is an *a priori* good

---

1 See Plato's *Protagoras*, 320d-322e.

2 We remind our readers that *modus ponens* is the Latin term for the following valid inference: from the two premises, i) if p then q, and ii) p; it follows that iii) q.

3 See his "Justice as Fairness," *The Philosophical Review*, vol. LXVII, 1958, and his book, *A Theory of Justice*, ch. 1, Harvard University Press, 1971.

in itself apart from the social and utilitarian values it so eminently serves. Even in those cases when it may not serve a utilitarian value, one still feels the compelling call of the Biblical command, "Justice, justice shall you pursue!"[4] Another integral element that composes this sense of morality is the compassion we feel for the suffering of another human being. These two—the sense of justice and the sense of compassion—comprise what I mean by the sense of morality and in this chapter I want to discuss these two senses. There may be other elements that enter into morality, but these are the primary ones.

The first thing I want to call attention to is the emotions one instinctively feels when one witnesses acts of injustice or suffering. They are called, respectively, righteous indignation and compassion. Why do we have these emotions? Injustice is really an act or a fact about human relations and suffering is a state of human existence. Why is it that these facts call forth these emotions? There is no necessity in our feeling these emotions and indeed we may know individuals or have read about certain people for whom the appropriate situations do not call forth such emotions. We call such people insensitive or lacking in moral feelings. Though they may not yet be said to be evil or cruel, it is nonetheless the *sine quo non* of being a morally good person that one *feels* indignation and compassion on the appropriate occasions.

I believe there is something innate about these feelings such that we find it quite 'natural' to have them and think it unnatural when we do not. This is particularly true of cruelty, which is so unnatural we call perpetrators of cruel acts 'inhuman.' Being a human being implies that one should feel compassion for the suffering of another human being and a decent person will feel indignant when he sees injustice.

These feelings are as natural as laughing at a joke. It is silly to ask why one laughs at a joke if it is truly funny, and it is just as odd to ask why one feels indignation and compassion on the appropriate occasions. How else should one react to injustice and suffering? It is difficult to imagine reacting in any other way, just as we would find it difficult to react to a funny joke other than by laughing. If one doesn't laugh at a Jack Benny joke, one lacks a sense of humour which is a significant flaw in one's personality. If one feels no indignation or compassion, this is a sign of something seriously amiss with one's humanity or

---

4 Deuteronomy 16.20.

goodness. The association of moral character with these feelings is so intimate that we are inclined to say that a decent person would never knowingly consent to injustice and a compassionate person could never inflict unnecessary pain or suffering on anyone. The "would never" and "could never" here is a 'logical' one in that what one *means* by a moral person is someone who would never act unjustly and could never bring oneself to cause unnecessary pain or misery to anyone. To say that someone is morally good but acts unjustly or is cruel is a 'logical' contradiction in the same sense in which it is a 'logical' contradiction to say that a bachelor is married.

The reason the term 'logical' is flagged here is that it is being used a bit differently from the way it is ordinarily used by logicians. Logical contradiction is usually applied to statements that negate logically valid inferences. Thus if *modus ponens* is a valid inference, then to say i) if p then q, and ii) p, but iii) not q, is a logical contradiction. The contradiction in saying that x is a bachelor and is married contradicts no valid inference. What it contradicts is how we use words in English. It has to do with our understanding of concepts or ideas. What ordinarily is meant in English by the term "bachelor" excludes the possibility that a bachelor could be married. To ask of someone to whom you have been introduced as a bachelor, "Are you married?" shows that either you do not understand English very well, or that you are trying to be funny, or that you are an imbecile. One might imagine other ways of explaining how or why someone might ask such a nonsensical question, but the point is that it is nonsensical, given the common meaning of the term "bachelor" in English. In a similar way, I think it is nonsensical to ask whether someone, unjust or cruel, is morally good or decent. I want to say that what one *means* by a good person is at least a person about whom one would say that it is unthinkable that this person could act unjustly or cruelly.[5] There might be other traits that define our concept of moral goodness, but certainly justice and compassion are necessary aspects of this concept and perhaps even sufficient aspects. In any event, they are crucial, such that anyone who lacked these qualities would not be said to be a

---

5 It goes without saying that no one is morally perfect. We are all prone to weakness and temptations. Occasionally we are unjust or lose our tempers and are mean. If we are morally decent, we will recognize these backslidings and regret them.

morally good person. If it is true, as we claim here, that these feelings
are innate or that all human beings are born with them, how is it that
some people feel them more strongly than others and some seem to
lack them altogether? I do not think these are counter examples to
our point. People get side-tracked through bad nurturing or training
from parents or teachers. It is a matter of education as is any kind of
character or emotional development. This is Plato's point that the evil
that men fall into is inadvertent and unintentional. No one willingly
sets out to become evil. Some people are raised in an environment that
is hostile to the basic moral feelings. The moral growth of such people
becomes stunted much as musical talent is stunted by an environment
that fails to nurture and develop that talent. The difference between
a talent for music and the sense of justice and compassion is that lack
of the latter is a more serious character fault than the former. One
who lacks a talent for music or a sense of humour is missing out on
something important that adds to the value of human life. Someone
who is unjust or cruel should be ostracized from human society. Such
people are cancerous. They destroy the trust and friendship that is
the glue holding society together. Sometimes these moral sentiments
shine through the thick skin of the most hardened criminals or those
whom one would ordinarily consider cruel or inhumane.[6] In *Kabbalah*
the term for evil is 'shell' or 'covering' (*kelipa*). The idea here is that
the world and man are essentially good, but an external layer of evil
covers and conceals this good. One simply has to peel back this layer
to reveal a basic underlying goodness.[7] No one is all good or all evil.

---

6 A close friend of mine who survived the infamous death march from
   Auschwitz was saved by a Nazi guard who, along with shooting straggling
   prisoners on the way, would come over to my friend every day and share
   his canteen of coffee with him. When they reached the railroad junction
   after days of marching and they boarded the cattle cars that transported
   them to Bergen-Belsen, the guard disappeared and my friend never saw
   him again. Why the guard showed my friend this kindness and who this
   person was has remained a mystery to this very day.

7 A similar idea was expressed in a lecture I once heard from Robert Frost
   who described what a poem was by the following metaphor: the ancients
   thought that the black sky at night was a curtain that was stretched over the
   heavens when the sun set. Beyond that curtain was a supernal light which

Each of us is a mixture of both, varying in the degree that goodness is able to shine through the shell of egoism that encrusts us all. This is the dark curtain that conceals the supernal goodness concealed in the soul of every person and the bad and evil among us are simply those unfortunate ones who, for whatever reason, have been unable to unearth this goodness. From time to time on rare occasions, it manages to poke a hole through the mire of our entanglements.

However we come by this sense of morality, we do not come by it as a result of G-d's commands, though the commentators on the Bible tells us that in pursuing morality we are emulating G-d.[8] Man naturally feels compassion with or without G-d. Furthermore Abraham actually challenged G-d for not displaying a sense of justice in dealing with the wicked people of Sodom and Gomorrah. "Would you (G-d) destroy the righteous with the wicked? Suppose there are fifty righteous men in the city, would you still destroy it and not spare the place for the sake of the fifty righteous living in it? G-d forbid that you should do a thing like this—to destroy the righteous with the wicked—that you should treat the righteous as you treat the wicked. G-d forbid that the judge of the whole world should not do what is fair!"[9]

G-d had to acquiesce to Abraham's logic. It would not be fair for G-d to treat the righteous as He treats the wicked. G-d did not ask Abraham for an argument why treating people unfairly is wrong or unjust. It is simply *prima facia* obvious that it is wrong and conse-quences are irrelevant. G-d had to admit the correctness of Abraham's position and promise not to destroy the cities if there were righteous men found among them. The fact that there were none, sealed their

---

we could not see. Powerful archers would shoot arrows at the curtain and sometimes they would pierce it and pinpoints of the supernal light would shine through. The ancients thought that was a star. Robert Frost said it is a poem. Kabbalah proclaims it a ray of that elemental goodness which is the essence of man and the world. The mysterious kindness shown by the Nazi guard mentioned in the previous footnote was a fleeting glimpse of that goodness in the midst of evil.

8 See the commentary of Rashi on Deuteronomy 11.22.

9 See Genesis 18.23-25. (My translation)

fate and Abraham had to resign himself to the destruction of these wicked cities.[10]

The interesting thing about this story is that it is taken for granted by both G-d and Abraham that it would not be fair to treat righteous men and wicked men in the same way, and that it is unthinkable that G-d could act unfairly. Suppose G-d had challenged Abraham to produce an argument why it is morally wrong or evil to treat people unfairly. What could Abraham have said? I do not know of any argument that Abraham could have produced. I doubt if G-d would have been impressed by either a Kantian or a Nietzschean argument, and certainly not a utilitarian one. Abraham, as a matter of fact, had pre-empted the question. "G-d forbid, that the judge of the world should not do what is fair!"[11] If G-d indeed had answered by saying something like, "What is so terrible in treating the righteous and the wicked in the same way? Why is this wrong?" we would then have to throw up our hands in despair for all would be lost. If the judge of the whole world is not just, G-d have mercy on us! If a fellow human being of flesh and blood would have asked this question, we would put him in an institution for he is obviously demented. How can any decent person ask why it is good to be fair?

A similar thing can be said about the sense of compassion. Why should one feel compassion at the suffering of another human being? The only possible answer is that if you don't, you are morally insensitive. You are probably capable of cruelty yourself. There is no answer to the question, What is so bad about being cruel? One simply throws up one's hands in horror and stays as far away as one can from such people. This is the only proper response. Such people do not deserve an argument! If G-d Himself were cruel (and there is no contradiction to His being an omniscient, omnipotent Creator of the world, etc. and also cruel), could one go on living? If the ultimate end of the righteous as well as the wicked is eternal damnation, what is the point of it all? Kierkegaard wrote a book (*Fear and Trembling*) in which he imagines how the Biblical story of the binding of Isaac might have been written a bit differently had Abraham not been the

---

10   See further in Genesis 18.26-33.
11   Genesis 18.25.

true Knight of Faith that he was. He might have pleaded with G-d, complained against G-d, held in repressed anger or disappointment, etc. It never occurred to Kierkegaard to rewrite the story as if G-d were not G-d but an Evil Demon. The Evil Demon would not only not have saved Isaac at the last moment, he would have gloated over his sacrifice and laughed at Abraham's suffering in gleeful joy. If He had said to Abraham, "You fool—the only reason I created you and tested your faith is that I should have the enjoyment of watching you suffer!" the only proper response to this is, as we suggested in Chapter 7, that Abraham plunge the knife into himself, for there would be no point in going on living. If G-d is cruel, that is the end—the world gets turned upside down. This shows how fundamental is the idea that the world and G-d are good.

This fundamental role that moral goodness plays in human life, however, is derived from man, not from G-d. It is not that we consider moral goodness crucial because G-d has commanded it—rather we consider it crucial because we cannot imagine living without it. In some ways, it is even more fundamental in our thinking than is G-d. Many people claim they can live without G-d, but no one can say honestly they can get along without goodness. This attests to the efficacy with which Zeus (according to the Greek legend) implanted it within us. One should not forget, however, that according to the legend it was *Zeus* who implanted it. That is, it did not come about by chance or through some evolutionary process. This certainly adds to our responsibility. If one has a talent, one should try to develop it if it enhances one's life, etc. However, one has no *responsibility* to develop it unless it is 'G-d-given.' If the Creator of heaven and earth has given someone a talent that enhances the value and the goodness of human life, then one has a categorical responsibility to nourish this talent. That is, it is not up to one's individual choice to decide whether one should develop it. How much more does this apply if we are talking about one's 'talent' for goodness, i.e. one's sense of compassion. This is nothing else than the emulation of G-d. "As I am merciful, shall you be merciful." The sense of compassion in man is a reflection of G-d's image in us. As G-d is good, so are we, or rather our dependency on goodness is due to the fact that that is how G-d made us, and the development of our talent for goodness is an emulation of G-d. The only difference is that this is a talent that every human being has, by right of the fact that one is a human being. This talent was not reserved for a select few. The exhortation by G-d that we should be merciful is not a command as such. It is more of an encouragement. "I know it is difficult," he says, "but you can do it—you have it in you—I know—I put it there!"[12] It is similar to G-d's exhortation to be holy. "You shall be holy because I am holy."[13] At first, this does not sound like much of an argument. If G-d had said, "You shall be omnipotent because I am omnipotent," we would think it a joke. The difference is that G-d has given us the ability to attain a degree of holiness or goodness, but *no* degree of omnipotence. Don't let it go to your head. Just because G-d shares with man some of His attributes, man does not, therefore, become G-d.

That goodness is a G-d given talent is significant. It implies that man has a categorical responsibility to develop that talent, which otherwise he would not have.[14] If one's feeling for justice and compassion for suffering are evolutionary traits that evolved in the course of man's cultural development, there is no moral duty or obligation to nurture them except for prudential reasons. They help stabilize society or lead to pleasure and happiness, but then we are no longer talking about morality but about prudence. In order for righteous indignation and

---

12   See the *Protagoras* 322D where Zeus says to Hermes that the sense of justice should be given to all alike.

13   Leviticus 19.2.

14   Kant assumed that one has a categorical responsibility to develop whatever talents one might have, but he never argues for this in any convincing fashion. He simply says that "… as a rational being, he necessarily wills that his faculties be developed since they serve him, and have been given to him for all sorts of possible purposes." (*Fundamental Principles of the Metaphysics of Morals* pp. 49-50 in original German edition, ed. Rosencranz and Schubert, 1838.) I do not see how reason can dictate the necessity of developing our talents unless it is on the basis of prudential or utilitarian considerations, which Kant actually suggests here. However, the duty then becomes hypothetical and not categorical as Kant would like. If one has no desire to develop his talent for music, why should he feel obliged to do so just because he has it?

compassion to be a genuine barometer for morality, one needs G-d. Man's compassion is a moral feeling because G-d is compassionate. Justice is a moral trait because G-d is just. Without G-d, the feeling we all have that righteous indignation and compassion are the *sina quo non* of morality could be 'explained' as some kind of evolutionary development that has survival value. The only way one can say that these feelings constitute morality as we know it, is not because that's the way we have been taught or nurtured, but because the moral life is some form of emulation of G-d. To be what it is, morality must be 'G-d-like.'[15]

When Plato asked his famous question in the *Euthyphro* about whether something is holy because G-d desires it or does G-d desire it because it is holy, the answer was a bit of both.[16] When we say that something is moral or that one has a categorical responsibility to it, we mean that this is so because this is what G-d Himself is, and man desires it because G-d implanted it in him. Without G-d, man might still desire it but there is no way he can justify its categorical demands. G-d and morality are essentially one and the same thing, and this dimension of human life that distinguishes mankind from animals disappears with the view that there is no G-d and man has no peculiar virtue other than being at the top of the evolutionary process. What we call morality would be nothing more than the end point of evolution but that does not make it moral but simply successful. Should the evolutionary process some day replace our present moral feelings

---

15   Thus the Bible says one must "… walk in His ways" (Deuteronomy 28.9). Various Rabbinic commentators interpret this to mean that one must emulate the characteristics that G-d Himself displays. To quote Maimonides, "Just as He (G-d) is called kind, so you should be kind. As He is called merciful so you should be merciful. As He is called holy, so you should be holy." (*Mishneh Torah, Hilchos Daos*, ch. 1, paragraph 6). One of the interpretations of the Biblical statement that man was made in the image of G-d is that the feelings we call the moral feelings are such as they are and have the categorical demands that they do because they are the feelings that G-d has also, insofar as it makes sense to talk of G-d as having feelings similar to those of human beings.

16   See *Euthyphro*, 10a. For our purpose, we can substitute "good" for "holy." The logic of the question is the same.

with others, then man would simply have outgrown morality and the evolutionary value of survival will have replaced the moral feelings and values with others which we might then call the 'new' morality.[17]

In a word, the categorical element in moral judgement has no basis without G-d. The main inspiration of this view has been the Hebrew Bible, and in particular the prophets. Indeed the purport of this chapter could not be more succinctly expressed than it is in a single sentence from Micah. "He has told you O man what is good, and what G-d requires of you: only to do justice, and to love mercy, and to walk humbly with your G-d" (Micah 6.8).

In reply to the question, "How do we know that this is really what G-d has told man?" we answer that the question is irrelevant. The point is that without the first part of the sentence quoted from Micah, the exhortation "… to do justice and to love mercy …" ceases to be a categorical imperative and becomes hypothetical as are all prudential imperatives. The power and inspiration that the Hebrew prophets have had on the history of mankind for so many hundreds and thousands of years is due precisely to the fact that the appeal to the human heart for justice and mercy in our dealings with our fellow man *is* a command of G-d and does express G-d's very dealings with us. As we should treat others so does G-d act towards us. If one is willing to grant that it is rational to believe there is a mind behind the orderliness of the world that is at the same time a necessary and eternal Being as well as single and absolutely infinite which created the world from nothing, and who is just and compassionate, it seems a small step to accept the notion that G-d wants man also "… to do justice and to love mercy … ."

If there is no G-d, there is no morality; and if the Creator of the world is not just and compassionate, all is lost in any event. The only rational alternative is that there is a G-d who is just and compassionate who created the world for some good purpose that man is supposed to fulfill.[18] The world need not be rational and may indeed be non-rational, serving no purpose whatever—any more than a shooting

---

17   One can well imagine that if Hitler had won the second World War and established his dream of the thousand year *Reich*, he might indeed have created a 'new' morality.

18   See Chapter 6, p. 83.

star. However, barring some proof or convincing argument that the world is not rational, it is more rational to take the prophet Micah at his word than not.

There is, however, another question, which may sound odd to some but which some eminent contemporary philosophers have seriously posed. The question is: Do we have a categorical duty to obey or emulate G-d if we have made no specific promise to do so? This is another way of asking why G-d's commands are categorical any more than the commands of people of flesh and blood, or why should we try to emulate G-d? Though this question may sound peculiar, it is not easy to answer. I believe some light can be thrown on an answer by raising it in a different form. The question arises in a discussion of the meaning of life, and how one deals with it in this context can shed light on why one should (categorically) obey G-d. We turn therefore in Chapter 9 to the question of the meaning of life.

9
THE MEANING OF LIFE

The notion that the categorical element in morality can be justified only by G-d, which we argued in our previous chapter, is similar to another view that I want to argue in this chapter—namely that there is a sense in which life can be meaningful only in the eyes of G-d. In this sense, a G-dless world is essentially a meaningless world. Both Sartre and Camus held such a view as did many other writers, ancient and modern. It is essentially the view expounded in the Biblical book of Ecclesiastes, attributed to King Solomon, the second sentence of which reads, Vanity of vanities, saith the Preacher, vanity of vanities; all is vanity.[1]

The difference between Sartre and Camus on the one hand and the author of Ecclesiastes on the other is that the former did not believe in G-d, while the latter did. Thus Sartre and Camus thought the world and human life were indeed meaningless. Since human beings by nature pursue meaning in life, such a life is doomed to failure—a life in the pursuit of what is unattainable. Camus called such a life 'absurd' and likened it to the life of the hapless Sisyphus who was condemned by the gods to spend eternity rolling a stone up a hill only to have it roll back down again.[2] Sartre called the G-dless man 'forlorn': "When we speak of forlornness ... we mean only that G-d does not exist and that we have to face all the consequences of this." There are numerous consequences, one of which is that life is meaningless, "... because all possibility of finding values in a heaven of ideas disappears along with Him ... ."[3] The author of Ecclesiastes certainly did believe in G-d. Furthermore, after describing human life as no different from that of an animal, ending as it does in death, the great equalizer, he came to

---

1 Ecclesiastes 1.2.

2 See Albert Camus, *The Myth of Sisyphus* (Random House, Vintage Books, New York, 1955).

3 Jean-Paul Sartre, *Existentialism*, trans. Bernard Frechtman (Philosophical Library, New York, 1947). Reprinted in part in Jones, Sontag, et al., *Approaches to Ethics* (McGraw-Hill, New York, 1977), p. 402.

the conclusion that the whole purpose of life is to fear G-d and obey His commandments for it was for this purpose that man was created.[4] The implication is that without G-d, life is certainly meaningless no matter how great one's accomplishments.

A concrete example of this can be seen in the life of Tolstoy. After having attained fame and fortune, at the pinnacle of his powers, Tolstoy considered his life a failure for there was a sense in which his life had no meaning. The question presented itself in the form of his death. What would all his talent, achievements, wealth, etc. amount to after his death? No one lives forever and sooner or later he and all his loved ones die. "… and there would be nothing left but stench and worms. All my affairs, no matter what they might be, would sooner or later be forgotten, and I myself should not exist."[5] It seemed to Tolstoy that the mortality and fleetingness of human life rendered any seriousness one might give it, a kind of bad joke. The poetical expression of that joke was penned by Shelley in his sonnet "Ozymandias," quoted here in full:

> I met a traveller from an antique land
> Who said: Two vast and trunkless legs of stone
> Stand in the desert. Near them, on the sand,
> Half sunk, a shattered visage lies, whose frown,
> And wrinkled lip, and sneer of cold command,
> Tell that its sculptor well those passions read
> Which yet survive, stamped on these lifeless things,
> The hand that mocked them and the heart that fed.
> And on the pedestal these words appear:
> "My name is Ozymandias, king of kings;
> Look on my works, ye Mighty, and despair!"
> Nothing beside remains. Round the decay
> Of that colossal wreck, boundless and bare
> The lone and level sands stretch far away.

---

4 Ecclesiastes 12.13.

5 See Leo Tolstoy, *My Confession*, reprinted in *The Meaning of Life*, eds. Steven Sanders and David R. Cheney (Prentice-Hall Inc., Englewood Cliffs, N.J., 1980): p. 17.

Death and destruction is the final end of man and all his great feats. When one contemplates this, one might well come to the conclusion of Ecclesiastes that all is vanity.

There is, however, something paradoxical in this view. Namely, that in a perfectly good sense of the word "meaningful," one can say that one's life was meaningful if it produced something of significance. One need not be a Shakespeare, Rembrandt, Beethoven, Einstein, or Tolstoy to live a meaningful life and no one would doubt that the lives of these great men were meaningful in the sense that their accomplishments gave great pleasure, enjoyment and increased understanding to human life. One can also point to the ordinary person who lives a decent life, raises a family, and contributes his or her fair share to society, as having lived a meaningful life. If one can look death in the face without fear, as did that atheist David Hume, with the conviction that his life was spent with an honest devotion to what he saw as the truth, why isn't that a meaningful life?[6] Sisyphus himself would be the first to testify that the most horrible punishment imaginable was that of his own—being given the task of doing something that was of absolutely no benefit to anyone, man or god, for an eternity. There is more to living a meaningful life than living eternally. How does one reconcile this notion of a meaningful life with Tolstoy's dilemma and the pessimistic utterances of Ecclesiastes? Is it true that all is vanity, and that the life of a Beethoven or an Einstein is ultimately no more meaningful than that of an ant crawling on the ground?

It seems to me there are two senses of "meaningful" here, and I think that most people have an appreciation and understanding of both. The problem is that one word is used to carry both of these senses, and so it appears as if there is some disagreement in its use. I do not think this is true though many writers on this topic seem to think so.[7] What I do think is that people who write on this subject see the forcefulness of one of these senses but not the other. They appear to be blind to what the other is talking about. The truth is that there is validity to both senses of the 'meaningfulness' of life mentioned above

6 See his autobiography, "My Own Life," reprinted in his *An Inquiry Concerning Human Understanding*, ed. Charles W. Hendel (The Liberal Arts Press, New York, 1955): pp. 3-11.

7 See the debate on this subject in the volume, *The Meaning of Life*, eds. Sanders and Cheney, Prentice-Hall, 1980.

and the seeing of one of these senses conceals our view of the other. It is difficult to 'see' them both at the same time. It's like the well-known picture of the duck-rabbit. You can see the picture at one moment as a duck and at another moment as a rabbit, but you cannot see the picture as a duck *and* a rabbit at the same time. Similarly, it is possible for someone to view one's life as meaningful, if one sees that one is accomplishing something that is significant for oneself and for others. It is also possible for that same person to 'stand back' and view his accomplishments in terms of eons of time that stretch back into the past and into the future, and to realize that in the eternity of time, no one's accomplishments are of any worth or significance. The question is why should one 'stand back'? What is the point of it? Most of the time we do not reflect on the 'ultimate' significance of what we do. We climb the mountain because it is there, as the mountain climbers are wont to put it. It is an apt phrase, however, for it describes why we live and act the way we do even if we are not climbing mountains. We live life and we strive to accomplish our goals because our lives and goals are before us. We have no choice. We may have freely chosen these goals, but we cannot live as human beings without goals of some sort if we are to live meaningful lives. A good example of a 'meaningless life' is precisely one that is lived without any goals and purposes. This is one of the chief characteristics of human life that distinguishes it from animal life. No matter how intelligent or adept an animal may be at solving problems, animals do not set goals for themselves and therefore can achieve nothing. The life of an animal is in this sense 'meaningless' but this does not seem to bother them. They simply do what comes naturally from instinct, much as a machine functions the way it was manufactured. There is no striving to achieve in animals any more than there is in a machine, and in this sense, animals are no more than machines that have organic life. Descartes was wrong in thinking that animals were not living beings, if that is what he meant by calling them 'machines,'[8] but he was not far wrong in calling animals machines if what he meant was that they do not pursue goals. Only humans do that, and only humans think of their lives as meaningful or meaningless. In this sense, the lives of humans are meaningful in a way that the lives of ants are not. Though the ant seems to be

---

8 Descartes, *Discourse on the Method*, part V.

pursuing a goal—see how it so tenaciously carries a stick or a piece of food back to its colony that contributes to the common welfare of the other ants—it really is not. It acts from instinct or 'mechanically.' It might as well be a machine as far as meaningfulness is concerned. In this sense it is wrong to say that the life of a Beethoven is no more meaningful than that of an ant. Look what Beethoven accomplished! Though ants build a colony, they accomplish nothing. The fact that both ants and Beethoven will die and within time nothing will remain of what they have done is irrelevant. The fact that a thousand years from now, no one may have any awareness of Beethoven or his music in no way detracts from the meaningfulness of Beethoven's life in the sense in which we are discussing it. Without Beethoven and the myriads of people who have enjoyed his music, the world would have been much poorer. Meaningfulness does not depend on our efforts or accomplishments enduring forever. This view has been persuasively argued by Kurt Baier. He writes,

> It is now quite clear that death is simply irrelevant. If life can be worthwhile at all, then it can be so even though it be short. And if it is not worthwhile at all, then an eternity of it is simply a nightmare. It may be said that we have to leave this beautiful world, but it is so only if and because it is beautiful. And it is no less beautiful for coming to an end. I rather suspect that an eternity of it might make us less appreciative, and in the end it would be tedious.[9]

This is one view of meaningfulness and if one is deeply committed to it, one will be unable to see the other view. If one constantly sees the duck-rabbit as a rabbit, one will never see it as a duck. There is, however, a perfectly valid way of seeing meaningfulness in a different light which is incompatible with the view expressed above. The remainder of this chapter will be taken up with expounding this view. It is the 'duck side' of our duck-rabbit analogy.

It may well be that an eternity of meaningless existence is a nightmare, but that death is irrelevant is a case of philosophically 'whistling in the dark.' Death does make a difference, particularly when death is the absolute end of our existence as Baier supposes. One may face

---

9 Kurt Baier, "The Meaningful Life," the Inaugural Lecture at Canberra University College (1957). Reprinted in *The Meaning of Life*, eds. Sanders and Cheney, p. 61.

it with bravery and courage or even defiance, but this is appropriate only when there is a genuine reason for fear.[10] What we all instinctively fear is that we might cease existing altogether and it is this fear that is behind our drive for self-preservation.[11] The fear may be instinctive, but the resolution of this fear is philosophical or religious. It is the conception that human life partakes in some sense of eternality. What is eternal is G-d, and thus the resolution of the fear of death in the sense of the fear of the cessation of one's existence is to be found in G-d.

It is appropriate to repeat at this point something we said in conjunction with our discussion of morality and G-d's goodness. Though we argued for the rationality of the belief in G-d's goodness, we did not base the rationality of belief on G-d's existence or on G-d's goodness. That is, we did not argue, as many argue, that because we need G-d to bolster our morality and we cannot live decent, human lives without it, it is therefore rational to believe in G-d in order to live decent lives. Our argument for the rationality of G-d is outlined in Part I of this book, which mentions nothing about morality. We argued in Chapters 7 and 8 that once one has accepted the rationality of belief in G-d, it is rational to accept that G-d Himself is good and not evil or perhaps amoral, i.e. a Being for whom good and evil is irrelevant.[12]

---

10 People who bear testimony to what is called 'near-death experiences' say they no longer fear death.

11 It can be that sometimes our lives are so painful and miserable that our instinct for self-preservation is overcome and we actually wish for death or at least the cessation of our pain and misery. At that point it may take courage and bravery to go on living. If we knew that by committing suicide, we were condemning ourselves to an afterlife of even greater misery than our present painful one, no rational personal would commit suicide under any conditions.

12 If the Creator of the world is a being for whom moral good and evil is irrelevant, we humans who must fight the battle of good and evil every day of our lives, the outcome of which determines the 'meaningfulness' of our lives, must view such a being as an unwitting contributor to all the evil in the world. The most charitable thing one could say about such a Being is that it is 'insensitive.' A truer description of this Being would be that it is just dumb. In any event, such a Being can hardly lay claim to satisfying the 'job description' of G-d. As we argued in Chapters 7 and 8, a Being who is not just and merciful as we humans understand this, is not G-d.

Similarly, here we argue that sharing in G-d's eternality adds meaning to our lives in a way we can never attain without G-d, but this
is not an argument for the rationality of G-d's existence in the first
place. Sartre and Camus were both correct in thinking that without
G-d, life is in some important sense meaningless or 'forlorn.' This fact,
however, is no reason to believe in His existence. Indeed both Sartre
and Camus based a good part of their philosophies specifically on the
rejection of G-d. If the arguments of Part I are persuasive, there is
no reason why anyone should reject G-d on rational grounds alone.
Here we argue that G-d adds a dimension to the meaningfulness of
life that satisfies our yearnings for eternity. Those who see only the
'rabbit side' of the meaningfulness of human life may never accept
the point of view of the 'duck-side' but this is the result of a kind
of blindness to what is staring them in the face. There may be some
people who just do not like ducks and thus shy away from seeing the
duck in the duck-rabbit picture. However, for someone who has no
'hang-up' about ducks, the picture can be seen as a duck. It could be
that our duck fancier does not like rabbits and refuses to see a rabbit
in the duck-rabbit picture. One can be so obsessed with eternity that
one enjoys nothing that is transitory. Why should one rejoice at the
birth of an infant? Don't we all know that someday this infant will
die? To find nothing meaningful in life because it is transitory is also
a kind of blindness. Life to be truly meaningful must bring together
both of these conceptions that life can be meaningful in itself and that
somehow our lives do partake of eternity. The duck-rabbit picture in
reality *is* both a duck and a rabbit.

It is sometimes said that our lives are meaningful in the sense that
G-d created the world and put man in it for a purpose. The Baal
Shem Tov[13] went so far as to say that not only does every human being exist in the world for a purpose, but that every blade of grass has
a purpose and, one might add, every sub-atomic particle. One may
never discover the purpose of a blade of grass or an atomic particle,
but one can discover one's own purpose in life through some connection one may find between one's life and G-d. How one comes to this
is not the subject of this chapter. I mention this here simply because

---

13   The founder of the Hasidic movement within Judaism. He lived from
     1698-1760.

it is a well-known and commonly accepted view that meaning can be found in discovering the purpose of our existence as it has been determined by G-d.

Kurt Baier in the article alluded to above (see footnote 9) considers it an insult to humans to suppose that G-d created them for a purpose in that they thereby become slaves to G-d, lacking any significance or meaning in themselves. We are reduced "… to the level of a gadget, a domestic animal, or perhaps a slave."[14] This misconstrues the relationship that man has with G-d as conceived in our religious tradition. Namely, that there is a relationship of love and awe that connects one with G-d. G-d loves every human being as a father loves a child and when one truly recognizes G-d's greatness, one cannot but stand in awe of Him. Similarly, if one loves G-d in return, one will not consider it a menial task to fulfill His wishes any more than one would consider it menial or degrading to fulfill the wishes of anyone we love. Furthermore, if we can stand in awe of a Beethoven or an Einstein, should we not stand in awe of the Creator of music and the entire realm of science and nature? Of course, one must first think that the world of music and nature does have a Creator and did not come about by accident before one can stand in awe of that Creator or come to love Him. Baier, no doubt, does not believe that G-d exists and therefore would find it difficult to imagine loving or standing in awe of Him any more than one could stand in awe of UFOs which one does not think exist.

A more fundamental problem is raised by Thomas Nagel in one of the most serious challenges to the view that G-d can be the source of ultimate meaning for human life.[15] Nagel argues that even if one believed in G-d, and there was no question about the purpose of life because of the acceptance of some religious tradition, one could still 'stand back' and ask why such a life has any ultimate meaning or purpose. Nagel's argument for this paradoxical view depends upon a certain kind of skeptical philosophy he promulgates which we must discuss. Someone unfamiliar with this type of philosophy will find it difficult to understand Nagel's argument and our evaluation of it. Such

---

14 Sanders and Cheney, p. 52.
15 See Thomas Nagel, "The Absurd," *The Journal of Philosophy* (October 21, 1971): pp. 716-27. Reprinted in Sanders and Cheney, pp. 155-165.

a reader should feel free to skip this discussion, as it assumes a familiarity with some subtle points in contemporary, skeptical philosophy. I do, however, feel obliged to take up Nagel's argument as I think it is the most interesting and subtle argument in all of the philosophical literature that discusses the meaning of life.

The best way of presenting Nagel's argument is to return to Hume, for Nagel, I believe, is the quintessential Humean. Let us recall Hume's discussion of induction which we touched on in Chapter 2. Though Nagel himself uses as his example of a skeptical challenge to our beliefs, the doubt that we may be dreaming all the time,[16] it makes no difference which form the skeptical argument takes. The point of every skeptical argument is to deny that there is anything anyone can know.

Recall that Hume argued that the ultimate ground or foundation of all our empirical knowledge of the world is our instinctive acceptance of the belief that the future will be like the past. We expect the sun to rise tomorrow because it always has done so in the past. Hume, however, challenged the rational validity of this belief. He argued, successfully I believe, that this belief is neither logically necessary nor empirically verifiable and that therefore there could be no proof of its truth. Every rational person, however, does as a matter of fact believe that it is true and could not live or function in the world without it. Nonetheless this does not demonstrate the truth of the belief but simply the fact that we can't live without it. Nagel would argue that in spite of our unquestioned acceptance of the belief that the sun will rise tomorrow, we can 'stand back' from it and ask for its justification. When none is forthcoming and when we realize that we cannot live without it, we return to it, but this time our acceptance of it has a tinge of irony. As Nagel says, "… we return to our familiar convictions with a certain irony and resignation."[17] The irony is that we have somehow evolved (or have been created) in such a way that we intuitively accept all kinds of beliefs that cannot be rationally justified. This was precisely Hume's point that our rational beliefs are no more 'rational' than the belief of Pavlov's famous dog that it would be fed when it heard the bell ring. The difference between us humans and Pavlov's dog is that we can 'stand back' and ask questions about whether what we do is

---

16   See his article in Sanders and Cheney, pp. 161-63 (Section V).

17   Sanders and Cheney, p. 168.

rational. Nagel's point is that it *always* makes sense to stand back and ask such questions, though the question may sound silly or absurd. For example, Nagel says,

> … we can ask not only why we should believe there is a floor under us, but also why we should believe the evidence of our senses at all—and at some point framable questions will have outlasted the answers. Similarly, we can ask not only why we should take aspirin, but why we should take trouble over our own comfort at all. The fact that we shall take the aspirin without waiting for an answer to this last question does not show that it is an unreal question. We shall also continue to believe there is a floor under us without waiting for an answer to the other question. In both cases it is this unsupported natural confidence that generates skeptical doubts; so it cannot be used to settle it.[18]

Just as Nagel thinks there is some sense in which the skeptical questions in the above quoted paragraph are meaningful, so likewise he thinks that once one 'stands back' and asks the question, "Why is life meaningful?," there is *no* answer to this question. Even if G-d Himself were to come down and tell us in no uncertain terms the purpose He had in mind when He created a world with human beings, according to Nagel we could still 'stand back' and say to G-d, "So what, that does not necessarily make my life meaningful." This would be so, if that purpose did not appeal to us or suit our lifestyle. Thus the question, "Why is life meaningful?" has no answer but we have no choice but to return to our daily routine like ants going about their business as if the whole world depended on what we are doing. Now, however, any seriousness that we may have about what we are doing "… is laced with irony,"[19] for we know that the natural confidence in what we are doing stands on sand.

The above, I think, is a fair presentation of Nagel's argument. There are, however, two things wrong with it. One is his claim that it makes sense to 'stand back' and ask skeptical questions about anything one claims to know. The second thing is that while it does make sense to 'stand back' and ask why is life meaningful, it is wrong to say, as Nagel does, that there can be no answer to this question—not even if G-d

---

18 Ibid., p. 162.

19 Idem.

Himself would tell us why He created the world. We shall take these two points up respectively.

The first error in Nagel's thinking is to suppose that the skeptical questions he raises about our knowledge make sense. They don't. It makes no sense to ask, as you sit in your study writing a paper on philosophical scepticism, whether you are justified in thinking there is a floor under you because you might be dreaming, any more than it makes sense to ask whether the sun will rise tomorrow because you don't know whether the future will be like the past. Both these questions are equally nonsensical and the claim of certain philosophers that they do make sense is, I believe, based on a confusion. The confusion can be pithily expressed as follows: If there is, literally, nothing you can know, then one cannot ask any questions, for *all* questions, even skeptical ones, presuppose there is something you *do* know.[20]

The crux of this argument turns on a unique feature of what it means to know something. 'Knowing' is different from any other term that describes what is going on in our minds. Let us illustrate this from the claim that we may be dreaming all the time and therefore can always doubt what we instinctively believe as true. Namely that we are awake and not dreaming.

Let us imagine we have just awakened from a nightmare in which we thought we were being chased by a lion. We might even say that in our dream we were convinced without any doubt that we were being chased by a lion. We might go on to say that in our dream, we were hoping it was all a dream from which we would soon, mercifully, awaken. What we could not say after we woke up is that we *knew* we were being chased by a lion, although we might say that we *thought* we were being chased by a lion or that we *dreamed* we were being chased by a lion. There is a difference between thinking something and knowing something. You can entertain the possibility that something you are thinking might be wrong, but you cannot entertain the possibility that something you claim to know might be wrong, because knowing something entails that you think what you know is true. A person who says he knows something when he thinks he might be

---

20 As Wittgenstein put it, you can't doubt something unless it is possible to first know something. See his *On Certainty*, paragraphs 20-35, 117-128, and 524, among others.

wrong is simply lying. This is a unique peculiarity of the word "know." It follows that if someone *always* had a doubt about what he was thinking, he could never know anything.[21] The skeptical questions that philosophers such as Nagel pose raise this very point—namely there is *nothing* we can say we really know. If that were true, however, there are no questions, not even skeptical ones, that philosophers can ask, for questions like, "Are we really awake when we think we are?" imply we can at least know the difference between dreaming and being awake. Otherwise, the question would be unintelligible. It would be like holding up a color card in front of a blind man and asking if the card is red or green. For a blind man, the question is unintelligible for he cannot see colors at all.[22] Similarly, if a person could really not know the difference between having a dream and being awake, the question of whether one is dreaming or awake would be unintelligible.

However, everyone *can* understand this question, even the skeptical philosopher, because we all *know* when we have dreamt and when we are awake. If, however, one can only surmise or think one is awake but can never know this, and if one can never know that one was dreaming but can only suspect or think one was dreaming, there would be no difference between wondering whether you are awake or dreaming, and wondering whether you were dreaming or awake. We, of course, can sometimes be mistaken about this as when we think we are awake when we are only dreaming, and sometimes we think we are dreaming when we are awake, but there is a way of discovering this mistake, and so the question is intelligible.[23] Since it is not possible to distinguish

---

21 Thus, if anyone ever said he knew anything, he would be lying if he were a sceptic.

22 This is quite different from being color blind, where you think you can tell the difference between certain colors and so the question is at least intelligible to you. It's just that you are mistaken in thinking you can answer the question correctly.

23 Many philosophers throughout the history of philosophy thought that one could not really know something unless it were impossible to be mistaken about it. If one looks carefully at the situations in which one thinks it perfectly proper to say one knows something, they are *always* situations in which it is possible to be mistaken. In fact, the *primary* use of "know" is to emphasize the fact that though this is a situation in which it might be possible to be mistaken, nonetheless, you are *certain* that in this case you

these two states of mind, we would be unaware of the difference, as the blind are unaware of the difference between red and green, and the question would be unintelligible to us. The philosopher who asks the skeptical question is aware of the distinction between dreaming and being awake (otherwise he could not ask the question) which means that he also *knows* when he is awake. The skeptical question, which implies that one cannot know when one is awake is therefore unintelligible, for if the question succeeds in its purpose, the question itself would disappear. All such skeptical questions might be called 'self-destruct' questions—they can succeed only by undermining what makes the question intelligible in the first place. Such questions literally pull the rug out from under themselves.

This is why I think Nagel is mistaken when he says that 'standing back' and asking skeptical questions throws doubt on the validity of human knowledge, and therefore our pursuit of knowledge in daily life should be tinged with irony. That is, in the back of our philosophical mind, there should be a lingering doubt that when we spend our time in the pursuit of knowledge we are spending it in vain because there is no such thing. I am arguing here that there is nothing to worry about, for human knowledge is possible. What is not possible is philosophically 'standing back' from it.

The second thing that is wrong with Nagel's analysis of the meaning of life is that while he is perfectly correct in thinking that it does make sense to 'stand back' from life and ask what is it all worth, even when that life is a happy and meaningful one, it does not make sense to say that this question cannot be alleviated even by G-d. Camus and Sartre were not mistaken in thinking that if they could believe in G-d, the problem of the meaning of life would be resolved, and Tolstoy was not misled in thinking that if he could find faith, he would find meaning

---

are not mistaken. This is why Wittgenstein thought G.E. Moore was using this term improperly when he pointed to his hand and said, "I *know* this is my hand." This is not what one would ordinarily say one knows, because it is not something about which one could be mistaken. One might be tempted to ask Moore the skeptical question, "How do you know you are not dreaming now and therefore not pointing to your hand?" The reply that is being argued here is that all such skeptical questions are unintelligible.

in living he could not find in wealth or literary success.[24] There is this desire in the heart of man for eternality, and failure to achieve this can make one wonder about the ultimate value of life. This is not a frivolous question or one that can be ignored or chalked up to man's *hubris* or arrogance. Furthermore, only some relationship with G-d can satisfy this desire. Aristotle thought it could be achieved through procreation, thinking that the world and the species were eternal. Even if this were true, it is not what we seek, which is not that mankind be eternal but that our unique lives and accomplishments in some sense partake of eternality.

In Chapter 6 we argued that given the facts of an absolutely infinite and eternal G-d and a finite contingent world, it is more rational to suppose that G-d, a knowing Being, created the world rather than that the world eternally coexists with G-d. Assuming this argument and the truth of Creation, it is more rational to suppose that G-d had a purpose in creating the world and not that it was an absent-minded doodle. Insofar as man has a role in furthering this design or fulfilling this Creation one could say that one's life is meaningful in some eternal sense. According to the view mentioned earlier, that there is a purpose for every sub-atomic particle in the universe to say nothing of a human being, what more meaningful life could one imagine than fulfilling the purpose of one's unique existence in the world.

As far as the remarks of Baier that such a view turns man into nothing more than a lackey or a slave of G-d, this assumes that the relation of G-d to man is analogous to that of a slave and a master. Nothing could be further from the truth. The relation between G-d and man as conceived of in all three monotheistic religions is that G-d has given man free will to choose or reject Him. G-d does not force Himself on anyone. He remains hidden behind the scenes (some say He is too hidden) and man must seek Him in order to find Him. He is very modest and retiring and rarely makes public appearances.

Secondly, the true bond between man and G-d is love. G-d loves man and man in return, seeks G-d out of love. Love indeed is the most powerful and meaningful force in human life. If there is anything in this temporary veil of tears that gives meaning to life, it is human

---

24   Leo Tolstoy, *My Confession*, originally published by J.M. Dent and Sons, 1905, reprinted with omissions in Sanders and Cheney, pp. 15-24.

love. Love is the strongest bond that can connect one human being with another. The poets of all ages bear witness to this and they are not wrong. The greatest of them proclaim that such love is eternal and dies not in the grave.

> Let me not to the marriage of true minds
> Admit impediments. Love is not love
> Which alters when it alteration finds,
> Or bends with the remover to remove.
> Oh, no! it is an ever-fixed mark
> That looks on tempests and is never shaken;
> It is the star to every wandering bark,
> Whose worth's unknown, although his height be taken.
> Love's not Time's fool, though rosy lips and cheeks
> Within his bending sickle's compass come;
> Love alters not with his brief hours and weeks,
> But bears it out even to the edge of doom.
> If this be error and upon me proved,
> I never writ, nor no man ever loved.[25]

This certainly touches a sympathetic chord with anyone who has every truly loved another person, but we all know that this is nothing more than poetic license and that death does separate loved ones at least in this world. If there really could be eternal love this would render eternality, eternally meaningful. This is exactly what is meant by love of G-d. Love of G-d truly dies not in the grave but simply grows and waxes as the soul draws closer to G-d in death. One cannot 'stand back' from love of G-d and ask why it has ultimate meaning. To ask such a question is an even greater absurdity than asking how we know that when we are awake, we are not dreaming. Not only is love of G-d the ultimate meaning of life in this world, it is the gate whereby one enters into the realization of the oneness and unity of G-d and the world that transcends human understanding.

There is a story about two tzadikim (righteous men) who lived in the early 19th century. They were very close friends and had great admiration and love for one another. One was Yisrael of Ruzhin and the other was Menachen Mendel of Lubavitch, commonly referred to

25 William Shakespeare, Sonnet CXVI.

as the Tzemach Tzedek.[26] Yisrael of Ruzhin, praising his friend Menachem Mendel, is reported to have said, "Mendel did better than I
did. His service of G-d began with intellect and later descended into
the heart, whereas I began with the heart and from there rose to the
intellect. The intellect, however, is limited while the heart is infinite,
so Mendel's service of G-d is infinite and eternal, while mine remains
finite and limited."

The 'heart' here is a symbol for love of G-d and the capacity of the
heart for love is limitless, but understanding comes to an end at some
point. The mystical union of the soul of man with G-d through love
is the ultimate meaning of life, not only in this life, but in the life of
the soul after it leaves the body. That there is such a thing as life after
death or as it is more fittingly described, 'life after life,'[27] is documented
by a multitude of 'near-death' experiences, as they are called. In our
next chapter we shall discuss two of these experiences and we will try
to point out why it is absurd to 'stand back' from them and ask why
they determine the meaning of life. These experiences are only arrows
that point to the main topic of our final chapter which is the oneness
and unity of G-d with the world. The realization of this oneness is the
meaning of life because it is the origin of all existence, and the search
for this mystical union is the basic drive of the human soul.

These experiences satisfy both the 'duck' and 'rabbit' criteria of
meaningfulness. Not only are they meaningful in themselves in a way
that transcends anything we experience when our souls are connected
to our bodies, but the state that the soul enjoys in near-death experiences will ultimately be the eternal state of the soul after it leaves the
material world. Thus meaningfulness and eternality are merged in a

---

26   Yisrael of Ruzhin was the leader of the Ruzhiner dynasty (1797-1851)
     and the Tzemach Tzedek was head of the Lubavitcher dynasty in his day
     (1789-1866).

27   In Judaism the name for a cemetery is :"*bais hachaim*," which in Hebrew
     means, paradoxically, "house of the living." This is not meant as a kind of
     joke or wishful thinking but expresses precisely what Judaism means by
     life. The source of life is G-d just as the source of light is a fire. The closer
     one comes to the fire, the brighter the light; and the closer one comes to
     G-d, the more intense is life. This is the spiritual life of the soul which
     is intensified when the soul leaves the body and comes closer to G-d in
     'near-death' experiences.

unity that can never be completely achieved while the soul is in the body. The question is, how is this connected with a meaningful life *in this world*? The answer to this lies in the fact that life in the world is not divorced from the life of the soul after it leaves this world and goes to the celestial world of spirit. These are not two different lives, but a single continuous life that simply is raised a notch. There is a continuum from the lowest level of life in this world to the highest level in the life of spirit and at some point in this continuum, the soul leaves the body and enters into the world of spirit. This is the dividing line between physical life and spiritual life. The point here is that the meaningfulness of life is defined in terms of the highest level the soul can attain in the realm of spirit and lower levels of spirituality represent a continuum that determines a relativity of meaningfulness as it measures up to the highest level of which the soul is capable.

There is a dividing line that separates the life of the soul in the body from its life apart from the body, but the meaningfulness of life is still measured in terms of the highest level attainable. Thus a life in this world devoid of all and any spirituality is a meaningless life. Most human beings enjoy some degree or form of spirituality as love and compassion that they share with family, friends and loved ones. This love and compassion that we feel not only for other human beings, but also animals and nature in general is a form of spirituality that is part of the continuum that continues after the soul departs the physical world. This is the picture of the soul we get from near-death experiences. The question is how reliable is this picture? This is the question to which we turn in our next chapter.

10

NEAR-DEATH EXPERIENCES

David Hume writes in Section X of his *An Inquiry Concerning Human Understanding* that "... no testimony is sufficient to establish a miracle unless the testimony be of such a kind that its falsehood would be more miraculous than the fact which it endeavours to establish."[1] Hume gives an illustration of what he means by a miracle.

> When anyone tells me that he saw a dead man restored to life, I immediately consider with myself whether it be more probable that this person should either deceive or be deceived, or that the fact which he relates should really have happened. I weigh the one miracle against the other, and according to the superiority which I discover I pronounce my decision, and always reject the greater miracle. If the falsehood of his testimony would be more miraculous than the event which he relates, then, and not until then, can he pretend to command my belief or opinion.[2]

Hume considers a dead man coming back to be a miracle for his definition of a miracle is that

> Nothing is esteemed a miracle if it ever happens in the common course of nature. It is no miracle that man, seemingly in good health, should die on a sudden, because such a kind of death, though more unusual than any other, has yet been frequently observed to happen. But it is a miracle that a dead man should come to life, because that has never been observed in any age or country. There must, therefore, be a uniform experience against every miraculous event, otherwise the event would not merit that appellation. And as a uniform experience amounts to a proof, there is here a direct and full *proof*, from the nature of the fact, against the existence of any

---

1 David Hume, *An Inquiry Concerning Human Understanding* (The Liberty Arts Press, 1955): p. 123.

2 Ibid., pp. 123-24.

miracle, nor can such a proof be destroyed or the miracle rendered credible but by an opposite proof which is superior.[3]

Hume's discussion of miracles in these passages makes no mention of G-d *per se*,[4] and according to his definition, what is necessary to prove a miracle is that there should exist evidence for a miracle such that the evidence is more likely true than that the miracle be false.

---

3 Ibid., pp. 122-23.

4 However, Hume's footnote 7 (p. 123) which comes immediately after the passage quoted above in our footnote 3 makes the point that if there is a suspicion that a breakdown in the laws of nature was an 'accident' and not due to G-d's intervention, it would not be considered a miracle. As he says in this footnote, "A miracle may be accurately defined, *a transgression of a law of nature by a particular volition of the Deity, or by the interposition of some invisible agent* (Hume's italics). A miracle may either be discovered or not. This alters not its nature and essence." (p. 123).

This is not entirely consistent with his definition of a miracle quoted above in which a miracle is said to be the occurrence of an event for which there is no prior evidence in the entire course of human history. The question of how one could determine whether or not such an event be due to "... a volition of the Deity," is not addressed by Hume. Whether G-d is behind an event, the like of which has never before been experienced in human history, is irrelevant to the force of the evidence upon which Hume's acceptance of the miracle depends. Thus, in our example of the discovery of the constancy of the speed of light (mentioned on the next page), the acceptance of such a 'miracle' should depend on the reliability of the Michelson-Morley experiments which has nothing to do with G-d. In footnote 7, Hume argues that the reliability of a miracle *depends* on the existence of G-d, and therefore cannot be used to prove G-d's existence. This seems clearly at cross purposes to his main argument in this chapter that there is no reason to accept the truth of a miracle on grounds independent of G-d, i.e. on the basis of empirical evidence.

Even more puzzling is Hume's rider to his definition of a miracle, quoted above, in which he describes a miracle as an interruption of a law of nature due to a volition of G-d, "... or by the interposition of some invisible agent." What does Hume mean here by an "invisible agent"? Whatever he means, what he says should apply also to the force of gravity, which might well be described as an incomprehensible, invisible force. Taking Hume at his word here would transform the force of gravity into a miracle as great as a dead man coming back to life! All in all, footnote 7 of Hume's chapter on miracles would have been better off, had it never been written.

Hume seems to think such a proof of a miracle is impossible in the nature of the case because he did not think there could be evidence that supports an event the like of which no one has ever experienced.

Hume is clearly wrong about this as evidenced by the well-known Michelson-Morley experiment in 1881 that showed the speed of light to be constant. No matter how fast or slow the source of the light is travelling, they discovered what according to Hume was a miracle, for it had never before been observed in the entire course of human history that the speed of anything was not effected by the speed of the origin of that motion. Thus if you threw a spear at an enemy while galloping towards him on a horse, the spear would strike your enemy with the force of the spear travelling at the speed with which you threw it plus the speed of the horse. If you shot an arrow at your enemy while galloping away from him, the arrow would strike him with the force of the arrow travelling at the speed with which you shot it minus the speed of the horse. If your enemy was galloping after you at the same speed that your horse was galloping away, the effect would be the same as if you were both stationary. Every scientist up until 1881 thought the same thing applied to the speed of light. The Michelson-Morley experiment revealed the 'miracle' that the speed of light was constant, or always the same no matter what speed the source of the illumination. If Hume had been around to comment on this puzzling and astonishing phenomenon, he would say there is no reason whatever to believe a miracle like this, and furthermore there can *never* be a proof for this miracle. As time went on, however, and evidence for this miracle mounted which culminated in Einstein's Special Theory of Relativity in 1905, Hume would have had to admit that the falsity of the evidence for the truth of this miracle was more unlikely than the falsity of the miracle.

In a similar way, I believe that the evidence from near-death experiences, or NDEs as we shall henceforth call them,[5] are of sufficient weight that their falsity is less likely than the falsity of the miracle of life after death that they support. In other words, there is sufficient

5 This abbreviation was coined by Dr. Raymond A. Moody, Jr. in his ground-breaking book, *Life After Life*, first published by Mockingbird Books, 1975. We will use the following abbreviations throughout: NDE near-death experience; NDEs near-death experiences; NDEer near-death experiencer; NDEers, near-death experiencers.

evidence today that makes it rational to think that the life of a person continues in some sense after the demise of the body which is called 'death,' and that our evidence for this is that people who appear to have died, have come back to life and have described what life after death is like.

The first part of this chapter will be concerned with substantiating this claim. The second part describes how NDEs support some of the conclusions of the previous nine chapters of this book, though the forcefulness of our arguments in the first five chapters of this book that support these conclusions in no way rests on NDEs. In this second part, I focus on the NDE of two remarkable accounts which have been put in book form by their NDEers. The first is that of Dannion Brinkley and the second is that of Rachel Noam. Above all, the most profound and interesting aspects of these experiences tend to confirm the central thesis of this book, namely the oneness and unity of all things with G-d. Furthermore, the binding force of this unity or the 'glue' that holds it together is love. This is the ultimate truth of mysticism: everything is one and nothing exists outside this oneness. It is bonded by love and behind it all is what we call G-d. Let us turn now to the first part of this chapter and NDEs.

I. NEAR-DEATH EXPERIENCES (NDES)

Since all NDEs are anecdotal, I will begin with a story of how I first became aware of this amazing phenomenon. In the summer of 1976 I was teaching a course in philosophy offered by the Faculty of Part-Time and Continuing Education of our University in a small town on the Georgian Bay in south western Ontario. I was expounding Aristotle's argument that sight could not exist without an eye to see, nor hearing without an ear to hear, etc. This argument had always impressed me as very persuasive and I was explaining it with gusto, revelling in its persuasiveness and power. One woman raised her hand and asked how I, or Aristotle, could explain the fact that some people who have been resuscitated from cardiac arrest or other critical situations, report that they have 'floated" out of their bodies and could see and hear everything going on around them from a vantage point of a few feet above their 'unconscious bodies'? I stated quite flatly that I did not believe this, being the first time I had ever heard of such a thing. At that time, I was satisfied that in this case, Hume's criterion of accepting the truth of a miracle could not be proven. I consoled myself with Hume's pronouncement that I had as strong an argument as anyone could possibly have for not believing something; namely, the uniform experience of all mankind known throughout history, in which nothing like this was ever reported (as far as I knew).[6] The next day the student brought to the class a newspaper report of such an experience. I still did not believe it, even though the paper was a 'reputable' one.[7] I again took heart from Hume's warning not to believe a miracle as long as the probability of the falsity of this rather slim evidence was greater than the probability of the truth of the miracle. Flying out of one's body and observing 'yourself' from a distance still seemed to me an improbable miracle in spite of the newspaper report. I more or less forgot about this incident, though in all truthfulness I stopped presenting Aristotle's argument against eyeless sight or earless hearing with the same enthusiasm that I once did. Then I heard about this phenomenon again and that there was actually a paperback Bantam book out about it by a Dr. Raymond A. Moody, Jr. I bought the book and spent the next twenty-four hours reading it. I couldn't believe what I was reading. I had never heard of anything like this before. I wondered if it was really as common as Moody claimed. He had said that in any random group of thirty people, there will be at least one person who has had such an experience.[8] I found this hard to believe and decided to test it. I was at that time teaching a course in philosophy of religion, again for the Faculty of Part-Time and Continuing Education of my University in a small city seventy miles west of London, Ontario. On a proper occasion I mentioned that a student in another class had called my attention to the fact that in critical health situations, people can float out of their bodies and be aware of what is going on around them while they (their bodies) are unconscious, thus refuting Aristotle's argument that sight without an eye is impossible. I asked if anyone in the class had ever heard of such a thing. No one raised a hand. I thought to myself that it is not as common as Moody makes out. After the class was over, one of the

---

6 See Hume's *Inquiry* quoted above, pp. 122-23.

7 It was not the *National Enquirer* or any such sensationalist newspaper.

8 Moody, *Life After Life*, p. 15.

young ladies in the class came up to me after everyone had left and confided that she, herself, had had such an experience, but she was reticent to talk about it in public, as people always treated her as if she were a little cuckoo. I asked her if she minded telling me about it, as I considered this a very important phenomenon to talk about if it were true. This is the story she told:

She was pregnant with her second child and haemorrhaged. She fainted from loss of blood and the next thing she knew she was out of her body looking down at it, while her husband was slapping her wrists in an attempt to revive her. She could see an ambulance backing up in the driveway and watched as the two attendants prepared the ambulance to receive her. She even noted the license plate of the ambulance. She felt herself moving upwards and then realized that she might be 'dead' and was leaving her family behind. She looked into the next room where her two year-old child was sleeping and felt a desire to return to her body to take care of him, and the next thing she knew she was back in her body looking up at her husband who was slapping her wrists.

She later told her husband the entire story, but he refused to believe her until she described how the ambulance was backed up in the driveway, and the license plate of the ambulance which she remembered. Her husband later checked with the ambulance company to see if the number tallied, and it did. That's when he began to believe the reality of what his wife was describing. There was nothing 'flaky' about this student. She was a mature woman with a family, highly intelligent, and she went on to earn an 'A' in the course.

I was beginning to feel that Hume's dividing the line between rejection and acceptance of a miracle was about to be crossed. Now, twenty years after my first encounter with NDEs and some twelve books I have read on the matter that have been written since then, I definitely believe that the evidence contained in those books is more believable than the falsity of NDEs. To my mind it is not only rational to accept the truth of NDEs, but actually irrational not to accept them in the light of all the evidence. I will try to recount a bit of that evidence not only to support the statements I have just made but also to give a more adequate description of NDEs so that they can serve as some kind of support for the metaphysical theses presented in the previous nine chapters. As metaphysical theses, I do not think they can be *confirmed* by empirical evidence for the reasons we have discussed in chapters one and two. NDEs, however, do give us a view of the nature of reality which points to metaphysical truths about the nature of reality for which we previously had given purely philosophical arguments. NDEs, though they may not confirm the truth of our metaphysical theses, certainly are consistent with them and lend them support .

So far, all we have mentioned about NDEs are the out-of-body experiences with which many NDEs begin. It is, however, only the beginning of the NDE. The most interesting aspects of these experiences are yet to come. We begin with the out-of-body experience here because, 1) that is where they often begin and, 2) out-of-body experiences are the best refutation of the view expressed by doctors and others—that these NDEs are a form of hallucination or the effects of drugs or traumas, and do not show that one can 'float' out of one's body and see and hear things being said while one's 'body' is unconscious. Here are some documented examples of out-of-body experiences that, to my mind, refute any such a view of the matter.

A most remarkable one is recounted in a chapter of a book by Kimberly Clark Sharp. The chapter is entitled, "The Shoe on the Ledge."[9] Sharp was a social worker at Harborview Medical Center in Seattle, Washington. As she knew a little Spanish, she was called in to help 'settle down' a female hispanic migrant worker called Maria. Maria had suffered a massive heart attack and was brought to Harborview's CCU. She was in the CCU unit and on the fourth day she suffered another cardiac arrest. She was resuscitated and when she regained consciousness she became almost uncontrollable, flailing her arms and speaking Spanish excitedly with a wild look in her eyes. She began to sob with frustration at not being able to express herself in a way anyone could understand. Sharp tried to calm her down and when she became more relaxed and able to talk coherently. This is the story she told.

> Maria pointed to a corner of the ceiling and said she had been up
> there watching people work over her body. She told me precisely,
> and correctly, who had been in the room, where they stood, what

9 See Kimberly Clark Sharp, *After the Light* (Avon Books, 1995). The passages quoted on the following pages are from Sharp's book, pp. 9-11.

they did, and what they said. She described the placement of machinery and all the paper that had been kicked around on the floor during the resuscitation, paper that the electrocardiogram machine had been continuously feeding out. Next, with a snap of her fingers to show me how fast she had moved, Maria told me she suddenly found herself outside the hospital room, looking down at the emergency room entrance. She described the curvature of the driveway, the vehicles all going in one direction and the doors opening automatically. Everything was absolutely accurate...

Maria wasn't through yet. She said she had been distracted by something in a different part of the hospital, and she next remembered staring closely at an object on a window ledge about three stories above the ground. It was a man's dark blue tennis shoe, well-worn, scuffed on the left side where the little toe would go. The shoelace was caught under the heel. Maria was upset, she explained, because she desperately wanted someone to go get the shoe. Not to prove to herself that it was there; Maria knew she was an honest woman and she was telling the truth. No, she needed to prove it to others—that she really had been out of her body, floating free, outside the hospital walls. That she wasn't crazy...

Clark went looking for the shoe. She first went outside and walked around the hospital looking up at all the third story windows for the shoe, but couldn't find it. She then started going into all the patients rooms on the third floor and looking down at the window sills from inside the room. She examined the north side of the hospital but found nothing and was four rooms into the west side of the building when she found the shoe.

Out on the narrow ledge below the window was a man's dark blue tennis shoe. It was well-worn, with the end of the lace tucked under the heel. I couldn't see if the little toe area was scuffed, because that side was facing away from the window. My gaze fell away from the tennis shoe, far away, toward the Olympic Mountains to the west and Elliott Bay spread out beneath them, forming a scenic backdrop for a lone high-rise building about a half-mile away.

There was no conceivable way that Maria could have seen that shoe either from the inside or the outside given her physical condition. Clark took the shoe from the window sill and brought it back to show

Maria. Maria became so excited when she saw the shoe that the nurse at the monitoring station rushed in to find out why Maria's heart was jumping like a Mexican jumping bean. When she was told about the shoe she promptly told the rest of the staff and as Clark describes in her book, my mind raced through a dozen different explanations and settled on three possibilities.

> By the next morning, every nurse in the CCU knew Maria's story, and by afternoon, a parade of doctors and nurses and other staff members had dropped in to pay their respects to the humble shoe. Maria displayed the shoe on a side table in her room, and received her many visitors with gracious hospitality. They saw, they touched, they left. No one, at least in the company of Maria or me or members of her resuscitation team, disputed a word of her account. Too many knew the seriousness of Maria's condition, and realized how impossible it would have been for her to have had detailed foreknowledge of the shoe.[10] [11]

I will now quote a passage from Raymond A. Moody's most recent book on NDEs entitled *The Light Beyond*, first published in 1988 and is Dr. Moody's most mature writing on NDEs. He attempts to answer various 'explanations' of NDEs given by theologians, medical personnel, and psychologists, who try to explain away NDEs as not being real but abnormal, mental phenomena due to drugs or stress, etc. He cites four cases of out-of-body experiences which he thinks refutes all such explanations. I quote them here in full.

> 1) A forty-nine year old man had a heart attack so severe that after thirty-five minutes of vigorous resuscitation efforts, the doctor gave up and began filling out the death certificate. Then someone noticed a flicker of life, so the doctor continued his work with the paddles and breathing equipment and was able to restart the man's heart.
>
> The next day, when he was more coherent, the patient was able to describe in great detail what went on in the emergency room. This surprised the doctor. But what astonished him even more was

10   Ibid., pp. 9-14.

11   A critical assessment of Kimberly Clark Sharp's account of the Shoe on the Ledge appeared in the *Sceptical Inquirer*, July/August, 1996, pp. 27-33. It is entitled "Maria's Near-Death Experience" authored by Hayden Ebbern, Sean Mulligan, and Barry L. Beyestein. A detailed discussion of their arguments is attached as an appendix at the end of this chapter.

the patient's vivid description of the emergency room nurse who hurried into the room to assist the doctor.

He described her perfectly, right down to her wedge hairdo and her last name, Hawkes. He said that she rolled this cart down the hall with a machine that had what looked like two Ping-Pong paddles on it (an electro shocker that is basic resuscitation equipment).

When the doctor asked him how he knew the nurse's name and what she had been doing during his heart attack, he said that he had left his body and—while walking down the hall to see his wife—passed right through nurse Hawkes. He read the name tag as he went through her, and remembered it so he could thank her later.

I talked to the doctor at great length about this case. He was quite rattled by it. Being there, he said, was the only way the man could have recounted this with such complete accuracy.

2) On Long Island, a seventy-year old woman who had been blind since the age of eighteen was able to describe in vivid detail what was happening around her as doctors resuscitated her after a heart attack.

Not only could she describe what the instruments used looked like, but she could even describe their colors.

The most amazing thing about this to me was that most of these instruments weren't even thought of over fifty years ago when she could last see. On top of all this, she was even able to tell the doctor that he was wearing a blue suit when he began the resuscitation.

3) Another amazing case that says NDEs are more than just tricks of the mind was relayed to me by a doctor in South Dakota.

Driving into the hospital one morning, he had rear-ended a car. It had been very upsetting to him. He was very worried that the people he had hit would claim neck injury and sue him for a large sum of money.

This accident left him distraught and was very much on his mind later that morning when he rushed to the emergency room to resuscitate a person who was having a cardiac arrest.

The next day, the man he had rescued told him a remarkable story: "While you were working on me, I left my body and watched you work."

The doctor began to ask questions about what the man had seen and was amazed at the accuracy of his description. In precise detail, he told the doctor how the instruments looked and even in what order they were used. He described the colors of the equipment, shapes, and even settings of dials on the machines.

But what finally convinced this young cardiologist that the man's experience was genuine was when he said, "Doctor, I could tell that you were worried about that accident. But there isn't any reason to be worried about things like that. You give your time to other people. Nobody is going to hurt you."

Not only had this patient picked up on the physical details of his surroundings, he had also read the doctor's mind.[12]

4) After a lecture to doctors at the U.S. Army base in Fort Dix, New Jersey, a man approached me and told about his remarkable NDE. I later confirmed it with his attending physicians.

I was terribly ill and near death with heart problems at the same time that my sister was near death in another part of the same hospital with a diabetic coma. I left my body and went into the corner of the room, where I watched them work on me down below.

Suddenly, I found myself in conversation with my sister, who was up there with me. I was very attached to her, and we were having a great conversation about what was going on down there when she began to move away from me.

I tried to go with her but she kept telling me to stay where I was. "It's not your time," she said. "You can't go with me because it's not your time." Then she just began to recede off into the distance through a tunnel while I was left there alone.

When I awoke, I told the doctors that my sister had died. He denied it, but at my insistence, he had a nurse check on it. She had in fact died, just as I knew she did.

These are only a few of the cases that prove to me that NDEs are more than just hallucinations or 'bad dreams.' There is no logical explanation for the experiences of these people. Although tunnel experiences and beings of light can easily be chalked off as mere 'mind play,' out-of-body experiences baffle even the most skeptical in the medical profession.[13]

In addition to the cases documented here, and many other similar cases, there are other arguments that are distinctive and unique to

---

12 It is not unusual that people after having a NDE will show psychic abilities, as reading people's minds, that they did not have before. One of the most striking examples of this is Dannion Brinkley. See his *Saved by the Light* (Harper Paperback, 1994): pp. 185-87.

13 Moody, *The Light Beyond*, pp. 170-73.

NDEs that also speak to the fact that these experiences are unlike dreams or hallucinations in fundamental ways.

First and foremost, NDEs are uniformly experiences that people having them are convinced are real *after* they 'come back' to their bodies. The *sine qua non* of a dream or an hallucination is that at some point one discovers that it's just a dream or an hallucination. One wakes up in the case of dreams, or finds that the oasis dissolves into sand in an hallucination. In fact the whole notion of a dream or an hallucination feeds on the fact that it is unreal. A dream from which one never wakes up would not be a dream, nor would an hallucination that is never revealed as a deception be an hallucination. Endemic to the meaning of the words "dream" and "hallucination" is the idea that they are false and not real. At no point in the life of an NDEer does one feel that the experience was in some sense false and not real. Quite the contrary, one comes back to the physical world with a feeling that it is the physical world that is false and unreal. The NDE introduces people to a reality that is permanent, eternal and desirable (some say ecstatic) and generally NDEers do not want to return to their bodies and the material world they have left behind. They are often forced to return against their will or feel that they must return to fulfill some duty or purpose. When a doctor or friend tells them that their experience was unreal they rarely convince the person. The NDEers live the rest of their lives with the conviction that they saw and experienced a realm of reality far superior to the physical world and one to which they look forward to returning to when their time comes to really 'die.'[14]

Some might argue that drugs do the same thing. They give one a 'high' from which one does not want to 'come down,' etc. There is, however, a major difference between the effect of drugs and NDEs and that is when you do finally come down from drugs you are worse off than you were before. In the 1960s when the effect of drugs was praised by some as equivalent to mystical insights and/or as a sub-

---

14   It is true that before Moody published his book, NDEers were isolated from one another and perhaps began to think that they were hallucinating or were just crazy. As soon as they came to realize that others had had experiences similar to theirs, their wavering conviction that they had experienced a reality that was far superior to their life in the physical was reinforced and became unshakable.

stitute for religion, and as having no harmful influence on the drug user, there were many who believed this. The world now knows of the manifold disasters that drugs have upon the individuals who take them and their disastrous effects upon society as a whole. Today, drugs are public enemy number 1.

In sharp contrast to this, people who have any kind of NDE are better for it. They are more mature, more caring, more compassionate and more loving than before. The NDE changes their life for the better. If everyone were able to have an NDE, the world would be a kinder, better, and more humane place to live—not one fraught with narcissism, violence, and mayhem that characterizes the sub-culture of the drug world. Anyone who 'bought into' drugs thinking that they were entering a better life than they had before (no matter how bad it might have been) was deceived, and the great majority of these people regret this fatal step as do their relatives and friends.

On the other hand, there is at least one case recorded by Raymond Moody in his book, *The Light Beyond*, in which the life of a criminal has been transformed in a dramatic fashion. Here is Moody's description of this remarkable case:

> One of the most startling examples that I've seen of personal growth through an NDE was the case of a man I'll call Nick. He was a con artist and an outright criminal who had done everything from bilking widows to running drugs. Crime had provided a good life for Nick. He had nice cars, fine clothes, and new houses, and no problems with his conscience to annoy him.
>
> Then his life changed. He was golfing on a cloudy day when a thunderstorm suddenly developed. Before he could get off the greens, he was struck by lightning and 'killed.'
>
> He hovered above his body for a moment and then found himself speeding down a dark tunnel toward a spot of light. He emerged into a bright pastoral setting where he was greeted by relatives and other people who were glowing like Coleman lanterns.
>
> He met a being of light that he still haltingly describes as G-d, who graciously led him through a life review. He relived his entire life, not only seeing his actions in three dimensions, but seeing and feeling the effects of his actions on others.
>
> That experience changed Nick. Later, while recovering in the hospital, he felt the full effect of his life review. With the being of light, he had been exposed to pure love. He felt that when he re-

ally died, he would have to undergo the life review again, a process that would be very uncomfortable if he failed to learn from his first life review.

"Now," says Nick, "I always live my life knowing that someday I'll have to go through another life review."

I won't tell you what he does now for a living, except to assure you that it's an honest and helpful profession.[15]

I doubt if anyone was ever reformed by drugs.

Intimately connecting with the change that NDEers go through is a review of their life which is administered to them by a 'being of light' or a spiritual power that communicates with them through some process of telepathy.

> When they see the review of their life, NDEers realize that the being of light loves and cares for them. They realize that (it) is not judgmental, but rather wants them to develop into better people. This helps them eliminate fear and focus instead on becoming loving people.[16]

Moody found eight characteristic changes that take place in NDEers, all of which enhanced their lives when they returned to their bodies. Moody in his book quotes these NDEers which we reproduce here in their original italics.

I. NO FEAR OF DYING

> *For the first fifty-six years of my life, I lived in constant fear of death. My focus was on avoiding death, which I regarded as a terrible thing. After my experience, I realized that by living my entire life in fear of death, I was blocking my appreciation of life.*[17]

---

15 Moody, *The Light Beyond*, pp. 35-36.

16 Ibid., p. 39.

17 Ibid.

2. SENSING THE IMPORTANCE OF LOVE

You know, this experience has a hold on your everyday life, from then on. Walking down the street is a different experience entirely, believe you me. I used to walk down the street in my own little world, with my mind on a dozen different little problems. Now I walk down the street and I feel I am in an ocean of humanity. Each person I see, I want to get to know, and I am certain that if I really knew them I would love them.

A man who works in the office with me asked why I always had a smile on my face. He didn't know about my experience, so I told him that because I almost died I was happy to be alive and let it pass. Someday, he'll find out for himself.[18]

3. A SENSE OF CONNECTION WITH ALL THINGS

The first thing I saw when I awoke in the hospital was a flower, and I cried. Believe it or not, I had never really seen a flower until I came back from death. One big thing I learned when I died was that we are all part of one big, living universe. If we think we can hurt another person or another living thing without hurting ourselves, we are sadly mistaken. I look at a forest or a flower or a bird now, and say, "That is me, part of me." We are connected with all things and if we send love along those connections, then we are happy.[19]

4. AN APPRECIATION OF LEARNING

Doctor, I have to admit to you that before this cardiac arrest, I had only contempt for scholars. I worked my way up with little schooling, and I worked hard. There is a university nearby and I used to think those professors were just lazy, doing nothing of any practical value, and living off the fat of the land. I let more than one of them know that I resented it, that I thought that I was laboring at my business sometimes seven days a week, ten or twelve hours a day so they could do research and write books that didn't have a thing to do with anything real. ...

Now that was a humbling experience for me. You can say I don't scorn professors any more. Knowledge is important. I read everything I can get my hands on now, I really do. It's not that I regret taking the path I did in life, but I'm glad that I have time now for learning. History, science, literature. I'm interested in it all. My wife fusses at me about my books in our room. Some of it helps me understand my

---

18 Ibid., pp. 41-42.
19 Ibid., p. 42.

experience better, I would say. All of it does, in one way or another, because, as I say, when you have one of these experiences, you see that everything is connected.[20]

5. A NEW FEELING OF CONTROL

The most important thing I learned from this experience was that I am responsible for everything I do. Excuses and avoidance were impossible when I was there with him reviewing my life. And not only that, I saw that responsibility is not bad in the least, that I can't make excuses or try to put my failings off on somebody else. It's funny, but my failings have become very dear to me in a way, because they are my failings, and darn it, I am going to learn from them, come hell or high water.

I remember one particular incident in this review when, as a child, I yanked my little sister's Easter basket away from her, because there was a toy in it that I wanted. Yet in the review, I felt her feelings of disappointment and loss and rejection.

What we do to other people when we act unlovingly! But it is wonderful that we are destined not to be allowed to remain unconscious of it. If anybody doesn't believe me about this, okay, I'll meet them in the afterlife when they've had a chance to encounter this and then we can discuss it...

Everything you have done is there (in the review) for you to evaluate, and as unpleasant as some parts of it are for you to see, it feels so good to get it all out. In life, you can play around and make excuses for yourself and even cover up, and you can stay miserable, if you want to, by doing all this covering up. But when I was there in that review there was no covering up. I was the very people that I hurt, and I was the very people I helped to feel good. I wish I could find some way to convey to everyone how good it feels to know that you are responsible and to go through something like this where it is impossible not to face it.

It is the most liberated feeling in the world. It is a real challenge, every day of my life, to know that when I die I am going to have to witness every single action of mine again, only this time actually feeling the effects I've had on others. It sure makes me stop and think. I don't dread it. I relish it.[21]

---

20   Ibid, pp. 44-45.

21   Ibid., pp. 46-47. There is a warning in the Rabbis of the *Mishnah* that sums this up neatly in *Ethics of the Fathers* (2.1): "Rabbi Judah the Prince (the redactor of the *Mishnah*) said, 'Consider three things and you will never sin. Know what is above you: 1) an eye that sees, 2) an ear that hears,

6. A SENSE OF URGENCY

Moody quotes no NDEer on this point but sums it up in the following words:

'Sense of urgency' is a phrase that comes up again and again when I talk to NDEers. Frequently, they are referring to the shortness and fragility of their own lives. But they are often expressing a sense of urgency about a world in which vast destructive powers are in the hands of mere humans.

Why they have these feelings I don't know. But these factors seem to keep people who have had the experience in a state of profound appreciation of life. After the NDE, people tend to declare that life is precious, that it's the 'little things' that count, and that life is to be lived to its fullest.

One woman told me that the life review doesn't show just the big events of one's life, as you might think. She said that it shows the little things, too. For instance, one of the incidents that came across very powerfully in her review was a time when she found a little girl lost in a department store. The girl was crying, and the woman set her up on a counter and talked to her until her mother arrived.

It was those kinds of things—the little things you do while not even thinking—that come up most importantly in the review.

Many people are asked by the being, "What was in your heart while this was going on?" It's as though he's telling the NDEer that the simple acts of kindness that come from the heart are the ones that are most important because they are most sincere.[22]

7. BETTER DEVELOPED SPIRITUAL SIDE

My doctor told me I 'died' during the surgery. But I told him that I came to life. I saw in that vision what a stuck-up ass I was with all that theory, looking down on everyone who wasn't a member of my denomination or didn't subscribe to the theological beliefs that I did.

A lot of people I know are going to be surprised when they find out that the Lord isn't interested in theology. He seems to find some of it amusing, as a matter of fact, because he wasn't interested at all in anything about my denomination. He wanted to know what was in my heart, not my head.[23]

---

3) and all your deeds are written in a book." (One might modernize this last into "all your deeds recorded on video tape.")

22   Ibid., pp. 47-48.

23   Ibid., p. 49.

8. REENTERING THE "REAL" WORLD

*When I 'came back,' no one knew quite what to make of me. When
I had my heart attack, I had been a very driven and angry type A. If
things didn't go right for me, I was impossible to live with. That was
at home as well as work. If my wife wasn't dressed on time when we
had some place to go, I would blow up and make the rest of the evening
miserable for her.*

*Why she put up with it, I don't know. I guess she grew accustomed to
it over the years, though, because after my NDE she could hardly cope
with my mellowness. I didn't yell at her any more. I didn't push her to
do things, or anyone else for that matter. I became the easiest person
to live with and the change was almost more than she could bear. It
took a lot of patience on my part—which is something I had never
possessed before—to keep our marriage together. She kept saying, "You
are so different since your heart attack." I think she really wanted to
say, "You've gone crazy."*[24]

The point here is that the general effect of having an NDE is that you
become a better person than you were before. This is so unlike the effect
of drug experiences as to be almost at opposite ends of the pole. The
argument here is that an experience that makes one a better person
has more reality to it than other experiences that have no such effect
or the reverse effect. What I mean by "reality" here is that it touches
something deep within us as does great music like Beethoven's 7th
symphony compared with some fashionable 'pop' music. This is true
of all great art as compared with entertainment. So too, the NDE
touches something profound within the spirit and wakens a deeper
love not only for our family and friends, but for life generally, the world
at large and for that ultimate source of all existence we call G-d. To
call NDEs hallucinations is to call love itself an hallucination. It is a
sad comment on the way of life to which we are accustomed to call
such feelings 'hallucinations,' and think of reality as the narcissistic,
indulgence of one's own selfish desires. It may be that this describes
how most people feel about life, but such an attitude leads not to
happiness and contentment but to anger and frustration. To call the
latter reality and the former an hallucination is like calling evil good,

---

24   Ibid., pp. 51-52.

and good evil. The most charitable thing one can say about such an attitude is that it is false.

Some have argued that while the NDE may indeed have a salutary effect and inspire a new-found attitude to life which is superior to the one previously held, this is no argument that the NDE glimpses a reality that transcends the material world. In other words, the NDE is not evidence for life after death. The NDE is better understood as the effect of some poetic imagination and its significance is merely 'symbolic.' Its value does not depend on it being taken as veridical, any more than the value of a poem or a novel depends on it being an accurate description of events or things existing in reality. The novel or poem has 'symbolic' meaning and it is a mistake to suppose that the value of such meaning depends upon it being true.

In the words of one writer,

> In every respect, our defence of near-death reports depends on treating them as symbolic expressions that can never be translated into direct observations or exact concepts. This will disappoint those who wish to have their doubts about life after death resolved. It has positive religious implications as well, however, for it requires us to give up our insistence on objective verification (which has been a source of so much grief throughout history) and in its place to cultivate an appreciation of symbol.[25]

This supposed defence of the validity of the NDE is a left-handed compliment, or to use a more apt metaphor, it takes away with the right hand what it gives with the left, for one of the great advantages of the NDE is that 80% of people who experience a core NDE no longer have any fear of death.[26] The reason for this is that they are totally convinced that their NDE was of a reality that in addition to being pleasant, spiritually satisfying and filled with love and compassion, was

25 Carol Zaleski, *Otherworld Journeys* (Oxford University Press, 1987), p. 199.

26 This figure is quoted in two books that purport to be statistical and scientific studies of NDEs. They are Kenneth Ring, Ph.D., *Life at Death: A Scientific Investigation of the Near-Death Experience* (Coward, McCann and Geoghegan, 1980), pp. 174-180, 204; and Michael B. Sabom, M.D., F.A.C.C., *Recollections of Death: A Medical Investigation* (Harper and Row, 1982), pp. 60-61, 125-126, 212-213.

also a reality that was eternal and deathless. The author quoted above would tell them that all this is an illusion and is no more real than a play on a stage. A play may be symbolic of the love of one person for another (as the play *Romeo and Juliet*) but it would be a mistake to suppose the actor playing Romeo really loves the actress playing Juliet. The actors on the stage were merely acting. When NDEers come back to their bodies and enter into everyday life, they often say how their relationship with people around them has changed. They feel a genuine love and compassion for people, even strangers, and they feel good about this in a way they never felt before. If, as our author suggests, the feelings of love and compassion experienced in the NDE are not 'real' but only symbolic, why do these people consistently say that their feelings were more powerful and real than the weaker 'watered down' versions of love one feels in the world. After all, when one watches a play, the emotions of love, anger, etc. displayed in the play are only symbols or portrayals of love and anger, but are not genuine expressions of these powerful emotions. In the case of the NDE, this experience, which is the supposed symbol of love, is more powerful and impressive that what it is supposed to be a symbol of, i.e. genuine love between two people in the physical world. This is paradoxical.

Furthermore, if one has a dream or an hallucination, when one wakes up or when the hallucination is spent, one knows that it was not real and this knowledge itself tends to lessen the impact this dream or hallucination will or should have on real life. If one would have a dream or an hallucination that in all respects resembled an NDE, if, when one wakes or 'sleeps it off,' the knowledge that this was a dream or an experience due to too much vodka, should itself diminish the influence of this dream or hallucination.

For example, if a woman had a dream that she was Jewish, when in fact, as far as she knew, neither she nor anyone in her family was Jewish, a rational person would discount this as a crazy dream and forget about it. However, a woman who was adopted into a Baptist fundamentalist family in the Deep South and whose grandfather was a Baptist minister, had an NDE in which a being of light told her (telepathically) that she was Jewish. She thereupon set out on a serious and determined investigation of her past life. After much effort she finally tracked down her biological mother who turned out to be

Jewish.²⁷ It is understandable that her family was greatly disturbed by this revelation, but in spite of their opposition, she insisted on converting to Judaism and ultimately divorced her husband and established what was virtually a new life for herself.

Such a course of action would be unlikely if this woman was not utterly convinced that in her NDE she had met a real spiritual being in a realm of reality superior to this one, such that she was willing to take the mere suggestion of this being as a guide that radically changed the course of her future life in this world. To my knowledge, everyone who has ever had an NDE is convinced that it was true and real and that this experience was a glimpse into a higher reality that awaits the life of every human being upon the death of their bodies. Upon this conviction rests the complete lack of fear of death, and changes of lifestyle, evidenced in the lives of many NDEers upon resuscitation. In other words, what is taken as the positive side of the NDE is gounded in the fact that the experience is true and not just 'symbolic' of something else. Similarly, if I would wake up some morning happy that the Detroit Red Wings had just won the Stanley Cup the evening before, this happiness would be grounded in the fact that I remember clearly having watched the final game the evening before, together with the ceremony following the game when the captain, Steve Yzerman was presented with the Stanley Cup. There is no doubt about this in my mind and that is the reason I am so happy. If there were the least doubt that what I remember from last night was not true, but some dream, visionary wishful thinking or something 'symbolic,' I would not be happy. Instead I would open up the morning newspaper with a beating heart and trembling hands to see if the Red Wings really did win the Stanley cup, as I dreamed or imagined. If NDEers are so absolutely certain of the truth and reality of what they experience to the extent that in many cases their entire lives are redirected or transformed for good, why should anyone go to such outlandish lengths to try to convince the NDEers otherwise? It does not take much of a perusal of the literature to see that the psychological, pharmacological, physiological or even 'symbolical' explanations of NDEs are not

27   For a fascinating account of this case, see Kenneth Ring, *Heading Toward Omega* (William Morrow, 1984), pp. 110-114.

very convincing.[28] The most plausible explanation of NDEs is simply unpalatable to the modern, scientific-oriented mind, namely that somehow the NDEers floated out of their bodies and after observing it, in some cases travelled down a tunnel and had the kinds of experiences they actually described. Given the evidence we now have, there is almost as good a reason to take the NDEers at their word on the matter as there is to believe a friend who had gone downtown and had returned to describe where he had been and what he had seen. The main difference being that in the case of the NDE you cannot take a trip 'downtown' to confirm whether what was said was true.

Thus far, we have been trying to establish the claim that the life of a person can continue after death without a physical body and that sometimes the soul can return back to the body after it (the body) has 'died.' Death here has to be viewed as the point at which the soul leaves the body or the point at which an 'out of body experience' takes place. If one accepts this definition of death, we claim that at the present time there is sufficient evidence for a dead person coming back to life such that the truth of the evidence is more probable than the falsity of the miracle, and that on Hume's stated grounds, it is more rational to believe that the dead have come back to life than not.

---

28   See particularly Kenneth Ring, *Life and Death*, pp. 206-217 and Michael Sabom, *op. cit.*, pp. 151-178. Most recently, there has been research undertaken in England by Dr. Peter Fenwick, a neuropsychiatrist at Southampton General Hospital and a consultant at the Institute of Psychiatry in London, which he thinks demonstrates conclusively that the phenomenon of the NDE could not possibly be the effect of a collapse of brain function due to lack of oxygen, or to drugs administered during the course of resuscitation. The reason for this is that, in some cases, at the time of the near death experience the patient was judged to be clinically dead with no brain function of any kind. Under these circumstances it would be impossible for the brain to record any experiences whatsoever. These experiments were performed in Southampton General Hospital's cardiac unit on 63 patients who experienced a cardiac arrest. Of those, 56 had no recollection during their period of unconsciousness. Seven had some recollection or memory, but of those, only four passed the Grayson scale which is the medical criterion of assessing a near-death experience. No doubt, the medical profession will be able to better evaluate this research when it is published.

One could, of course, redefine death as a person who has died and who has never been resuscitated, thus excluding a person who has been resuscitated from the category of one who has died. In this case, having been resuscitated is the *sine qua non* of not having died. The fact remains, however, that all the vital signs of life are absent from someone who 'appears' to have died but who has been resuscitated, as they are from someone who really dies and is never resuscitated. The only distinction in the medical description of the two is that one is resuscitated and the other, not. There are, in fact, recorded cases of patients coming back to life after the doctor has signed a death certificate. In such cases, one might consider that the person did not really die but only appeared to. If this is what Hume had in mind when he said that no one ever came back from the dead to tell us what it is like 'on the other side,' then it is logically impossible (analytically false) that this should ever happen, as it is logically impossible (analytically false) that a triangle not have three sides. Hume, however, could not have meant this, as he appears to argue that there has never been *any* evidence in the entire course of human history, strong enough to justify the belief that someone has come back from the dead. However, if it were logically impossible that such a thing could ever happen it would be nonsense to argue that in the entire course of human history a thing like that has never happened, as it would be nonsense to argue that in the entire course of human history no one has ever seen a triangle without three sides. I conclude that Hume's argument that there is the strongest possible argument against believing in a miracle as a dead person coming back to life, has been refuted. According to a Gallup poll, "… eight million adults in the United States have had an NDE. That equals one person in twenty."[29] To discount this evidence is simply not rational. Let us turn then to the second and more important part of this chapter, which argues that the actual content of a large number of NDEs supports some of the basic points made in previous chapters—above all the oneness of G-d and the world.

---

29   Moody, *The Light Beyond*, p. 6.

II. THE LESSON OF NDES

DANNION BRINKLEY

I will illustrate what I take to be the primary lessons of NDEs as far as what we can learn about life and reality, from the stories of two individuals who have written books about their NDEs. The first is that of Dannion Brinkley, a young man of twenty-five when in 1975 he was struck by lightning in his hometown of Aiken, South Carolina. Brinkley was actually pronounced dead and his body was on the way to the morgue when he suddenly 'came back to life.' Brinkley 'died' a second time some fourteen years later in May, 1989, and had a second NDE, in some ways even more remarkable than the first. The second story is that of a young Israeli woman, Rachel Noam, raised on a communist kibbutz in Israel, who, in 1973, was struck on the head by a beam falling from a construction site in Tel Aviv.

The reason I have chosen these two, as models of NDEs is that 1) each of these individuals was in no way 'religious' or raised in a religious orientated family or environment; 2) each came from a very different culture or background; 3) each was transformed by the NDE into what I would call a deeply religious person in which they came to understand that G-d is represented by a light, that love and kindness is the essence of life, that each had a purpose to fulfill in life, and finally, they both felt compelled to write a book about their NDE and tell the world about it.[30]

The story of Dannion Brinkley begins on September 17, 1975, in Aiken, South Carolina, the day he was struck by lightning. He was talking on the phone with a friend of his when a thunderstorm approached suddenly and he was struck by lightning through the phone. The nails of his shoes were welded to the nails in the floor boards and he was thrown out of his shoes up towards the ceiling. He felt excruciating pain throughout his entire body. From this pain he suddenly found himself engulfed in peace and tranquility free of all pain which he described as a "glorious calmness." As he further described it, he looked down from a height of the ceiling and saw his body draped over the bed. His wife was giving him CPR. He thought he must be dead and then suddenly he was back in his body feeling horrendous

---

30   For another good example of a person who wrote about a truly remarkable NDE, see Betty J. Eadie, *Embraced by the Light* (Bantam Books, 1994).

pain. By the time the ambulance arrived Dannion was out of his body again. He described how the ambulance attendants put him in the ambulance. He continued to hover over his body in the ambulance while his wife, Sandy, sat at his side weeping. The ambulance technician put a stethoscope to his chest, declared him dead and pulled the sheet over his face. Brinkley then went on to describe one of the most detailed and amazing near-death experiences ever recorded. He looked towards the front of the ambulance and he saw a tunnel forming. As he watched, the tunnel approached him, he heard the sound of chimes as he entered the tunnel. He was engulfed by the tunnel and saw in the distance a spot of light towards which he was moving, the chimes ringing all the time in rhythmic succession. The light became larger and brighter as he approached it until he was out of the tunnel surrounded by the brightest light he had ever seen. Though it was much brighter than the sun, the light did not hurt his eyes. Brinkley looked at his hand as he appeared to have some kind of body but it was not the kind of body he had when he was 'alive'. In his own words, "It was translucent and shimmering and moved with fluidity, like the water in the ocean. I looked down at my chest. It, too, had a translucence and flow of fine silk in a light breeze."[31] He then noticed a 'Being of Light,' as he called it, approaching him. It had no human form, and no gender, just a presence of power that emanated love and compassion. This Being of Light engulfed Brinkley and as it did, Brinkley began to experience his entire life from his earliest memories to the moment he was struck by lightning. It was as if he was looking at a replay of his life on T.V. except that it passed by very quickly and with absolute clarity. He was what you call a 'bad kid,' constantly getting into fights, being expelled from school and the cause of much grief to his parents. He estimated that from the fifth to the twelfth grade, he had at least six thousand fist fights. Now he was reliving each one of those fights, but this time he was experiencing not the physical pain, but the shame and humiliation his victims had felt, the grief he had caused his parents, and the frustration and mental pain he brought to his teachers. He even felt the pain he had caused his dog when he once beat it for having chewed a rug. Generally speaking he had led a

---

31   Dannion Brinkley, *Saved by the Light* (Harper Paperback, 1994): p. 10.

pretty egotistical life, not caring about anyone else other than himself. In his own words, "I hadn't given a damn about my fellow humans.[32]

Brinkley had been an assassin in the Vietnam War, and after he left the service he was involved in distributing arms and weapons to forces fighting the communists in South America. In the review of his life, he relived his assassinations as well as the havoc and pain the weapons he distributed in South America caused to not only the victims killed by these weapons, but the pain and misery it brought to the bereaved families.

When the review was over Brinkley expected the Being of Light to give him some kind of rebuke. Instead the Being conveyed nothing but love and non-judgmental concern and forgiveness. "Any fear I might have had at the notion of being dead was quelled by the love that poured from the Being before me. His forgiveness was remarkable. Despite the horribly flawed life we had just witnessed, deep and meaningful forgiveness came to me from this Being. Rather than issuing harsh judgment, the Being of Light was a friendly counsel, letting me feel for myself the pain and the pleasure I had caused others. Instead of feeling shame and anguish, I was bathed in the love that embraced me through the light, and had to give nothing in return."[33]

In this communication, no actual words passed between Brinkley and the Being of Light, but a telepathy that was sure and unmistakable. The Being of Light conveyed to Brinkley some quite remarkable ideas. "Humans are powerful spiritual beings meant to create good on earth. This good isn't usually accomplished in bold actions, but in singular acts of kindness between people. It's the little things that count because they are more spontaneous and show who you truly are."[34]

Meanwhile, back at the hospital the attending doctor pronounced Brinkley dead, and called the morgue to come pick up the body. Brinkley, unaware of what was happening to his body, then began the most amazing part of his NDE which he describes in chapter four of his book, entitled *The Crystal City*.

Together with the Being of Light, Brinkley began to move upward. They moved like an airplane climbing in the sky and flew over mountains

---

32   Ibid., p. 24.
33   Ibid., p. 29.
34   Ibid., p. 25.

shimmering in mist like fog off the ocean. They swooped down on the side of a mountain range and floated into a city of cathedrals made of some crystalline substance that glowed from within. He entered the structure and as he did he looked around and the Being of Light who had accompanied him was no longer with him. Rows of benches were lined across the room and a radiant light made everything glow and feel like love. He sat down on one of the benches which faced a long podium. The room as well as the podium were empty but Brinkley said he had the strange feeling that other spirits were in the room though he could not see them.

Suddenly thirteen Beings appeared from nowhere on the podium. Each of them represented different emotional powers. One was intense and passionate, another artistic and emotional, another bold and energetic, etc., as Brinkley described them. He felt this was a place of learning and in the presence of these Beings of Light, he was to receive instruction the like of which he had never received before. Brinkley said he could feel a power of understanding he had never had before. "I had only to think a question to explore the essence of the answer. In a split second, I understood how light works, the ways in which spirit is incorporated into physical life, why it is possible for people to think and act in so many different ways. Ask and you shall perceive, is the way I sum it up."[35]

Brinkley then describes how each of these Beings in turn, flew at him in the form of a box that contained a television-like view of an event that was to take place in the future. Brinkley recounts how he later wrote down one-hundred and seventeen events that he witnessed in the boxes that gave him a peep into the future. In the eighteen years that followed his 'death,' Brinkley notes that ninety-five of these events have taken place, the most remarkable of which were the nuclear disaster at Chernobyl, the fall of communist Russia, and Desert Storm, the war with Iraq. The final vision of these boxes portrayed the Armageddon—World War III—which was not one single great war, but hundreds of small, local wars all taking place at the same time and fuelled by world famine due to numerous natural disasters and the pollution of the environment on a world-wide scale.

---

35   Ibid., p. 36.

What struck me, however, as the most interesting part of Brinkley's encounter with the thirteen Beings of Light were not the horrific events they foretold, but the lessons that were conveyed by these Beings when these visions of the future had ended. Here are Brinkley's own words:

> As these visions ended, I had the amazing realization that these Beings were desperately trying to help us, not because we were such good guys, but because without us advancing spiritually here on earth, they could not become successful in their world. "You humans are truly the heroes," a Being told me. "Those who go to earth are heroes and heroines, because you are doing something that no other spiritual beings have the courage to do. You have gone to earth to co-create with G-d."
>
> As I was presented with each of these boxes, my mind pondered the same questions, over and over: Why is this happening to me? What are these scenes in the boxes and why are they being shown to me? I didn't know what was going on, and despite the seemingly infinite knowledge that I had been given earlier, I was unable to find the answers to those questions. I was seeing the future and I didn't know why.
>
> After the final visions, the thirteenth Being of Light answered my questions. He was more powerful than the others, or at least I assume he was. His colors were more intense, and the other Beings seemed to defer to him. His personality was conveyed in his light and encompassed the emotions of his fellow Beings.
>
> Without words, he told me that everything I had just seen was in the future, but not necessarily cast in stone. "The flow of human events can be changed, but first people have to know what they are," said the Being. He communicated to me again their belief that humans were great, powerful, and mighty spiritual Beings. "We here see everyone who goes to the earth as great adventurers," he said. "You had the courage to go and expand your life and take your place in the great adventure that G-d created known as the world." ...
>
> Then the Being let me know what I was supposed to do back on earth. I was to create centers where people could come to reduce stress in their lives. Through this reduction of stress, said the Being, humans would come to realize "as we do," that they are higher spiritual beings. They would become less fearful and more loving of their fellow man.[36]

---

36 Ibid., pp. 57-59.

Brinkley was told that his purpose in life would be to build these stress-reduction centers to enable people to gain control of their lives. "'The purpose of all these rooms [centers] is to show people that they can be in control of their lives through G-d,' said the Being."[37] To this end, Brinkley would have to return back to his body and the physical world.

> I resisted the return. I liked this place. I had been there so little time, but already I could see that I was free to roam in so many directions that it was like having total access to the universe. After coming here, going back to earth would be as confining as living on the head of a pin. Still, I was given no choice.
>
> "This we ask of you. You must return to fulfill this mission," said the Being of Light.
>
> And then I came back.[38]

In Chapter 6 of his book, Brinkley gives an amazing account of how he returned to his body.

> I left the Crystal City by fading into an atmosphere that was a rich blue-gray color. This was the same place I had gone when I was first struck by lightning, so I can only assume that it was the barrier we cross when we enter the spirit world.
>
> I came out of this atmosphere on my back. Slowly, and without effort, I was able to roll over, and when I did, I could see that I was floating above a hallway. Below me was a gurney with a body on it, covered with a sheet and lying still. The person underneath the sheet was dead.
>
> Around the corner and down the hall I heard an elevator open. I saw two orderlies in white outfits emerge from the elevator and walk toward the dead man. They were talking like two guys who had just left a pool hall, and one of them was smoking, blowing clouds of smoke toward the ceiling where I was hovering. I sensed that they were there to take the body to the morgue.
>
> Before they reached the dead man, my buddy Tommy (his friend with whom he was talking when he was struck by lightning) came through the door and stationed himself next to the gurney. It was then that I realized that the man underneath the sheet was me. I was dead. It was me—or what was left of me—who was about to be rolled off to the morgue!

---

37 Ibid., p. 60.
38 Ibid., pp. 60-61.

I could feel Tommy's sadness that I was gone. He couldn't let me go. As he stood there and stared at my body, I felt the love coming from him as he begged me to come back to life.

By now, my entire family had arrived at the hospital, and I could feel their prayers, too. My parents, brother, and sister were sitting in the waiting room with Sandy (his wife). They didn't know I was dead because the doctor didn't have the heart to tell them. Instead, he said that I probably wasn't going to last much longer.

Love truly can give life, I thought, as I hovered in the hallway. Love can make the difference. As I focused on Tommy, I felt myself become denser. In the next instant, I was looking up at the sheet.

This return to my human body put me in possession of its pain. I was on fire again, aching with the agony of being burned from the inside out, as though acid was in all of my cells. A ringing started in my ears that was so loud I thought I was inside a bell tower. My tongue had swelled and filled my mouth completely. On my body were blue lines crisscrossing me, marking the path the lightning had taken as it surged from my head to the floor. I couldn't see them, but I could feel their burn.

I couldn't move, which is a bad state to be in when orderlies are coming to take you to the morgue. I tried to move, but no matter how hard I tried, I couldn't twitch a muscle. Finally, I did the only thing I could. I blew on the sheet.

"He's alive, he's alive!" shouted Tommy.

"Look, yeah," said one of the orderlies. He pulled back the sheet and there I was, my tongue lolling out of my mouth and my eyes rolling around. Suddenly I began to convulse like an epileptic having a grand mal seizure.

The orderly who was smoking threw his cigarette to the floor and pushed me back into the emergency room. "He's still alive," he shouted. The doctors and nurses sprang into action.[39]

The rest of the story of Brinkley's life recounts the very painful (physically painful) process of healing his body from the effects of the lightning bolt that had seriously weakened his heart and had virtually immobilized him. The most distressful part of his recovery and return to normal life, however, was coming to terms with his NDE and incorporating it into his new life. He became, virtually, a new, changed person. He was obsessed with his mission to build the stress centers and spoke constantly about it. His friends began to think he

39 Ibid., pp. 63-66.

had gone berserk and his personality seemed to have undergone a complete change. He was no longer the self-centered egotist he was before but began visiting hospices to comfort the dying and being kind and compassionate to anyone he thought he could help. Above all, he entirely lost his fear of death and tried to comfort the dying that they had nothing to fear and that the life they were about to enter was far superior and more desirable than the one they were leaving behind. Brinkley, however, was plagued by the fact that there was absolutely no one he spoke to who really understood what he was saying. Most of his friends thought he had gone mad. After a while Brinkley himself began to wonder if they were right.

The turning point in Brinkley's life came when he met Dr. Raymond Moody who was at that time completing his first book, *Life After Life*, which was the ground-breaking effort that introduced a new term, and with it, a stunning, original notion that crisscrossed over medicine, psychiatry, psychology, and sociology—namely the NDE, the near-death experience.

Dr. Moody was the first person that Brinkley met who took him seriously. He listened patiently to Brinkley's detailed and remarkable NDE, and when it was over, he leaned over and looking deep into Brinkley's eyes, said the following:

> "You aren't crazy," he said. "I have never heard a story as detailed as yours, but i have heard other stories with the elements of yours. You are not crazy. You have just experienced something that has made you unique. It's like discovering a new country with different people and trying to convince everyone that such a place exists."
>
> A hard spot inside me melted as what he said filled me with comfort. I realized I would now find others just like me who had seen this 'new country.' I felt a burst of fresh energy. I knew I was going to come back and that nothing was going to stop me.[40]

Dannion Brinkley did come back. For the next sixteen years he put every effort into completing the stress centers with a devotion and relentlessness that was all consuming. When people asked him why he was so determined to build the centers, he replied:

---

40   Ibid., p. 103.

Thirteen Beings of Light told me to build these centers. They put it on me. They didn't ask if I wanted to build them, they just told me that this is what I had to do. When I pass, I will be with them forever. Knowing that, I am determined to pull it off.[41]

Such commitment to an NDE bespeaks the reality and seriousness with which experiencers of this unique phenomenon hold it.

In May of 1989, Brinkley had a second NDE when he almost died a second time. He contracted an infection that settled in his heart already weakened from the lightning bolt. The doctors said the only way to save his life was to operate, but Brinkley refused to sign the consent forms. He said he wanted to die. He told his father: "For you it's like I am leaving and I'll never be back. ... For me it's like I am going home."[42] The family decided to call Dr. Moody to fly from Georgia to talk with their son. When Dr. Moody arrived, he asked Brinkley why he showed no fear of death. Brinkley replied: "Because living on earth is like being forced to go to summer camp. You hate everyone and you miss your momma. Raymond, I'm going home."[43] Dr. Moody pleaded with Brinkley to sign the forms if for no other reason than that he needed him to help him with his work. "You don't have to die," he said. "Stay for me. I need your help."[44] Brinkley could not refuse this plea. He felt wanted and needed. He signed the forms.

Immediately the surgical team took over. It was at this point that Brinkley had his second out-of-body experience, where he heard two surgeons making a ten dollar bet as to whether he would survive. He floated above the operating table watching the details of the operation with the detachment of someone watching a movie or a television show. Having heard the surgeons betting on his life, he did not have any expectations of surviving the surgery. Ever since he had been struck by lightning his body had been a source of pain and a burden for him. Now he was freed of that burden. For the second time in his life he was drawn up a black tunnel towards a light. The rest of Brinkley's NDE is described in his own words.

---

41 Ibid., p. 202.
42 Ibid., p. 180.
43 Ibid., p. 183.
44 Ibid.

At the end of the tunnel I was met by the Being of Light, the same one that greeted me the first time. People often ask if these Beings have faces. Neither time did I see a face, just a brilliantly glowing spirit that was firmly in charge of me and knew where I was supposed to go.

He drew me toward him, and as he did he spread out, almost like an angel spreading its wings. I was engulfed by these wings of light, and as I was, I began to see my life all over again.

The first twenty-five years passed as they had in my first near-death experience. I saw many of the same things: the years of being a bad child, my growing up and becoming a bad-assed soldier. Watching these early years again was painful, I won't deny that, but the agony was tempered by viewing the years since the first experience. I had a feeling of pride about these years. The first twenty-five years were bad, but the next fourteen were of a changed man.

I saw the good that I had accomplished with my life. One after the other, events both great and small were reviewed as I stood in this cocoon of light. I watched myself volunteering in nursing homes, performing even the smallest duties, like helping someone stand up or comb her hair. Several times I watched as I did jobs no one else wanted to do, like clipping toenails and changing diapers.

One time for instance, I helped care for an elderly woman. She had lain in bed so long that she was stiff and could hardly move. I scooped her out of the bed like a child—she couldn't have weighed more than eighty pounds—and held her while the nurses changed the sheets. To give her a change of scenery, I walked around the building with her in my arms.

I knew this meant a lot to her at the time because she thanked me profusely and cried when I left. Now, as I relived the event, the perspective I had in this heavenly place let me feel her gratitude at having someone hold her again.

I relived a time in New York when I invited a group of bag ladies to a Chinese restaurant for dinner. I saw these women in an alley scrounging through garbage cans and felt compassion for their situation. Escorting them into a small restaurant, I treated them to a hot meal.

When I saw this event again, I could feel their mistrust of me as a stranger. Who was this man and what did he want? They were unaccustomed to someone trying to do a good deed. Still, when the food came, they were grateful to be treated with humanity. We stayed in the restaurant for almost four hours and drank several large bottles of Chinese beer. The meal cost me more than a hundred dollars, but the price was nothing compared to the joy of reliving it...[45]

The life review that came with this second near-death experience was wonderful. Unlike my first, which was filled with mayhem, anger, and then death, this one was a pyrotechnic display of good deeds. When people ask me what it is like to relive a good life in the embrace of the Beings of Light, I tell them it is like a great Fourth of July fireworks display, in which your life bursts before you in scenes that are spiced with the emotions and feelings of everyone in them.

After the life review was over, the Being of Light gave me the opportunity to forgive everyone who had ever crossed me. That meant that I was able to shake the hatred that I had built up against many people. I didn't want to forgive many of these people because I felt that the things they had done to me were unforgivable. They had hurt me in business and in my personal life and made me feel nothing for them but anger and disdain.

But the Being of Light told me I had to forgive them. If I didn't he let me know, I would be stuck at the spiritual level that I now occupied.

What else could I do? Next to spiritual advancement, these earthly trespasses seemed trivial. Forgiveness flooded my heart, along with a strong sense of humility. It was only then that we began to move upward.

The Being of Light was vibrating. As we moved upward, that vibration increased, and the sound emanating from the Being became louder and higher-pitched. We moved up through dense fields of energy that changed color from dark blue to a whitish blue, at which point we stopped. Then the Being's pitch lowered and we moved forward. Again, as in the first experience, we flew toward a range of majestic mountains, where we dipped down and landed on a plateau.

On this plateau was a massive building that looked like a greenhouse. It was constructed of large panes of glass that were filled with liquid in all the colors of the rainbow.

As we passed through the glass, we also passed through all of the colors contained in the liquid. These colors had substance to them and felt like fog off the ocean. They offered a slight resistance as we entered the room.

Inside were four rows of flowers, long-stemmed beauties with cup-shaped petals the consistency of silk. They were every color imaginable, and on each of them were drops of amber-colored dew.

---

45   Ibid., pp. 187-189.

Among these flowers were spirit beings wearing silver robes. These were not Beings of Light. I can best describe them as radiant earthlings. They moved up and down the rows of flowers, emitting some kind of power that caused the flowers to become brighter in color as they passed. These colors would leave the petals and beam through the panes of glass, sending back a rainbow of colors. The effect was like being in a room surrounded by ten thousand prisms.

I found this environment to be tremendously relaxing. The colors and surroundings combined with the humming vibration of the Being to erase stress. I remember thinking: *here I am, either dead or dying, and feeling good about it.*

The Being of Light moved close to me. "This is the feeling you are supposed to create in the centers," he said. "By creating energies and tones in the centers, you can make people feel the way you feel right now."

I became aware of the fragrance of the flowers. As I breathed in the sent, I heard a chant resonating throughout the building. A-L-L-A-H-O-M went the chant, A-L-L-A-H-O-M.

This chant made me aware of everything around me, and I began to breathe the fragrance deeply and observe everything with such intensity that it was almost as though I were bathing in it. A-L-L-A-H-O-M, A-L-L-A-H-O-M, went the chant, and I became more and more absorbed in my surroundings. As I did I began to vibrate at a speed equal to everything around me. I became one with everything around me and could experience everything. At the same time, everything was experiencing me.

As I delved into this heavenly world, it also delved into me. There was an equality to the experience. Not only was I given a heavenly experience, I was *giving* one. As I was blending with this place I call the heavenly realm, it was also blending with me with the same amount of respect, courage, hopes, and dreams. I was an equal to all things there. I realized that true love and understanding make us all equals. Heaven is that kind of place.

I would gladly have stayed there. I had smelled the heavenly fragrance and had seen myself among the essence of all things. What more could I ask for?

I looked at the Being of Light, who knew without a doubt what I was thinking. "No, you're not staying this time," he told me telepathically. "You have to go back again."

I didn't argue. I looked around and took in a view that time will never erase from my mind. The room was crisscrossed with colors that radiated from the liquid-filled panes. In the distance I could see jagged mountains that were every bit as beautiful as the Swiss Alps. The chant that resonated through the room was as beautiful as a symphony. I closed my eyes and bathed my ears in the sound. The fragrance was wonderfully overpowering. I took a deep breath … and I was back in my body.

I passed through no transition zone this time, and change was very abrupt. It was like being in Buckingham Palace, blinking, and suddenly finding yourself in a garage.

I looked around the room and saw other people covered with powder-blue sheets. The room was very bright, and everyone in it had tubes in his body that were attached to bags or machines. I could tell there were tubes down my throat and needles stuck in my arms, and I felt as if there were lead in my head and an elephant sitting on my chest. On top of all this, I was freezing cold. Good G-d, I thought, I feel worse than before the surgery.

"Where am I?" I asked a nurse.

"You're in the recovery room," she said.

I closed my eyes and didn't remember anything for another eighteen hours.[46]

What is significant about this NDE of Dannion Brinkley which was lacking in his first NDE was the unity and oneness that Brinkley felt with the heavenly realm to which he had been lifted. "As I was blending with this place I call the heavenly realm, it was also blending with me with the same amount of respect, courage, hopes, and dreams. I was an equal to all things there. I realized that true love and understanding make us all equals."[47] This certainly borders on the experiences described by those who have the mystical experience of sensing the organic unity of all things as if all of reality was a single harmonious living thing. This bears witness to the philosophical conception of the unity of all reality which we described in Chapter Five as the ultimate, rational conception of reality. If Being and reality would not evidence this unity and oneness, it would not be as rational a world as it might have been. It is at this point that rationality and mysticism

46 Ibid., pp. 192-197.

47 Ibid., p. 196. This description of a unity and the oneness of merging with one's environment or objects and things in one's environment bears some resemblance with the I-Thou relationship Martin Buber describes in his book *I and Thou*, which is often said to be the essence of the mystical experience as it is expressed by mystics from diverse cultural backgrounds.

merge. This, together with the idea that love and compassion is the true meaning of life not only in heaven, but especially here on earth, is the lesson that Brinkley's two NDEs give us. We have argued for such a view in chapters seven, eight and nine on philosophical grounds alone. The NDEs of Dannion Brinkley, as well as many others we have not mentioned, is a phenomenological support for these arguments.

RACHEL NOAM

Let us now examine the remarkable NDE of a young Israeli woman who originates from a background as far removed from Dannion Brinkley as Israel is from South Carolina. Let us take a look at the NDE of Rachael Noam. In spite of the great cultural differences between her and Dannion Brinkley, the similarity and lesson of their experiences have much in common and had a similar dramatic effect upon her future life.

Rachel Noam was a young Israeli woman when she was struck on the head by an eighteen-foot long wooden beam that fell five stories from a construction sight, as she was walking on Bograchov Street in Tel Aviv just after the Yom Kippur war in 1973. It was a miracle that her skull was not crushed. Not a single bone in her body was broken but she was knocked unconscious. Rachel herself, however, was aware of everything going on around her body. Here is how she describes it.

> All at once, I felt I was outside my body, floating upward about twelve to fifteen feet above the sidewalk, watching the scene below. I did not know how I left my body, or how I got up there. Everything happened so suddenly that I was caught completely by surprise. I saw the big woman (whom she had noticed walking towards her just moments before she was struck by the falling beam) bending over my body, trying to detect a sign of life in my motionless form. Then she started screaming for help. Several passersby stopped and stared at my body. Reacting to the insistent cries of the woman, the people became alarmed and deliberated as to what to do.
> The woman, still kneeling beside me, looked up.
> "Where's the building contractor?" she yelled. "Where's the foreman on this job?"
> The other people joined in the shouting.
> On the roof, a young man emerged.

"What's going on down there?" he shouted. "What's all the commotion?"

The woman pointed at my body.

"I want to speak to the building contractor this minute!" she insisted.

The young man disappeared, returning a short while later.

"The contractor is up here," he said. "He won't come down, and he won't talk to anyone."

I could see my body stretched out on the sidewalk.

This is my body, I thought, but I am not inside it. I am looking at it from above. How is this possible? With what eyes am I seeing this, and where are my ears? How could I be hearing all this noise in the street?

It was strange to look at myself from the outside, knowing with certainty that this was my body. I was viewing it from a different perspective, since while I was inside my form I could not see it from the outside. Now I was looking at my body the way I used to look at other people. I was baffled. Obviously, I existed, I was real, I was conscious, but not inside my frame. I always thought that 'I' and my body were identical. I did not know that I was a being that was more than just a physical body.

I was not at all afraid. Quite the contrary, I felt fine. I felt no pain or bruising; I felt relaxed, buoyant, worry-free. I existed independently of my bodily functions. I did not need any physical organs to see, to hear or to think. All the while, my body was lying dead-still on the sidewalk, unable to function without my presence. All its faculties were now with me, outside my body, hence, my flesh-and-bone frame was unable to react or move. I was observing it from my external vantage point. When I was inside my body I saw with my physical eyes; now I perceived without them, and they—my eyes of flesh—saw nothing.

My sense of vision, thus, existed even without my physical eyes; the ability to reason existed even outside my brain. All my life, I had seen by means of my eyes, heard by means of my ears, reasoned by means of my brain. My consciousness had been fully integrated with my body into one inseparable unit. But now everything was different. Being separated from my body was an amazing, supernatural experience. I was surveying the scene from above, looking not only at other people but at myself, at my own material body.

A gradual change began to occur in my status of 'observer.' The events in the street began to fade away into darkness, and through this darkness, I perceived a glimmer of brightness. As the radiance came closer it grew in intensity, becoming a glorious, powerful light, radiating an abundant flow of exalted spirituality.

In harmony with this flow of illumination, the events in my life began to pass before my eyes. The images were three-dimensional, and I saw myself taking part in them. My entire life flashed by, from the day I was born until the very moment I fell to the ground.

The vision I saw was like a wide-screen film in which I had the starring role and was also the audience. The images streaked by very rapidly, yet not a single detail was omitted. It was like a video on which every incident is recorded, every musical note, every shade and color that enhanced my life, and now everything was being played back at high speed and with astounding sharpness. I do not remember the actual vision I saw. What endures in my memory is my surprise at the amazing vividness of the images, recalling long forgotten events and details. I wondered where this visual memory was coming from. How did I suddenly remember my entire infancy and childhood? These questions cropped up as I was watching the replay of my life. When the vision ended I asked myself whether it had really been my own life. I came to the conclusion that indeed it had been. The entire experience filled me with an indescribable sense of exalted happiness.

Once again, I saw the blinding luminescence, glowing in a soft velvety white, as if an infinite number of brightly flashing magic sparks were uniting in a burst of spectacular brilliance. I tried to compare this brilliant glow to the colors of light from various sources I had seen when I was inside my body, but even sunlight paled in comparison to this awesome superabundance of immeasurable brightness.

The magnificent stream of light was accompanied by a flow of sublime love, a kind of love I had never before experienced. It was unlike the love of parents toward their children, the love of friends and relatives or the love of Eretz Yisrael [the land of Israel]. Any love I had ever felt was nothing but a tiny speck compared to this exalted, powerful love. Even if all the sparks of love that abound in this world were to combine they could not equal the powerful, pure love I sensed.

Faced with this overpowering love, I felt incapable of remaining an independent entity; I simply melted away. I was too small to withstand the flow of goodness streaming toward me and into me. I tried to defend myself, to close my eyes, but I had no eyes to close! I had no way of hiding before the radiance. I had no body. I felt completely stripped of the outer shell that had protected me in this world. There was no possibility of evading the current of love that enwrapped me. No words can describe the enchantment, the wonder, the incomparable, infinite goodness. I discerned in it qualities of compassion, spiritual pleasure, strength, happiness and beauty, all in infinite profusion.

I was powerless. I had no way of expressing myself. My body was lying on the sidewalk, totally incapacitated.

I felt my very being dissolving. I knew that if I did not return to my body immediately it would be too late; my mortal being would cease to exist. I realized that the only reality was the reality of this light, the essence that prevails beyond the physical world. I thought, how can there be a 'self' inside a body How can a person have self-awareness? The instant I was swept up in the wonderful light, my 'self,' my 'I,' dissolved into nothingness. Any sense of independence, pride, anger and desire vanished. All selfish tendencies disappeared, since my ego was about to be absorbed into the great light.

I felt a powerful bond with this marvellous presence. This was the will of a higher Power, a Being of infinite might. I felt a strong pull to become part of this wonderful eternal flow. It attracted me like a magnet with the power of its goodness, just as the earth exerts its attraction on the physical body. This magnetic force consisted of a confluence of goodness, light, faith, pleasure, self-effacement, joy, love, compassion, beauty, hope and favor that drew me closer with its overwhelming magnetism.

Filled with awe and reverence I turned to the wonderful Being and told Him about the extraordinary attraction He wielded over me.

"I am drawn to following my inclination," I said, "but I ask to be returned to my body. I ask to be given another opportunity in this world."

I went on to relate about Uzi [her fiancé whom she had not seen since the beginning of the Yom Kippur war, when he was activated], about the long time we had not seen each other because of the war, about our devotion to each other, about the meeting that was slated for this afternoon. I resisted the attraction of the Higher Will. I asked Him not to separate us. I told Him about my doubts and my search for the truth, until I had found Uzi and knew that he was truly meant for me, about my feeling that we were one, heart and soul.

I had a sensation as if I were being torn away from Uzi, just like you rip up a piece of cloth or paper. It felt as though my soul was being torn away from his soul. My 'I' and Uzi's 'I' were in reality one and the same 'I' that was being forcibly shattered. I was surprised that I had not felt this way toward any of my relatives and friends.

I knew then why I had met Uzi and why we were together. I knew that we were essentially one single indivisible being.

My body and all I had done with it, that is to say, my life in the physical world, were described to me in the third person. There appeared before me a young woman who lived her life the way she was brought up, and I—meaning my soul—was not this woman. I was not the body that had been living in this world. Never before did I feel like this. I always saw myself as one personality, a fusion of body and spirit. Only now did I realize that my body and I were two distinctly different entities that have been united in this world for a certain purpose.

Looking at myself, I was overcome by a depressing thought.

Too bad, I thought. She was so young and did not have a chance to live a meaningful life.

The accident happened on my birthday. I was thinking about this young woman of twenty-two years of age whose lifeless body was lying in the street. I reviewed her/my life, a life without any real accomplishment. I felt as though I was waking up from a dream, the dream of my life. For the life I was living had flitted away; nothing was left of it. I sensed that I had not fulfilled my task in life, I knew that I had pursued false objectives. I understood that my soul had come down into my body to fulfill a certain assignment. I did not know what this assignment was, but I knew it had not been carried out. I was disappointed that the purpose of my life had not been accomplished.

The wondrous light did not interfere with my feelings and thoughts or influence them in any way. It was simply there; the absolute truth. It did not impose any demands on me, nor did it take responsibility regarding the purpose of my life. The light was simply present in my inner consciousness, and integral part of my feelings. It did not tell me the true meaning of life, what was its purpose or why I resided inside my body all those years. It did not express any judgement regarding my actions of the past, whether they were good or bad. But simply by being there, surrounded by the light, I intuitively knew with absolute certainty that I had not fulfilled the mission for which I had been joined with my body in the corporeal world, in the *olam haasiah*, the world of action.

I was overcome with a deep sense of regret for the time I had wasted. The time I had received as a gift had been frittered away without being put to good use. It became clear to me that presently, being outside my body, I could not do anything in the world of action. Becoming an integral part of the marvellous light did not ease the distressing feeling that I had squandered my life. I felt sorry for my body which had been my faithful companion, the body which I should have elevated but did not. I sensed that I had used my body improperly, and I wanted to set a new course for my life.

I was gripped by a powerful desire to come back and live a true life. I asked to return into my body that was sprawled on the street, to return to my loved ones, to life itself. I knew that only inside the body, in this world, can the will of the One Above be made real.

The pull of the powerful love of the benevolent light was almost irresistible. I felt my willpower crumbling and melting away. I knew that if I would not go back this very instant, I would not want to or be able to return any more. I would not be able to return, because I was losing my "self," my identity, my yearning to return to my body. Faced by this outpouring of goodness and love, I was losing my will to be a separate individual. It felt as though a loving mother embraced my individuality and pulled my 'I' toward a state of perfect happiness, toward an elevated state of being that ensured everlasting sublime delight. I was filled with great compassion for my loved ones who would remain in this world, for my body, for the life I had wasted. A wave of pity swept over me.

I felt that this force of compassion brought me back into my body. Overcome with tenderness, with a boundless sense of compassion, I bust into tears. The big woman bent over me, and grabbing my hand, she coaxed me to get back on my feet.

My soul returned to my body. I made it back. I do not know how I re-entered my body; everything happened so fast, and before I knew it, I had slipped back.[48]

The rest of the book is a description of how over the course of the next ten years Rachel came to terms with this NDE. It had a profound effect upon her and the main thrust of the book is not the recounting of the NDE but how it changed her life. To realize how dramatic an influence it had, one has to know something about Rachel's childhood and early education. Rachel tells us a little about her early life on an Israeli *kibbutz*:

> I was born on a *kibbutz* of Hashomer Hatzair, the leftist movement that is based on the socialist-communist theory of a classless society with public ownership of all property. The name Hashomer Hatzair

48 Rachel Noam, *The View from Above*. Trans. from the Hebrew by Avraham Yaacov Finkel (C.I.S. Publishers and Distributors, 1992), pp. 90-97.

means Young Guard, and its ideology of dialectical materialism denies the existence of G-d and rejects the Torah tradition that has guided the Jewish people since for more than three thousand years ago. Atheistic socialism ridicules the belief in a Creator. It considers material existence and possessions as the only reality. Communist ideology denies the existence of anything that cannot be perceived with the five senses and renounces all belief in spiritual reality.

In that society, people do not take death into account. The subject of death is taboo; it simply is not discussed or even considered. It is as though death does not exist. It is banished from the mind. People assume that after death there is absolute nothingness, that life reverts to empty non-existence. As I grew up, I often wondered how it could be that an individual, whose life had been filled with emotions, dreams, thoughts and actions, could suddenly evaporate and plunge into a black hole of total nothingness. It simply did not make sense to me.[49]

Rachel came to reject the philosophy of dialectical materialism, but she had nothing with which to replace it. She left the *kibbutz* when she was called to the army and never returned. Meanwhile, she had met Uzi and became engaged when the Yom Kippur war broke out. On the day she was supposed to meet Uzi after the war, the accident occurred.

The man in charge of the construction site from where the wooden beam had fallen, took Rachel to a clinic for x-rays. When Rachel walked out of the clinic after having had the x-rays that revealed she had no broken bones, things looked different:

Cheerfully I stepped out into the street. Things had never looked quite as rosy as today. The air was fresh and stimulating, and my body was whole. The images around me seemed uncommonly sharp and clear. The world seemed different somehow from before. People around me were busy and rushing about, their faces expressing unhappiness and discontent.

Everything seemed so bizarre, like a city of phantoms. Why don't they recognize the truth? Why do people live in misery, and without hope? It seemed as though they were all looking down at the ground, each fretting about his troubles. Why don't they lift their eyes toward the sun, toward the universe, toward the beauty of creation? I could not understand why people do not burst into

49 Ibid., p. 10-11.

song, into a mighty song of thanksgiving for the privilege of walking this earth. Why don't they show others the truth, the wondrous
eternal light, the joy of creation, and point out to them that there is
a spiritual world beyond the limits of the physical universe?

I knew I could not adequately describe this other reality. I rec-
ognized that my vocabulary was capable only of expressing finite
concepts, that it was unequal to conveying the totality of the supernal
perfection that transcends the confines of the material world... .

Was I the only person who ever experienced 'the other side'? Were
there other people who are aware of the Existence that envelopes
the cosmos, the Essence that is the source of all being, the Almighty
Who is concealed while He reveals Himself? It did not make sense
that I, a simple woman with no special qualifications, should know
something that no one else knew.

From a rational point of view, my out-of-body experience could
not have happened, yet I was certain that it was no hallucination.
I was also sure that I had not gone insane, that I was in my right
mind. Proof of this are the ensuing years of my life which I lived
in complete normalcy.

I had no doubt that there were other people who had had similar
out-of-body experiences and knew about the existence of the exalted
infinite light. Where could I find them? I found the answer after a
search that lasted for many years. After seven years of fumbling in
the dark, I established the connection with the light.[50]

Uzi returned from the war and he and Rachel were married. Rachel
had told Uzi about her out-of-body experience and the 'Great Light,'
as she called it. They decided to keep it to themselves for fear that
Rachel might be thought to be insane and committed to an institution. Rachel first told the story of her experience in public seven years
later, after studies of out-of-body experiences, etc., had been published
by Dr. K. Kovler-Cass and Dr. Raymond Moody in *Life After Life*.

The effects of the tremendous blow to her head gradually began to
manifest themselves. She was unable to concentrate for any length
of time and had to drop out of the university. She was plagued for a
long time with bouts of amnesia and would forget appointments and
things she had been talking about only minutes before. She developed
headaches that were so acute she could barely function. Sometimes
the headaches were accompanied with nausea which made her body

---

50 Ibid., pp. 106-108.

shiver all over. Subsequently, she visited two specialists and had a thorough examination. After a while the headaches and bouts of amnesia faded and Rachel was diagnosed as suffering ten to fifteen percent permanent disability. "Every doctor who examined me was amazed when I described the vehemence of the blow I received. They all agreed that it was impossible that I could have survived an impact of such magnitude."[51]

Rachel and Uzi came across meditation and together with some friends tried it as a way to achieve relief from their physical ailments. (Uzi was plagued by a stomach ulcer he had developed during the war). Ultimately they found it unsatisfactory and since the whole idea of religion was foreign to them and had been ridiculed by their friends and the community they had grown up in, it never occurred to them to look into Judaism or any other religion to find solace from their physical ailments or to help them come to terms with the Great Light.

Then one day Rachel decided to visit an old childhood friend, Esther, whom she had not seen for a long time. Esther had married and was raising a family in Jerusalem. The rest of the story of this visit, I will let Rachel tell in her own words:

> I arrived at their house early in the evening. We were thrilled to see each other again. ... As we were talking, I noticed that Yehudah was wearing a small *yarmulka* [head covering]. I expressed surprise.
>
> "Well," he replied forthrightly, "I made up my mind to adopt the religious way of life."
>
> We sat around the kitchen table, had dinner and talked late into the night. Yehudah and Esther were tired, and we decided to go to bed. I slept in the guest room on the second floor.
>
> Before going upstairs, I noticed a book on the dining room table. [The book was a prayer book called in Hebrew a *siddur*.] Since I was an avid reader, I decided to read a little before going to sleep. I took the book and went up to my room.[52]
>
> I put my things in place, went to bed and picked up the book. The title on the cover read: *Siddur Tefillat Yesharim*, the Prayer of the Upright.

51 Ibid., p. 118.

52 From the context of this passage it is obvious that this was the first time Rachel Noam had ever held a Hebrew prayer book in her hands. She had said earlier in the book that she had never yet been inside of a synagogue.

I started to read the Hebrew: "*modeh ani lefanecha*—I gratefully thank You—*Melech chai vekayam*—O living and eternal King—*Shehechezarta bi nishmati bechemlah*—that You returned my soul within me with compassion—*rabbah emunatecha*—abundant is your faithfulness!"

I was overwhelmed. I wanted to continue reading, and I realized at once that this book was unlike any other book I had ever read. This book I had to treat differently. Even the lettering was unusual. Some sections were in large print, while other parts were in smaller print. Occasionally, the type and the thickness of the letters alternated from normal type to boldface.

Very slowly, the images I had seen during the accident began to reappear in my mind's eye, as though emerging from a haze.

I continued reading: "*Elokai*—My Lord—*neshamah schenatata bi*—the soul You placed within me—*tehorah hi*—is pure—*ata beratah*—You created it—*ata yetzartah*—You formed it—*ata nefachta bi*—You breathed it into me—*ata meshamerah bekirbi*—You safeguard it within me—*ve'ata atid litelah mimeni*—and eventually You will take it from me—*ulehachazirah bi*—and restore it to me—*le'atid lavo*—in time to come."

My excitement soared. I had the urge to cry out, "That's right! I know that this is true!"

I wanted to tell people that I had personally experienced this. My soul was removed from my body, and it has been restored to it! But who would believe me? On the other hand, here it was, black on white, in the book that I had found on the dining room table, and obviously, people were reading it. What was going on here? Who had written this book? The questions kept coming in quick succession as I continued to read.

"As long as the soul is within me I gratefully thank You O G-d, my Lord, and the Lord of my forefathers, Master of all works, Lord of all souls—blessed are You, O G-d—Who restores souls to dead bodies."

At this point my emotions peaked. I was all choked up. Tears flowed freely down my cheeks. "Lord of all souls, Who restores souls to dead bodies ..." The thing I dared not speak about for so many years was written here plainly and lucidly.

I was enthralled with the *siddur* [prayer book]. On and on I read without stopping, as if I were reading a suspenseful mystery novel. For about two hours, I read prayers and several chapters of *Psalms*. While reading, tears were streaming from my eyes. I wanted to scream: "True! True! Whatever is written here is all true!"

I did not close my eyes all that night. Over and over, I browsed through the *siddur*, trying to digest in my mind what my eyes were reading. I realized that this was a book of commitment, of attachment to Hashem[53] and communicating with the *Shechinah* [G-d's Presence], a book of supplications, assurances and commandments. I did not understand the meaning of these commandments and how they were associated with the Great Light, but I felt intuitively that by dint of these commandments and abundant flow of goodness and kindness is drawn down from Heaven to our world.

The tears that were flowing from my eyes reminded me of the uncontrollable crying spell I had had after the accident. Once again, I was weeping irrepressibly, although by nature I am quite unemotional and unsentimental. In fact, for many years I hardly cried at all. But these were tears of a different sort. I asked myself: How is it possible that for thirty years I had not even once read the *siddur*? ...

Meanwhile, on that fateful night, I continued to read the pages of the *siddur*, following the prayers in their proper order. Over and over, I was struck by the wonder of it all.

"Let a person always be G-d-fearing privately and publicly, acknowledge the truth and speak the truth within his heart ..."

The simplicity and clarity of the words struck a responsive chord in me. I needed no explanations or commentaries; it was all there before me in its literal meaning.

With growing interest I continued to read: "Master of all worlds! Not in the merit of our righteousness do we cast our supplication before You, but in the merit of Your abundant mercy. What are we? What is our life? What is our kindness? What is our righteousness? What is our salvation? What is our strength? What is our might? Are not all the heroes like nothing before You, the famous as if they had never existed, the wise as if devoid of wisdom and the perceptive as if devoid of intelligence? For most of their deeds are desolate and the days of their lives are empty before You, and the pre-eminence of man over beast is non-existent for all is vain. Except for the pure soul which will have to give an accounting before Your Throne of Glory."

Who, more than I, knows that a person will have to give a reckoning, that death is not emptiness and void? I remembered the scenes from the 'film of from my life' as they unfolded before from my eyes when I was outside my body. I recalled from my feeling

---

53 The term "Hashem" is often used in Rabbinic writings as a synonym for G-d.

of anguish and disappointment over my wasted life and from my unfulfilled mission in this world.

I continued reading in the *siddur*: "But we are Your people, members of Your covenant ...Therefore, we are obliged to thank You, praise You, glorify You, bless, sanctify and give praise and thanks to Your Name. We are fortunate, how good is our portion, how pleasant our lot and how beautiful our heritage!"

I went over these words once more: "Our heritage." I was a Jew because of my heritage. But what was this heritage that made me Jewish? As much as I tried, I could not remember ever receiving any inheritance. But if this wonderful *siddur* states that we received a heritage then I am sure this heritage is in existence and all I must do is simply look for it.

The text continued: "We are fortunate for we come early and stay late, evening and morning, and proclaim twice each day: hear, O Israel: G-d is our Lord, G-d is One."

Master of the universe, how happy I was! Until now You were hidden, and now I have found You! Impulsively the words burst forth.

I went on: "Take to heart these instructions with which I charge you today."

I felt that this verse was speaking directly to me. I knew that it was my duty to do all these things, to bring them to fruition and to carry them out in practice.

I continued: "It was You before the world was created, it is You since the world was created. It is You in This World and it is You in the World to Come. It is You Who are G-d, our Lord, in heaven and on earth, and in the highest heavens. True, You are the first and You are the last and other than You there is no god. Fulfill for us, G-d, our Lord, what You have promised us. Give thanks to Hashem [G-d], declare His Name, make His acts known among the peoples. Sing to Him, make music to Him, speak of all His wonders. Glory in His holy Name, be glad of heart, you who seek Hashem. Search out Hashem and His might, seek His Presence always."

I thought back to the hours immediately after the accident, when I walked in the street thinking, Why aren't people singing and giving praise and thanks for the privilege of walking the earth? And here I was reading it!

I felt that my mind was opening up, as if I had been sitting in a dark room and someone suddenly turned on the light. For six long years, I had been searching, and now, in the seventh year I had finally found the answer.[54] My tears were not only tears of joy; I also felt a sense of deep bitterness and self-reproach. Why? Why did I have to suffer so much? So many years of physical and mental anguish, years of wandering and searching. The best years of my life had passed by in hollow emptiness. They had turned to nothing, and yet this book, the *siddur*, was within easy reach. How many times had I passed a synagogue, yet it never occurred to me to enter! How many times did I visit a bookstore or a library, and not once did I come across a *siddur*? Why?

"Blessed are You, Hashem ... Who forms light ... He who illuminates the earth ... with compassion ..."

Is there anyone who understands as I do the intense compassion with which the sun shines on this finite world of ours? Our finite body cannot absorb the radiant splendor of this Light. How great is Hashem's compassion when he restricts His essential infiniteness and withholds His endless light so the world may exist.

I reached the *Shemoneh Esrei* [the main prayer of 19 blessings said while standing]: "Hashem, open my lips, that my mouth may declare Your praise ... You nourish the living with loving kindness, You revive the dead with great compassion ..."

It was this 'great compassion' that brought me back into my body. I recalled the moment when my soul returned to my body and the abundant flow of mercy cascaded over me. I understood that it was through this stream of compassion that my life was granted me...

I continued reading in the *siddur*. I read it and reread it, over and over. I did not believe what I was seeing. At long last I made it! I have come home! I felt like a girl who came back from captivity, like a girl who returned from drifting about aimlessly.[55]

This was the beginning of Rachel's involvement in Judaism. Gradually she, as well as Uzi, began to adopt a religious life, practising the customs and traditions of religious Jews. Much of what Rachel writes in this book is colored by her involvement in and commitment to the practice of Judaism that developed later, just as she describes here, in retrospect, her experience of reading the Hebrew prayer book (*siddur*) for the first time in the home of her friend, Esther.

---

54 See P.M.H. Atwater, *Beyond the Light* (Avon Books, 1994). There Atwater writes, "I found that it takes the average near-death survivor *seven years* to even begin to integrate the experience," p. 218.

55 Noam, *The View from Above*, pp. 138-46.

As time went on and Rachel's involvement with Judaism deepened, she began to look for a philosophical or metaphysical outlook that would help assimilate her new-found Judaism with her NDE. She found it by pure chance in a religious bookstore in Haifa. Again, here are Rachel's words:

> On one of from my trips to Haifa, I entered a religious book store, looking for a special kind of book, an interesting book about Torah and Jewish thought.
>
> Scanning the books on the heavily packed shelves, one title caught from my eye. The book had a strange-sounding name: *Tanya*. I lifted it from the shelf and browsed through the pages. Although printed with Hebrew letters, it used a terminology that was baffling to me. I did not recognize any of the expressions the author used. Although it was very difficult to understand, there were a few passages that did make sense to me.
>
> The salesman was a young man wearing black clothes, a large black *yarmulka* and a beard that had barely begun to sprout. His piercing dark eyes, which were recessed in his lean and bony face, gave him an otherworldly look. I went over to him and inquired about the author whose name appeared on the title page: Rabbi Shneur Zalman of Liadi....
>
> I skimmed through the book and read a few random paragraphs. In Chapter Twenty-One I read: "Hashem hides Himself, withholding His endless light, in an act of Divine withdrawal, to the extent necessary in order that the world may exist, since within the actual Divine light nothing can maintain its own existence."
>
> I was stunned. I thought that this book was talking about the light I had perceived, the light that is hidden from mankind.
>
> I sensed that this book was something special, and I quickly paid the salesman and left the store. I wanted to get home as fast as possible and start reading this unique book.
>
> It took me forever to get home. The bus was delayed, and when it finally came, it moved very slowly. I did not want to read on the bus; I wanted to wait until I was home and could read in peace, alone. I wanted to try to understand it in depth.
>
> Uzi was not at home. I sat down on the easy chair and started to read. I reread the same sentence many times, trying to understand its meaning.
>
> Much as I tried, I could not fathom the meaning. Much later, after studying the *Tanya* with qualified teachers I gained a little superficial understanding of a few details.

In Chapter Two, I learned that the soul ... has a variety of spiritual levels. To begin with, the soul gives the body its life, movement and propagation of the species, the life force that vivifies all living creatures. On this primitive level it is called *nefesh habahamit*, "the animalistic soul." On a higher level—above this elementary soul—there exists the divine soul, or *nefesh elokit*. It is a particle, a spark of Hashem Himself, so to speak it is the "spirit in man," ...

I read that when a person contemplates the greatness of Hashem he arouses within himself a sense of awe and deep respect for Hashem's infinite exaltedness. As a next step, a powerful love of Hashem is ignited in his heart, a yearning to unite with the infinite Essence of Hashem, a state that is called *kelot nefesh*, "the craving of the soul," as it is written, "My soul thirsts for You, my body yearns for You." (*Psalms* 63:2)

As I was reading this, tears welled up in my eyes. I suddenly remembered the strong feeling I had of overpowering love for the Great Light, how the Great Light was beckoning me, and I recalled the urge I sensed to nullify myself and become one with the Great Light.

In Chapter Four, I read that every *nefesh elokit*, Divine soul, is clothed with three garments—thought, speech and action—and that the study of Torah and the performance of *mitzvot* [commandments] therefore clothe the soul, so to speak ...

Hashem's Divine Presence is everywhere. But in the material world His Presence is hidden. It is manifest only when the material is nullified. I understood why we cannot perceive the Divine Light inside our body. It is because our body is not nullified; it is a tangible entity. It is 'something.' Hashem is manifest only when there is complete self-renunciation.

In Chapter Nineteen, I read that a soul is like a flame of a candle which by its very nature moves upward, because the fire of the flame wants to free itself from the wick and unite with its universal root of fire above.

Like the flame, the soul, too, has an innate desire to depart the body and attach itself to its Divine Root, notwithstanding that in so doing it becomes null and void and loses its identity.

In Chapter Thirty-Six, I learned that Hashem created the universe so that He may have a dwelling place in the lower worlds, especially in our world which is the lowest world of all, where darkness reigns supreme and light is shut out completely. Hashem's intention was to turn this darkness into light. This is to be accomplished by virtue of the fulfilment of *mitzvot* [commandments]. To this end,

Hashem gave the Torah to the Jewish people. The Torah enables us to receive the Infinite Light, the *Or En Sof*, in its pure form. Thus when we study the Torah and perform the *mitzvot*, the darkness of this world is turned into light.

In the era of *Mashiach* [Messiah], the revelation of G-dliness will be manifest to all the nations of the world, as it is written, "Reveal Yourself in the majestic grandeur of your strength over all the dwellers of Your inhabited world." (from prayer for the New Year holiday). This is the culmination of the Creation of the world and the fulfilment of the purpose for which it was called into being ...[56]

This description of how Rachel's NDE led to her adoption of the philosophy of Chabad was not inevitable. This is just how it worked out for her. This is how she fit it into some metaphysical picture of the world that made sense of her NDE. It was not necessary that she interpret it within the context of Judaism. It might well be interpreted as a manifestation of any one of a number of other religions.[57] Nonetheless, there are some features of NDEs that uniquely fit important aspects of Judaism. One is an idea that occupies a prominent place in Kabbalah and Chabad philosophy which is that G-d's presence makes Itself manifest in the form of light. This is interpreted as the infinite light of G-d which mediates between G-d's absolute, infinite Being and the finite, created world.[58] The *tzimtzum* or diminishing of G-d's absolute, infinite Being takes place not in G-d Himself, but in an emanation called the infinite Light of G-d. The phenomena of a Light experienced in many NDEs can be interpreted as an awareness, in varying degrees, of this Supernal Light. This Light is not G-d Himself but a *tzimtzum* or contraction of His essence and true Being, as we described this in chapter VI. This is how I think the Light that plays such a dominant role in the NDE can be viewed by Kabbalah and Chabad philosophy.

56   Ibid., pp. 165-170.
57   See Betty J. Eadie, *Embraced by the Light* (Bantam Books, 1994), in which the remarkable NDE of the author is seen and interpreted within the context of Christianity.
58   According to this, the Light that G-d created on the first day of the Biblical account of Creation was this infinite light. It could not have been a natural light as the sun and other heavenly bodies were not created until the fourth day.

Secondly, another idea that I believe is unique to Judaism is expressed in other aspects of NDEs. This idea has two elements to it. One is that the ultimate purpose of Creation is to be found in human actions in the physical world, and the second, is that each person has a unique purpose and plays an important role in the history of the world. In our next and final chapter we will discuss both these ideas. First we will discuss the purpose of the physical world according to Kabbalah and Chabad philosophy, and connected with this, the role of the individual in the grand scheme of things. Secondly we will discuss the notion of the infinite Light of G-d. We will see that both these ideas converge in the end of days as this is described in the eschatology of the Kabbalah and Chabad philosophy when the unity of G-d and the world become revealed in a manner that never existed before and which introduces a new form of existence altogether. This end of days of the world completes the unity of G-d and the world which was sundered at Creation. This is not only the ultimate end of the world as described in Kabbalah and Chabad philosophy. It is also the attainment of the ultimate rational end of the world—an end that will witness the final revelation of the unity of G-d and the world which the human mind sees as the rational conclusion of all existence. Thus the end of this book comes full circle. What is predicted by Kabbalah and Chabad philosophy is precisely what the rational mind would have hoped for, i.e. the reuniting of the world with G-d such that what appears as two distinct existent things, G-d and the world, merge and become one not only in thought but also in a reality that is palpable and present. The end of this book is the best that could be hoped for by a rational mind and thus the suitable title for the last chapter is "The End."

Finally, the role of each individual in the attainment of this end is the meaning of life for that person in the unique role that person plays in the world. Each individual is sent into the world to achieve something that only that person could achieve which is necessary for the perfection of the world. In this sense, the 'meaning of life' is the purpose of that life, which is unique and different from the purpose of all other individuals in the world each of which is unique in the sense that no one else could achieve and do what that person can do. Secondly, the experience of the Light as attested to by all NDEers without exception conveys the ultimate experience which lifts the soul to such an elevated and rapturous state, that all who experience it have no doubt that this is the highest joy that any created being could attain and as such gives meaning to one's existence to whatever degree that state can be attained or maintained. This chapter then is the culmination of the question of the meaning of life raised in Chapter IX.

When the NDE provides one with the purpose of one's existence in this world, it also gives one a glimpse of the highest joy and happiness the soul can attain through love of G-d and the delight of basking in His radiance, as described so vividly in the NDE of Rachel Noam. Insofar as one can achieve something of this relationship with G-d does one achieve meaning in one's life. There is no doubt in the mind of any NDEer who has seen 'The Light' that these two aspects of the NDE constitute the meaning of life. At some point these two elements merge in the joy of the unity with G-d attained by the fulfillment of one's Divine purpose in this world.

APPENDIX TO CHAPTER 10:
THE CASE OF THE SHOE ON THE LEDGE

The article mentioned in footnote 11 (see Chapter 10, p. 139) was called to my attention by a friend of mine, Dr. Milton Blake, after I had completed the book. He suggested that it would be appropriate for me to make some remarks as to how I view it, as this article is commonly cited as casting skepticism on NDEs. Since my friend is a highly respected psychologist, I am following his advice. None of what follows, however, should be taken as expressing his views. They are solely my own.

First, the authors of the article in question freely admit that their intention in investigating the case of the shoe on the ledge was to try to question and undermine it. Given that attitude, it is quite possible that Kimberly Clark Sharp (whose name I will call "Clark" for the purposes of this Appendix) did not willingly cooperate with the investigators. This is suggested by the vagueness with which the authors refer to the room where they attempted to reenact the case of the shoe on the ledge. They placed one of their own shoes on a ledge of a room which is vaguely referred to as "... at the place Clark described" (p. 32). They then went down to see if they could see the shoe from the outside and to their surprise, the shoe was clearly visible. This is in contradiction to Clark's account in her book where she says that she could not see anything on the window ledges from the ground because "the tops of the ledges were largely blocked from view" (p.11).[1] This makes sense if one is standing close to the building. Perhaps if she had taken a few steps backward, she might have seen it as Ebbern and Mulligan saw their shoe. The lack of the construction that Ebbern and Mulligan mention as affording them a "better view" than Clark's might have contributed to Clark's not seeing the shoe in the sense that she might not have stood as close to the wall of the building than she would have, if the construction had been there earlier. This, of course, is all speculation and I have no way of explaining

---

1 In this appendix, all quotations from Clark are from her book *After the Light*, cited in footnote 9. Otherwise the pagination refers to the critical article by Ebbern, etc. cited in footnote 11.

the discrepancy between Clark and our authors regarding what can be seen from the outside of Harborview Medical Center.

One thing which remains a puzzle in all of this is the vagueness of the location of the window ledge upon which the authors of this article placed their shoe. "... It was described at the place Clark described." Why not on the ledge of the room in which the shoe was originally discovered by Clark? One would suppose that if one wanted to reenact the seeing of the shoe, one would put in *on the same ledge* of the room in which it was originally discovered. It is possible Clark could not remember which ledge that was, after so many years, but it would seem to me that an event of that magnitude in the life of Clark, as she herself describes it (p.12), would have been embedded in her memory forever. How could she have forgotten in which room the shoe was found? If she had not forgotten it why did she not tell Ebbern, etc. which room it was? If she actually told them which room it was, why do our authors describe it in this vague way as "... at the place Clark described"? That description might fit *any room* on the west side of the north wing. This suspicion that the authors did not know the precise room in which Clark discovered the shoe is reenforced a few paragraphs later when they describe how they placed a shoe "... on the ledge from inside *one of the rooms*" and claimed that the shoe was easily visible from any place inside the room. The authors claim it was not necessary for Clark to have pressed her face to the glass of the window to see the shoe, as she described in her book (p.11).

Both of these discrepancies between what was able to be seen on the window ledge outside the building and from inside the room are important for our authors' argument that it is quite possible that numerous doctors, nurses or hospital support staff might have known about the shoe for a while before Maria took her little 'trip' around the building.

I cannot explain this discrepancy between Clark's account and the authors,' concerning the visibility of the shoe, but I am puzzled why our authors travelled all the way to Seattle to investigate this matter without locating the precise room in which the shoe was originally found and do all their 'experiments' in that very room. Maybe the view inside or out was a bit different. Again I emphasize I am not denying the truth of the authors' investigations here, but I cannot fathom why they did not say that they used the very same room in which the shoe was found. If

Clark had told them that she could not remember exactly which room it was, but that it was one of the rooms on the west side of the north wing, one would have thought that our authors should have mentioned this, but that it really made no difference to their experiments because they had examined all the rooms on the west side of the north wing and the windows and everything about the rooms are exactly the same. This may be picking at unimportant details, but it does raise a question about the kind of cooperation the authors had from Clark which might have affected the outcome of their inquiries. The obvious disdain that our authors had for Clark and her support group, the Seattle International Association for Near-Death Studies (IANDS), might well have been reciprocated by Clark. The authors attended a meeting of IANDS and condescendingly described the atmosphere of these meetings as that of a "revival meeting" (p.33).

In any event, the fact that Clark claimed not to be able to see the shoe from the outside, and from the inside could see it only if she pressed her face against the window pane, doesn't appear to be directly relevant to the question of how Maria knew there was a shoe on a ledge of one of the windows of the hospital and was able to describe the kind of shoe it was, how it was positioned, that it was worn at the little toe and that the shoelace was caught under the heel. Even if the shoe was completely visible from inside the room, when could Maria have had an opportunity to get out of bed and walk around the hospital, peering into rooms, between the time she was admitted with a massive heart attack and four days later when she had her cardiac arrest and went 'flying' around the hospital? The authors, therefore, 'hypothesized' the following explanation. Since the shoe was clearly visible from the outside and from inside of the room, there was a good possibility that some of the doctors, nurses and other hospital personnel had seen the shoe and noted the kind of shoe it was, its exact position on the ledge, the scuff marks at the little toe and the shoelace tucked under the heel. (One might wonder how one could see such details from the ground! On the other hand, if someone had seen it from inside the room, why would they not have removed it?) Maria might have heard some of the nurses, doctors or orderlies talking about the shoe and describing all these details, and in spite of her meagre knowledge of English, understood everything with precision and accuracy notwithstanding the fact that she was recovering from a massive heart attack just a few days previously (see p.32).

Our authors think that such a scenario is distinctly possible, but it strikes me as highly unlikely for three reasons. The first is that even though some doctors or nurses might have seen the shoe from the outside or from the inside, it is unlikely that they would have taken the trouble to notice that it was scuffed near the little toe or that a shoelace was tucked under the heel. Secondly, even if they had noticed it, why would they have mentioned these details in their discussions with one another, which Maria was supposed to have overheard? It would have been natural to say something like, "Did you see that tennis shoe perched on the ledge of the window in the north wing? How in the world did it get there?" What would have been the point of saying something like, "By the way, I noticed that it was scuffed near the little toe and that the shoelace was tucked under the heel!"? Thirdly, and most importantly, if it was common knowledge to the extent that it became a conversation piece among the hospital personnel, why didn't someone remove it! It is not the best advertisement for the neatness and efficiency of a hospital to leave a clearly visible tennis shoe on a window ledge for any length of time. Indeed our investigators proved this very point. They left their shoe on the window ledge and when they returned a week later it was gone! (see p.32). Ebbern and Mulligan, however, don't seem to realize that this fact works against their hypothesis, for if the shoe was removed in less than a week from the time they placed it on the window ledge, isn't it unlikely that 17 years earlier a similar shoe could have remained on the ledge long enough for it to become a topic of conversation among hospital staff? Should it not have been removed by the first staff person to have seen it, and isn't it likely that it would have been seen by someone shortly after it was placed there if it was "clearly visible" as our authors say? (p.32). If our authors had really been interested in testing their hypothesis by scientific method, they should have worked this 'experiment' a number of times. They should have left the shoe on the ledge and not gone away for a week, but gone back each day to see if the shoe had removed. Having done this ten times, they could then have calculated the average time it takes for hospital personnel to notice such a shoe and remove it. They then could have determined by 'scientific method' if there was enough time for patients to find out about it. One would have to assume that even if the shoe had been removed, the hospital staff would continue talking about it in all its detail, i.e. that it was scuffed at the little toe and the shoelace was tucked under the heel!

Another fact about the story as it is told by Clark in her book, that is inconsistent with our investigators' hypothesis, is that after Clark had retrieved the shoe and Maria's story became known to the hospital staff, numerous doctors, nurses, etc. came to visit Maria to take a look at the shoe. They were all amazed by the story as much as Clark herself. How could they have been amazed by it if the existence of the shoe with all its detail was a topic of conversation among them? They should have said, "How could Maria have known about that shoe? She was so sick all this time."

I suspect one of the reasons our investigators were not troubled by this part of the story is that they really didn't believe it. I think that they thought that for some reason Clark had manufactured a good part of the story. They even suggest at one point that Clark wrote her book for profit (p.33). Did there exist a Maria who was admitted to the hospital after suffering a massive heart attack and who did undergo a cardiac arrest four days later? I suppose this can be confirmed by hospital records. It is also possible that Maria had the hallucination of taking her 'trip' during her cardiac arrest. Everything else in Clark's account that is inconsistent with the investigators' hypothesis is said by them to be due to Clark's unscientific method, lack of notes, and a poor memory.

I, myself, find our authors' hypothesis highly improbable for all the reasons I have given and am inclined to believe the truth of Maria's account not because Maria told it to a social worker in a state of extreme excitement seventeen years before our authors made their investigations, but because it is consistent with hundreds and even thousands of similar such accounts that exist in the near-death literature, some of which I have recounted in this chapter, and which I find impossible to believe are all hallucinatory.

Our authors, in preparing the groundwork for their investigations, give us the following definition of an hallucination: "... what we *mean* by the term *hallucination* is an internally generated experience so detailed, emotional and believable that it is indistinguishable from ordinary perceptions of reality" (p.29). Taken at its word, this would seem to make it impossible to tell the difference between real, veridical perceptions and hallucinations. Maybe what we call veridical perceptions are also hallucinations? René Descartes proposed more or less the same argument to cast doubt on our ability to tell the difference between dreams and real life. He argued that what we call waking life might really be a dream.[2] Descartes' argument, however, is as fallacious as our authors' argument that one cannot tell the difference between a real experience and an hallucination.

The oasis turns into a hallucination when you bend down to drink the water and get a mouthful of sand! You can also tell a dream from a waking experience by waking up from a dream. As far as real life being a dream from which we never wake up, what difference does it make?

What would make a difference would be to 'wake up' from real life to discover that it is not as real as we thought it was. If I am not mistaken, this is precisely what happens in cases of deep and profound NDEs, where one comes in contact with "the Light." This is nothing else than a 'wake-up call' from the passing, temporal unreality of what everyone calls 'real life'. People who experience this are never the same and the change is for the good. They are more loving, caring and better people than they were before and permanently lose all fear of death. How could they do that if they were not convinced that the NDE was a glimpse of a reality which is masked by 'real life'. That some investigator with a fallacious definition of an hallucination could talk someone who has had a near-death experience into thinking that his or her experience was an hallucination, is as absurd as someone who might try to talk us into thinking that we are dreaming all the time because he fallaciously thinks there is no difference between dreaming and being awake.[3]

---

2 See Descartes *Meditations* (particularly Meditation I).

3 In response to my email inquiry, Kimberley Clark Sharp, author of *After the Light,* responded via email (quoted below), thus confirming the truth of what I suspected from simply reading the article: "One item you might change is the reference to the *Skeptical Inquirer* article. I did not know of the article (or heard of the magazine, for that matter) until a relatively short time ago and am aghast at the content, which for the most part, is simply untrue. I have written a response to the article which will be published in an upcoming issue of the *Journal for Near-Death Studies....* Bottom line, the shoe on the ledge happened as told and I have corroborating validation from a few medical staff who were in attendance."

11

THE END

The Baal Shem Tov (1698-1760), founder of the Hasidic movement in Eastern Europe, said that when a leaf falls from a tree on one blade of grass rather than another, there is a specific reason for this that serves to fulfill the purpose of the Universe.[1] What this purpose is transcends human understanding, but nothing in the world is an accident. If this is true for a leaf or sub-atomic particle, how much more so does it apply to the life of a human being. There is some purpose that the life of every person serves that is unique and that purpose in some small but important way is necessary for the Universe, as a small bolt in a complicated piece of machinery. The world that G-d created is more complicated and intricate than any machine and it takes more than a bolt to put it out of commission, but there is a sense in which the world remains unfulfilled and incomplete as long as there is one person who has not fulfilled the purpose of his or her existence. In some mysterious way that no one can fathom, the fulfilment of all Creation including all the realms of spiritual existence is dependent upon what happens in the material, physical world. This is one of the primary teachings in the mystical writings of the Zohar and the Chabad Hasidic philosophy of the *Tanya*. This was also aptly expressed by Dannion Brinkley when he said that the souls of human beings are considered the true spiritual heroes of heaven and their descent into the material world, an act of bravery and courage of which no angel is capable.[2] One might draw an analogy with the soldiers of a nation at war, who fight on the front line. They are the true heroes, and all the others—the factory workers, quartermaster corps, etc., exist for the sake of the soldiers on the front line, where the war is either won or lost. Similarly, all the hosts of Heaven and spiritual realms above exist for the sake of the material,

---

1 In modern terms one could say this about the movement of a sub-atomic particle.

2 See the quote above in Chapter X, p. 158, from his book *Saved by the Light*.

physical world where the war between good and evil rages every day. This is the front line and every human being in the world is a front line soldier that is being cheered on and encouraged by all the hosts of heaven including G-d. Every act of kindness and compassion we show for our fellow human beings brings a cheer from Heaven above and moves the world one step closer to ultimate redemption. Every act of cruelty, egoism, selfishness, and lack of concern for our fellow man is a set-back in this cosmic war and for the individual personally.

G-d, Himself, is simply an interested observer. He is watching the game but he is not impartial. He is rooting for the side of goodness and is disappointed when evil scores a point. However, in the inimitable words of Yogi Berra, He is 'watching this one.'[3] G-d relegated Himself to this position when he gave man free will. According to some Rabbinic commentators, this is what is meant in the story of Creation when it is said that G-d created man in His image. The only other creature that has any semblance of free will is man.[4] It is not the same level of freedom that G-d enjoys. G-d's freedom is unconditional. There is *nothing* G-d cannot do (except perhaps destroy Himself),

---

3 See the story about Yogi Berra in footnote 8 in Chapter 3.

4 Angels lack free will as they have no desires to entice them to evil or ego-ism. The word "angel" is derived from the Greek *angelos*. This is a literal translation from the Hebrew "*malach*" which means a messenger or envoy. An angel is nothing more than a messenger of G-d. It cannot fail in its mission any more than a weight can fail to fall to earth when unsupported. It has no free will any more than a rock. It is, therefore, impossible for an angel to rebel against G-d as expressed in Milton's view of Satan (see *Paradise Lost*). According to Judaism, Satan is simply that angel whose Divine mission it is to tempt and entice man to evil. Were there no such temptation, or if there were no Satan, it would not be possible to choose between good and evil and there would be no free will.

   Animals also lack free will as they lack the ability to deliberate and choose between alternative courses of action. The Stoic's portrayal of a dog deliberating between two paths and then "choosing" one is an anthropomorphism. What the dog is probably doing is sniffing and following its nose. The dog can hardly be said to 'choose' which way it wants to go. In this sense Descartes was only partially wrong in describing animals as robots or machines lacking a soul (i.e. consciousness) altogether. What they lack is that crucial ability that every human being has of choosing a course of action that renders one a moral agent.

while man's freedom is limited to choosing between good and evil within the parameters of the conditions in which we find ourselves. We cannot choose who our parents shall be, nor the circumstances in which we are born, nor the personality traits that are encoded in our genes. What we do have control over and what we therefore must take responsibility for, is how we act when faced with the moral choice of good and evil. This is where the battle for the cosmos rages and we are the heroes and villains fighting this battle. The difference between real life and a movie is that in the movie, it is clear who are the heroes and who are the villains. In real life, however, one can be a hero one day and a villain the next. Sometimes we choose good and sometimes evil. The goal is to score higher on the side of good than evil. This is the general purpose of every human being in the world, but the circumstances of each of us is unique. It is as if the war between good and evil were not a single World War that engulfs everyone, but rather, it is more like a million or billion small, little wars going on simultaneously. Each of us is fighting a unique war, but the general effect is cumulative. We are all in the same boat—the one world that G-d created. The success or failure of each individual in his or her own personal battle has an effect on others. How each of us succeeds or fails in the world is the business of everyone. In a lifeboat, one cannot argue that if one wants to drill a hole under ones's own seat, this is his or her business and no one else's. We are all responsible for one another and therefore we are duty bound to encourage one another when the going gets tough and we see others faltering, as soldiers in battle rush to the rescue of a wounded comrade.

In the literature of Chabad Hasidus, there is an attempt to argue for the above account of the purpose of the world, based on the story of Creation in the Hebrew Bible. This argument goes as follows: When a person builds a house the first thing he does is dig a hole in the ground for the foundation. Then he pours the foundation, puts up the walls, the ceiling, installs the plumbing, heating, and electricity, furnishes it and finally he moves in and lives in it. The moving in and living in the house expresses the true purpose of the house. Before he can move in, however, he has to dig a hole in the ground for the foundation. The builder does not want the hole or the foundation *per se*. What he really wants is a house to live in. To achieve this purpose he has to dig a hole and pour a foundation. If it were possible to build a house without a foundation he would happily dispense with it as they do in California, southern Texas, and Florida where the ground never freezes. One can say this about every step in the building of the house until the house is completed and the builder moves in. None of the steps in the building of the house expresses the true will or desire of the builder. Only after the house is completed and he moves in, is his true will and desire satisfied.

Similarly when G-d made the world He created it as a person builds a house, except that we, being creatures on earth, constrained by gravity, build from the ground up. G-d, however, is not bound by this constraint and when He created the world, He built it, so to speak, from the top down. First He created the Heavens and all the spiritual realms of being of which, according to Kabbalah, there are myriads of thousands of levels, and then came to create the material physical world and finally, the existence of man. The formation of the world comes to an end with man in the physical world. The only thing left is for the Creator to dwell in the world that He created.

One might say that if G-d has created the world in order to dwell in it, He should dwell in it no matter what man does. The fact is, however, that G-d did not create the world for its own sake, but in order that man with his free choice should choose good over evil. G-d, therefore, dwells in the world only when man chooses good.

In the Bible, the first humans, Adam and Eve, were given this choice in the form of obeying G-d's command not to eat of the fruit of the tree of knowledge of good and evil.[5] Before they disobeyed G-d by eating of that fruit, G-d did indeed dwell with Adam and Eve in the garden and they lived a life untainted by evil. Upon their eating the fruit and thus making themselves susceptible to evil temptations, they introduced evil into the world for the first time and therefore G-d removed Himself from the world and now dwells in the world

---

5 In the Christian tradition, this fruit was said to be the apple. The Bible itself, however, does not specify what fruit this is. In Rabbinic tradition, there are four different opinions as to what fruit this was. They are 1) wheat, 2) fig, 3) a citrus fruit called esrog, and 4) the view expressed in the *Zohar* that it was grape. There is no opinion in Jewish tradition that it was an apple. I, myself, do not know the origin of the Christian tradition in this matter.

only to the extent that men and women succeed in overcoming evil in their own lives.

This idea is expressed in a Hasidic tale told by Martin Buber.[6] Once the Rabbi of Kotzk, the well-known Kotzker Rebbe, surprised a number of learned scholars who were visiting him by asking, "Where is the dwelling of G-d?" They all laughed and said, "What a thing to ask! Is not the whole world full of His glory?" The Kotzker replied, "G-d dwells wherever man lets Him in."

Indeed, the whole world is full of G-d's glory, but that is just His glory. Where is G-d Himself? The answer the Kotzker Rebbe gave was that G-d Himself goes only where He is invited. True, He made the world to dwell in, and did dwell in it for a while until Adam and Eve sinned. Since then, G-d dwells in the small acts of kindness and goodness that individuals do in the world, just as every act of pride, arrogance, greed, selfishness, and cruelty to a fellow human being or even to an animal removes G-d from the world. The purpose of man, then, is to invite G-d back into His world.[7]

---

6 Martin Buber, *The Way of Man According to the Teachings of Hasidism* (Routledge and Kegan Paul, London, 1950). Reprinted in Walter Kaufman, *Religion from Tolstoy to Camus* (Harper Torchbooks, 1964): pp. 425-441. Unfortunately both editions of this short but illuminating piece of writing are out of print.

7 These two ideas, 1) acts of kindness and 2) G-d's presence in the world are brought together in a *Midrash* (Rabbinic homiletical literature) which recounts how G-d chose a hill outside of Jerusalem as the Temple Mount, i.e. the place where the Temple of Solomon was to be built through which G-d's presence in the world would be revealed. This is the story told in the *Midrash*:

Two brothers inherited a field on a hill from their father. One had a family and the other lived by himself. At harvest time, the lone brother tossed about sleeplessly in bed. "How can I rest comfortably and take a full half of the yield, when my brother has so many more mouths to feed?" So he arose in the night, gathered bushels of produce and quietly brought them over to his brother's barn.

Meanwhile his brother across the hill also could not sleep. "How can I enjoy my full share of the produce and not care for my brother who is alone, without help and future support?" So he arose in the night and quietly brought over bushels of produce to his brother's barn.

The question still remains, why did G-d see fit to make a world from which He could be banished by man's evil, or why did He make a physical world in the first place? Why didn't He stop with the Heavens, where only good resides and the soul knows only love, peace, and harmony?

It is at this point that Jewish mystical philosophy introduces an idea that is unique in the annals of religion or religious philosophy. This is the notion that the physical world has greater potential for good than all the Heavens or spiritual realms put together. Man has an opportunity of drawing closer to G-d Himself in this world more than his soul will have in the eternal life it will enjoy in the spiritual worlds after it leaves the body. This surprising view is ensconced in a pithy but enigmatic statement in the *Ethics of the Fathers*, which is the ethical writing of the *Mishnah*.[8] "He (Rabbi Yaacov) used to say, One hour of repentance and good deeds in this world is better than all the life in the world to come."[9] The world to come is the life of the soul after it leaves the body and enters the spiritual realms of being described in the NDEs recorded in the previous chapter. The above quotation is immediately followed by what appears to be its contradiction: "One hour of bliss in the world to come is better than all the life in this [material] world."[10] How is one to understand this apparent contradiction?

One can readily understand the second part of this *Mishnah*. It expresses the view common to all religions. The life of the soul in Heaven is incomparably better than life in this world, fraught as it is with pain and suffering, misery, and unhappiness. Nearly all NDEers

---

Next morning, each brother found that which they gave away was replenished, so they continued bringing over produce to each other, night after night.

One night, the brothers met during their nightly trip, embraced and hugged. G-d looked down on this expression of brotherhood and said, "On this spot of mutual love I wish to dwell. Here I will build my Temple."

8 The *Mishnah* is the collection of laws comprising what is called the Oral Torah which was written down by Rabbi Judah the Prince in the year 210 C.E. It is the compendium of laws which provides the basis of the legalistic discussion in the Talmud.

9 *Ethics of the Fathers* IV, 17.

10 Ibid.

will testify to this. What, however, could possibly be the explanation of the enigmatic first part of this saying? Rabbi Schneur Zalman,[11] explains in his work, the *Tanya*, that all understanding and delight that the soul derives from the Heavenly light of the spiritual realms of Being is not delight in G-d Himself, but is rather a mini-glow or a radiance of the Divine splendour.[12] No finite mind or soul can grasp the essence of G-d Himself or delight in His presence. If G-d were to reveal His true essence, the soul would simply cease to exist, being unable to abide the intensity of such a revelation, as the earth would burn up if it were too close to the sun. The sun instead of being the source of warmth and life on earth would destroy it. Similarly G-d, when He created not only the material world but also all the hosts of Heaven, had to contract and lessen the power of His light in order to create a Heaven and a material world that could exist apart from Him. There is only one place in all of Creation where His true essence dwells and that is, oddly enough, in the material world. The reason for this is that only in the material world is the purpose of Creation fulfilled. G-d did not create the world so that the soul, after overcoming the tests and travails of this veil of tears, should be able to enjoy eternal bliss in Heaven. Rather, G-d created the Heavens because it was a necessary step in making the material world, much as a builder has to dig a hole and pour a foundation in order to build a house. In this case, the House that G-d built for the purpose of dwelling in was not Heaven but Earth. Heaven is simply the foundation for the material world. It was necessary to have a Heaven in order to have the kind of physical world that G-d desired. It was a means to an end, not the end itself. A proof of this is that after the Heavens were complete, the act of building continued until the earth was formed and finally man. Only then did the formation of world came to an end, after the ultimate goal was reached an autonomous soul inhabiting bodies in the material world. Only then could the real action begin.

---

11   Rabbi Schneur Zalman, commonly called the Alter Rebbe, the author of the *Tanya* which is the central work of Chabad philosophy, was the founder of the Chabad-Lubavitch movement within Hasidism. He lived from 1745-1813.

12   See Schneur Zalman, *Tanya* , bilingual edition (Kehot Publication Society, Brooklyn): p. 17.

The free will of man could now be tested by the temptations of the garden of Eden. The first test was a failure, but the 'game' was not over. Mankind had to pick itself up and try again. G-d sits on the sidelines and cheers. When His side overcomes the forces of darkness and evil, He cheers and runs over to his players and pats them on the back. When they fail, he does not take them out of the game. They have to try again. Angels are simply water boys or bat girls that keep the players supplied with whatever they need to stay in the game. The real action, however, is on the playing field—the physical world, while the water boys and bat girls stand on the sidelines. When a player is exhausted, G-d sends a water boy over to refresh him. Before a player steps up to the plate, the bat girl hands him the right bat, chosen by G-d Himself. All the substitute souls sitting on the 'bench' in Heaven can't wait to get into the game, for that is where they have a chance to excel, become a hero and win the plaudits of the 'coach' who runs the team. When, for whatever reason, a player is removed from the game, he is sent to the showers, relaxes and takes a rest. After being refreshed he is anxious to get back into the game and waits expectantly for his turn to play again.[13]

The enigmatic saying from the *Ethics of the Fathers* quoted above now becomes clear. Repentance, or regret for one's past misdeeds which spurs one to future good deeds, is better than going to Heaven and basking in the radiance of G-d's glory. The reason it is better, is that while the life of the soul in the body is more difficult and fraught with all kinds of dangers, nevertheless, when it succeeds in overcoming the hindrances that stand in the way of doing a simple act of kindness for another person, G-d Himself comes and stands beside him. One may not know this and indeed it is impossible to know G-d or be aware

---

13   Apropos this metaphor, I quote here an excerpt from the daily diary of Hasidic thoughts compiled by the Lubavitcher Rebbe, of blessed memory, for the 15th day of the Hebrew month of Cheshvan: "The soul above awaits the time it will be privileged to descend into a body. For the soul senses how much it can accomplish here below (in this physical world); it can attain the level of 'delighting with G-d.' So what is everyone wait- ing for? (Why the procrastination in devoting ourselves to our assigned task—when our souls waited impatiently just for this very chance!)" See Rabbi Menachem Mendel Schneerson, *Hayom Yom—From Day-to-Day*, bilingual edition (Kehot Publication Society, 1988): p. 104.

of His presence any more than it is possible for the earth to exist next to the sun. Nonetheless, according to the teachings of Kabbalah and Hasidic philosophy, that small act of kindness fulfills the purpose of the entire Creation including all the worlds of spiritual bliss that exist in the Heavenly spheres of Being. This small act of kindness is what G-d had in mind when He created the world, and that act redeems the world from oblivion. Or rather it redeems the world and G-d's dwelling in it from oblivion, for without that small act of kindness and all the other such acts that people do in the world for others, the world could not exist. The reason for the entire Creation would cease to exist and along with it all the hosts of Heaven. When the 'game' is finally over and there is no action on the field, there is no need for a water boy or a bat girl. All the angelic beings above will be out of a job. This view of the role and purpose of the physical world in G-d's plan of Creation is, so far as I know, unique to Judaism generally and specifically to the teachings of the *Zohar*, Kabbalah, and Hasidic thought.

There is, however, one final point that has to be made. When the Torah scholars visiting the Kotzker Rebbe answered his question "Where is G-d?" by saying that the whole world is filled with His glory, they were not wrong. Neither was the Kotzker Rebbe, when he replied that G-d is found in the world only where man allows Him to enter. How does one reconcile this apparent contradiction? The clue is given in the difference between the 'glory' of G-d, and G-d Himself, as we suggested. The 'glory' of G-d is a ray of His presence. As a ray of light spreads out from its source but is in some sense separated from its source, so the manner in which G-d reveals Himself in the world cannot be a revelation of G-d's very Being but a watered down version where the essence of the Divine Being is diminished and shielded as the rays of the sun are diminished and shielded from earth by the distance and an atmosphere that filters out the harmful rays. G-d's revelation must not destroy the world but maintain its existence the way G-d intended. Thus the Heavenly realms receive varying degrees of G-d's light. The higher realms receiving a more intense and concentrated degree of G-d's revelation than the lower realms. The literature of Kabbalah and Chabad Hasidic philosophy contains volumes and whole libraries describing the various levels of Heavenly worlds and the degree to which each level is receptive of the Divine radiance. The daily prayers in the Hebrew prayer book are designed to lead the worshipper through each of these levels to whatever degree the worshipper is able to follow. Isaac Luria, who lived in Sefat in the latter part of the sixteenth century, designed special acts of meditation to lead the worshipper through all the levels of heaven if one could only follow. Only the pious elite can follow this course. The Baal Shem Tov, the founder of Hasidism, emphasized that while the meditations of Isaac Luria were important for a few select righteous men, what G-d really wants is the sincere calling out to Him from even the simplest person. The soul of every human being has deep within it the desire and the need to reach out to G-d as an infant or small child reaches out for its mother, the source of its life and very existence.[14] G-d answers such prayers in the

---

14   This is illustrated by the following story. The Baal Shem Tov was praying with his congregants in the synagogue at the close of Yom Kippur (Day of Atonement). The time for concluding the prayers and going home to break the day-long fast had long passed, but the holy Baal Shem Tov was still engrossed in his prayers. His face was stern and showed concern and anxiety. Everyone knew that something very serious was taking place at that moment and began beseeching G-d for mercy. Suddenly the countenance of the Baal Shem Tov broke into a smile. He quickly concluded his prayers, and after the blowing of the shofar, which signalled the end of the fast, told all the congregants they should go home and break their fast in a joyous frame of mind, for G-d had certainly bestowed upon them blessings.

Later the students of the Baal Shem Tov who were close to their master questioned him about the sudden change from his stern and serious countenance to one of joy and happiness. The Baal Shem Tov replied that in his devotions as he was travelling through all the palaces of Heaven, he saw that a harsh decree had been passed in Heaven against a community. No matter how hard he prayed that this decree should be lifted, he was unable to influence the Heavenly court to nullify it. Then suddenly, the prayer of a simple peasant boy who knew no more than the letters of the Hebrew *aleph beit* (alphabet), but was unable to put the letters together to make words, reached up to the highest levels of Heaven and nullified the decree. The prayer of this simple young boy went something like this:

G-d, I see everyone around me praying with all their heart and soul and the holy Baal Shem Tov looks so stern and worried. Surely something very serious is at stake. I wish I knew more so that I too could join in praying to You for mercy, but I am just a poor, peasant boy and all I know is the

form of whatever enlightenment these prayers call forth. However, all these varying degrees of Divine revelation from the highest Heaven to the lowest person who turns to G-d with simple faith and sincerity as the peasant boy in the story of the Baal Shem Tov is all part of what is called the 'glory' of G-d. It is not the presence of G-d Himself. G-d Himself is found in Creation only in the physical world, and He is found there only when man invites Him through an act of kindness or by obedience to his commands. G-d's presence in these cases are, of course, hidden. G-d's presence cannot be revealed, even in the highest Heavens above. If you want to have G-d Himself next to you, you have to be a soul embodied in the world, struggling to fulfill one's Divine purpose. This is what is meant in the *Ethics of the Fathers* when it is said that one hour in this world of sincere prayer and turning to G-d and acts of kindness unites one with G-d Himself, while the bliss and joy of the soul in Heaven is only of the radiance or light of G-d, but not G-d Himself. On the other hand, one hour of that bliss and joy far exceeds what little fleeting happiness and spiritual enlightenment one can derive in an entire lifetime in this world of materiality where ego, lust, greed, fear, and hatred seem to rule.

As Rabbi Schneur Zalman himself writes in the *Tanya*, "This world is filled with evil, and the wicked are triumphant."[15] In such a world, it is a wonder that mankind is not engulfed by evil altogether. The only saving grace is that G-d has hidden within the soul of every person a desire for goodness and G-dliness, and on those occasions when this goodness manifests itself, G-d Himself comes and saves the world from utter destruction.

---

aleph beit (alphabet). I will give You what I can—namely the letters, and You, G-d, take them and compose whatever prayer pleases You the most.

The boy then proceeded to name the letters: "*aleph, beit, gimel, daled* ..." until he had completed the entire *aleph beit*.

The Baal Shem Tov then told his disciples that those letters, because of the purity and sincerity with which were uttered, flew straight up before the very throne of G-d's glory and pleaded for mercy for that community whose fate lay in the balance, and this is what nullified the decree. When the Baal Shem Tov saw that, he smiled and quickly concluded his prayers and sent his congregation home with the promise that all was well.

15 See *Tanya*, Chapter VI, p. 20.

202 G-D, RATIONALITY AND MYSTICISM

What is the point of it all? Why does G-d need such an evil world? The answer is that by man's overcoming the evil of this world, G-d will ultimately reveal Himself to all Creation. This will not be a revelation of His glory or radiance of varying degrees as exists now in Heaven. Rather it will be a revelation of G-d Himself. How, then, will the world be able to withstand this revelation without being destroyed? This will be the miracle of the messianic age which, according to Jewish tradition, will usher in an age of love, peace and harmony in the world, when all evil will be removed. This great revelation of G-d, Himself, will reveal the holiness that is hidden in the material matter of the universe. Then the soul will live from the body, not as it is now when the body lives from the soul. All the souls that have lived in the world and have fought the battle of good and evil will return to their physical bodies and death will cease. The highest revelation that now exists only in Heaven will pale in comparison to the revelation of G-d at that time on earth, and as the prophet Isaiah predicts, "The earth will be filled with the knowledge of G-d as the waters cover the sea."[16]

This quotation from Isaiah is puzzling. How can the waters cover the sea? The sea and the waters are the same thing! What the prophet means is this: this physical world now seems far away from G-d or anything spiritual. Even if for some unknown reason deep inside, you find yourself reaching out for G-d, you might still explain it away as a weakness or superstitious hangover of a bygone era, or perhaps an 'opium' of some sort. What about evil and, if you are a Jew, the holocaust? Who can explain that? The Mezritcher Magid[17] once told his disciples, the youngest of which was Rabbi Schneur Zalman, that a time will come in the future when faith in G-d will be as difficult as climbing up an ice wall without shoes. Nevertheless, he told them, "Don't despair, I promise you the messiah will come." At that time there will be a revelation of G-d in the world that far transcends His glory and radiance that now fill the Heavens.

The plethora of evidence from NDEs that are now appearing which bears testimony to this glory, does not come as any surprise

---

16 Isaiah 11.9.

17 The disciple of the Baal Shem Tov who succeeded his master in the leadership of the Hasidic movement. His birth date is unknown but he passed away in December of 1772.

to a student of Kabbalah and Hasidic thought. It is what would be expected. However, the ultimate revelation will go far beyond that. It will manifest itself primarily on earth and at that time the earth and the physicality of the body will no longer separate the soul from G-d. That revelation will reveal the ultimate truth, that the material world and G-d are not two different things but that they are truly one and inseparable. It is not that G-d is one thing and the world is something else and they are somehow connected like a carpenter and the house he builds. Rather G-d and the world are one and the same as the waters and the sea. The knowledge of this oneness will fill the entire world and everything in it, including animals and plants down to the smallest sub-atomic particle. After all, the prophet does not limit this knowledge to man. He does not say, as he could have said, that *man* will be filled with the knowledge of G-d. It is the *entire earth* that will be filled with this knowledge. Perhaps the meaning here is connected with the statement in Maimonides' *Mishneh Torah*, mentioned earlier that the creative power that constantly keeps the world in existence is nothing else than G-d's knowledge of it.[18] That is, the knowledge of G-d that Isaiah proclaims will fill the world as the waters cover the sea, is the awareness of G-d's creative power that sustains the world at every moment and this power will no longer be concealed but made manifest in every tiny particle in the universe so that one will no longer see a distinction between G-d and the world—they will be one as are the waters and the sea.

It is no accident that this prophecy from Isaiah constitutes the last words of Maimonides' great work, *Mishneh Torah*, which is the only compendium of Rabbinic law that contains the entire gamut of Jewish law as well as a complete philosophy and ethics. Nor is it an accident that the last section ends with a description of the messianic age and the last words of this description is the quotation from Isaiah. This is nothing else than a realization of that proclamation which is the Clarion call of the Jew—"Hear O Israel, G-d our G-d, G-d is one."

This proclamation, however, is a statement of belief. It is not something we see with our physical or even spiritual eyes. It is an idea that defies human comprehension, even though it be the ultimate requirement of human reason that all reality form a unity, as we argued in

---

18   See Maimonides, *Mishneh Torah, Hilchot Yesodei Hatorah*, ch. 2: 9-10.

Chapter 5. If there is a Creator of the Universe, that Creator must be one with everything including the created world. That there is a Creator is the rational conclusion of reason as we argued in Chapter 6. Thus it is reason itself that leads us to the ultimate, mystical idea —the absolute unity of G-d with the world and thus the absolute unity of everything in the world with everything else.

The question, however, remains, how can G-d reveal His true essence in the physical world, and the world still remain a distinct finite world? If G-d could not reveal His true Being in Heaven without destroying the Heavenly worlds, how can He reveal His true Being in the material, physical world and the physical world still exist? The answer is that right now the physical world contains a greater capacity for holiness and G-dliness than do all the hosts of Heaven. That G-dliness is, however, concealed and the potentiality of its revelation will be fulfilled only in the messianic age. That revelation will right all wrongs, and justify the suffering of mankind throughout all the ages of man's cruelty to man. All the questions that we have of G-d will then be answered and G-d's justice and righteousness will reign throughout the physical world greater than that which now rules in Heaven. Death will cease and all the righteous throughout the ages will return to their physical bodies, and Heaven will basically close up shop. Rather, Heaven will move into nicer, more spacious quarters downstairs for there will be no limitations to G-d's revelation. There will no longer be degrees of revelation as there is now both in Heaven and on earth. There will be one, single Divine revelation for all existence, the revelation of G-d's creative power that maintains the existence of all things, both physical and spiritual. It will be a "new Heaven and a new earth."[19] There will no longer be a separation between the two. Both will be devoid of evil and creatures in both worlds will be aware of only the goodness of G-d. The revelation in the physical world will then be unique, for there will exist the revelation of G-d's true Being. At that time, as the prophet says, G-d will then be one and His name one.[20] "G-d" here is G-d's true Being undiminished and unrestricted. "His name" is His diminished power that created the finite, material world. Even though this creative act gave rise to a

19   Isaiah 66.22.
20   See Zacharia 14.9.

finite, material world that appears to exist in its own right apart from G-d, this itself is a sign that it was created by the True Being of G-d, which is the only thing that exists independently of all other things. All the spiritual beings in the spiritual worlds are profoundly aware that their existence at every moment depends upon G-d. This is because their source in G-d is not as high as that of the material, finite world. The source of the creation of the Heavens required some element of contraction of G-d's light, but the source of the finite, material world coming as it does from G-d's essential will is rooted in G-d's pure Being unconstricted in any fashion. This is why G-d is hidden in the physical world in a way that we are, for the most part, unaware, and the world gives the appearance of existing in its own right.[21] This very fact that the physical world gives no external appearance of depending on G-d indicates that this world is indeed created by the very essence of G-d's true, unconstricted Being.[22]

Just as man in the world is the only creature in all of G-d's creation that shares with G-d some modicum of free will, so the physical world is the only world in all of G-d's creation that shares with G-d some modicum of independent existence. In this case, however, the independence is illusory and only appears this way in our empirical experience of the world. In truth, however, reason will lead one to understand that nothing that exists can have absolute independence other than G-d. This was the conclusion of our arguments in chapters IV and V. That G-d's existence is not caused or dependent on any other thing, and that He created a finite world from His absolute free will that defies all comprehension, was our conclusion in chapter VI. It follows from the goodness of G-d, for which we argued in chapter VII, that all the evil that has existed throughout the history of the world will somehow find its conclusion in an ultimate state of goodness that could never have been achieved without that evil. All evil

---

21   Such an appearance is lacking altogether in the spiritual worlds of Heaven where all heavenly creatures are aware of their dependency on G-d at all times.

22   See the Hasidic discourse delivered by the Lubavitcher Rebbe, Rabbi M. M. Schneerson, of blessed memory, on the occasion of his acceptance of the mantle of leadership of the Lubavitcher movement, on the first anniversary of the passing of the previous Lubavitcher Rebbe, of blessed memory, January 17, 1951.

will be seen as leading up to that ultimate state of goodness in which the unconstricted Being of G-d will be revealed in the physical world from whence evil originated.

This revelation in the end of days will be unique in that it will not obliterate the existence of the world, and finite souls in bodies will witness this revelation. At that time no difference will be seen between G-d's true Being, and the finite creatures of this world created originally by His name or G-d's constricted Being. Then there will be fulfilled the prophecy of Zacharia, "... on that day G-d will be one and His name one."[23] G-d's primary creation—the finite, physical world, will then not only be understood as one with its Creator, but one will see this with open eyes. It will be as obvious as the ground on which we stand. Thus the ultimate end of Creation is precisely what rational thought should have hoped for but could never understand how it could come about. Furthermore, this ultimate revelation of G-d and goodness, the like of which no creature in Heaven has ever witnessed, will in fact be witnessed by finite human beings all of whom have suffered in the world and whose acts of goodness and kindness have ultimately merited the removal of evil and suffering and brought the world to that ultimate revelation that defies all understanding in which justice and goodness triumph. Above all, the greatest miracle will be that all this, though witnessed by finite beings living in a finite world, will survive this great revelation in order to bear testimony to the goodness and justice of G-d which will affirm His absolute unity and proclaim that indeed on that day, "... G-d is one and His name one." This is not a vague, mystical hope. It is the projection of what the rational human mind has a right to expect of G-d and the world, if indeed it is rational.

---

23   Zacharia 14.9.

INDEX

A

abortion 95, 96
Abraham 73, 99, 105-107
absolute infinity 81
absolutely infinite 12, 13, 67, 70,
    71, 74-77, 81, 110, 126
absolutely infinite being 70
After the Light (Sharp) 137, 185
Aiken, Henry David 85
Albritton, Rogers 52
analogy 41, 79, 81, 82, 117, 191
ancient Hebrews 12
anomaly 23
Anselm 52, 56
anthropic principle 46
a posteriori 30, 31
a priori 27, 30-32, 34, 35, 42, 61,
    65, 95, 97, 98, 101
a priori beliefs 34, 61
argument from finitude 78
argument, the skeptical 121
argument, teleological 35, 37, 38,
    40-43, 45, 46, 48, 50, 51, 71,
    75
argument from unity 35, 71
Aristotle 12, 31, 37, 38, 52-55,
    57, 65, 67-69, 73, 75, 77, 78,
    126, 134
a sense of urgency 147
astrophysicist 48-51
atheism 11, 13, 35, 48
atomism 55
atoms 54, 55, 73
Auschwitz 85, 104

B

Baal Shem Tov, the 119, 191,
    200-202
Baier, Kurt 117, 120
become a better person 148
Beethoven, Ludwig 115, 117, 120,
    148
Being of Light, the 156, 159, 163,
    164, 165
Benjaminson, Rabbi Yerachmiel 78
Bergen-Belsen 104
Blake, Dr. Milton, 9, 185
Brief History of Time, A 51
Brinkley, Dannion 134, 141, 154,
    155, 161, 166, 167, 191
Buber, Martin *The Way of Man*
    According to the Teachings of
    Hasidism 195
by accident 37, 38, 42, 47, 49, 56,
    120

C

Camus, Albert 113, 119, 125, 195
categorical value 93, 97
cathedrals 157
cause of itself 52, 53
causes 17, 41, 42, 80
celestial world of spirit 129
Chabad Hasidus 193
    Chabad Hasidic literature 72
    Chabad Hasidic philosophy
    13, 191, 199
    Chabad philosophy 78, 79,
    182, 183, 197
chaos 38, 39, 42, 43
Chelm 14
Christianity 11, 12, 54, 72, 182
clarion call 92, 203

co-create with G-d 158
co-eternal 54, 59, 75
cockroaches 46
Collected Papers (Peirce) 45
commit yourself 20
common course of nature 131
compassion 92, 102, 103, 105-
      108, 129, 150, 155, 163, 167,
      170, 172, 179, 192
confirmable 21, 27, 33
confirmed by empirical evidence
      137
consequences 93-100, 106, 113
contingent existence 12, 61, 69, 75
continuity of space 34
contraction 98, 183, 205
corollary 44
cosmological argument 35, 43, 50-
      54, 56, 58, 59, 69, 71, 75, 76
cosmology 55
Creation 12, 50, 72-77, 80-83, 85,
      126, 182, 183, 191-193, 197,
      199, 201, 202, 206
creation 13, 41, 55, 72-74, 76, 83,
      174, 205
criterion 25, 33, 52, 94, 135
Crystal City, the (Brinkley) 159
cumulative 15, 193

D

darkness 73, 169, 182, 198
death 19, 40, 88, 89, 94, 104,
      113-115, 117, 118, 127, 131,
      134, 139, 141, 144, 145, 149,
      151-153, 157, 161, 164, 173,
      178, 190, 202
Demea 41
Democritus 55
Descartes, René 85, 116, 190, 192

Desert Storm 157
Detroit Red Wings 151
Diary of Anna Frank, The 88
disconfirmable 21
Divine, 42, 72, 74, 90, 180-182,
      184, 197, 199-201, 204
    Divine purpose, 72, 184, 201
    Divine radiance, 200
    Divine revelation, 74, 201, 204
dreams 79, 81, 82, 141, 142, 165,
      166, 173, 190

E

Eadie, Betty J. 154, 182
Eastern religions 54, 74
Ebbern, Hayden 139, 185, 186,
      188
Ecclesiastes 113, 114, 115
Einstein, Albert 61-63, 66, 115,
      120, 133
Ellington, James 91
elucidate 11
emanation 78, 183
Empedocles 38, 55
empirical confirmation 26, 61, 62,
      63
empirically verifiable 32, 121
Ethics of the Fathers 146, 196, 198,
      201
evidence 17-23, 25, 27-31, 35, 36,
      47, 49, 65, 66, 80, 122, 132-
      136, 149, 152, 153, 167, 202
evil 13, 24, 35, 41, 50, 85-90, 92,
      94-96, 100, 102, 104-106,
      118, 149, 192, 194, 196, 198,
      201, 202, 204
evil Demon 85
evolution, theory of 46, 55
existence of G-d per se 74
existentialism 113

eyewitness testimony 18

F

Fear and Trembling (Kierkegaard) 100, 106
fear of death, no 162
finitude, argument from 78 100, 106
force of gravity 27, 47, 132
forgiveness 156
form 11, 13, 21, 24, 37, 40, 54, 55, 57, 61, 63, 64, 68, 77, 101, 109, 111, 114, 121, 129, 134, 137, 155, 157, 167, 168, 182, 183, 194, 201, 203
formal consistency 87
Frechtman, Bernard 113
freedom 192
Frost, Robert 105
functions 97, 116, 168
Fundamental Principles of the Metaphysics of Morals (Kant) 108
future 17, 20, 23, 28-30, 32, 87, 88, 95, 116, 121, 123, 151, 157, 158, 167, 195, 198, 202

G

G-d as a necessary being 58
G-d as Creator 12, 59, 72, 74, 83
G-d Himself 12, 23, 24, 79, 106, 109, 118, 122, 123, 183, 195-199, 202
G-dless man 113
Gallup poll 153
general theory of relativity 62, 63
genocide 96
Gerson, Safran, 12
glowing spirit 163
green-house effect 18

Grounding for the Metaphysics of Morals (Kant) 91
Guide for the Perplexed (Maimonides) 72, 75

H

hallucination(s) 137, 141, 142, 148, 150, 174, 189, 190
Harborview Medical Center 137, 186
Hasidic 11, 83, 119, 191, 195, 198, 199, 202, 205
  Hasidic thought 198, 199
Hawking, Stephen 51
Heading Toward Omega (Ring) 151
Hebrew Bible 12, 24, 54, 73, 74, 83, 110, 193
Hitler, Adolf 87, 93, 96, 110
hit man 95
HIV virus 98
Holmes, Sherlock 61, 62
hologram 24
hosts of Heaven 191, 197, 199, 204
human history 28, 132, 133, 153
human rights 97, 98
human will 93
Hume, David 27-32, 35, 40-43, 56, 86, 90, 115, 121, 131-133, 135, 136, 152, 153
hydrogen atom 38, 46, 54
hypothesis 18, 19, 44, 188, 189

I

I and Thou (Buber) 166
ideal circumstances 89
idolatry 24
inalienable rights 99
incompatible 11, 63, 64, 117
incontrovertible 91

ineffable 13
infallibility 85
     infallible 20
infinite, the 70, 73, 181-183
*Inquiry Concerning Human Under-
     standing, An* (Hume) 115, 131,
     135
inscrutability 14
instinct 29, 31, 89, 116, 118
     instinct of survival 89
     instinct to expect the future to
     be like the past 29
Institute of Psychiatry in London
     152
intelligibility 41, 43, 45, 50, 74
interfaced 45
inviolate 93
irrational 12, 17, 19, 22, 26, 27,
     34, 35, 43, 66, 86, 88, 89, 136
Isaiah 202-204
Islam 11, 12, 54, 72
Israel 83, 154, 167, 169, 178, 203

J

jargon 11
Judah the Prince, Rabbi 196
Judaism 11, 12, 54, 72, 73, 79,
     119, 128, 151, 175, 180, 182,
     183, 192, 199
justice as fairness 101

K

K.G.B. 97
Kabbalah 11, 13, 78, 83, 104, 182,
     183, 194, 199, 203
     Kabbalah & Hasidic thought
     203
Kant, Immanuel 56, 88, 90-92,
     97, 108
Kenny, Sir Anthony 53

Kierkegaard, Søren 100, 106
kindness, small acts of 195
King Solomon 113
Knight of Faith 107
knowledge 21, 25-28, 30-33, 35,
     44, 47, 59, 65, 66, 69, 71, 77,
     81, 82, 85, 86, 97, 121, 123,
     125, 150, 151, 158, 188, 194,
     202, 203
knowledge of G-d 202, 203
Kotzker Rebbe, the 195, 199

L

Leibnitz, Gottfried 77
life after death 128, 133, 134, 149
Life and Death (Ring) 152
life is precious 147
life review 143, 144, 147, 164
lifestyle 122, 151
Light, the, 63, 133, 136, 139, 143,
     154-156, 171, 174, 179-180,
     182-184, 190, 207, 213-214
     Light, the Being of 156, 159,
     163-165
     thirteen Beings (of Light), the
     158
Light Beyond, The (Moody) 139,
     141, 143, 144, 153
logic 27, 30, 36, 81, 97, 105, 109
     logical functions 21
     logically impossible 34, 43,
     77, 153
     logically necessary 30-33, 36,
     52, 56, 58, 121
     logically possible 37, 77
     logically possible worlds 77
Love of G-d 127
Luria, Isaac 78, 200

M

Maimonides, Moses 53, 72, 74, 75, 82, 83, 109, 203
Maimonides, *Mishneh Torah* 53, 74, 82, 109, 203
Maria (see Sharp, and "Shoe on the Ledge" 137-139, 186-189
mathematics 21, 30, 36, 97
    mathematical 21, 63
matter 12, 13, 17, 19, 23, 31, 34, 38, 42, 45, 47, 49, 54-56, 62, 63, 65, 68, 73, 75, 77-79, 82, 93, 95, 97-99, 104, 106, 114, 116, 121, 133, 136, 137, 143, 147, 148, 152, 160, 186, 194, 200, 202
matters of fact 30
meaningfulness of life 119, 129
meaning of life 13, 111, 121, 125, 127, 128, 167, 171, 183, 184
"Meaningful Life, The" (Baier) 117
Meaning of Life, The (Sanders & Cheney) 114, 115, 117
Meditations (Descartes) 85, 190
Mein Kampf (Hitler) 87
messianic age 202-204
metaphysical materialism 47, 65
metaphysical question(s) 48
metaphysical theses 136
    metaphysical thesis 47
Metaphysics 45, 54, 68
    Metaphysics Book VII 54
metaphysics 47, 48, 97
meteorologists 21
Mezritcher Magid 202
Michelson-Morley experiments 132
Midrash 195
mind 12, 13, 15, 17, 20, 24, 34, 37-45, 47, 50, 56, 64, 68-71,
75, 77, 81, 83, 86, 110, 122, 125, 136, 137, 139-141, 145, 151, 153, 158, 166, 173-177, 179, 183, 184, 197, 199, 200, 206
miracle(s) 22-24, 39, 40, 46, 49, 131-133, 135, 136, 152, 153, 167, 202, 206
miserable ease 93
Mishnah 146, 196
Mishneh Torah (Maimonides) 53, 74, 82, 109, 203
modus ponens 30, 86, 91, 101, 103
monotheism 13, 53, 71, 76
    monotheistic background 11
    monotheistic tradition 76
Moody, Dr. Raymond 133, 135, 139, 141-144, 147, 153, 161-161, 174
Moore, G.E. 97, 125
morality 96, 97, 99, 101, 105, 108-110, 113, 118
    moral agent 192
    moral decision 96
    moral disagreements 91, 96
    moral heroes 89
    moral ignorance 86
    moral integrity 90
    moral judgment(s) 91
    moral life 13, 109
motivation 94
Mulligan, Sean 139, 185, 188
murder 18, 19, 27, 94, 95, 99
My Confession (Tolstoy) 114, 126
"My Own Life" (Hume) 115
mystical 11, 13, 22, 59, 72, 128, 143, 166, 191, 196, 204, 206
    mystical awareness 13
    mystical side of G-d 59, 72
mythology 12

N

Nagel, Thomas 120
National Enquirer 135
nature of morality 13
Nazi guard 104, 105
Nazi party 93
near-death experience (NDE) 13,
    23, 118, 128, 133, 152, 155,
    161, 163, 164, 190
necessary being 50, 52-59, 61, 70,
    71
necessary existence 52, 53, 55, 72,
    75
necessary truth 30, 31
Newtonian mechanics 63
Nietzsche, Friedrich 90, 93
night 29, 73, 95, 105, 151, 175,
    177, 195, 196
Noam, Rachel 134, 154, 167, 172,
    176, 184
no fear of death 162
normative element 91
normative fact 88
nothing 20, 24, 25, 29, 32, 33,
    38, 43-48, 50-53, 55, 56, 58,
    59, 61, 62, 64, 65, 67, 68, 70,
    71, 73, 74, 76, 78, 83, 97, 99,
    101, 107, 109, 110, 114, 116,
    118, 119, 123-127, 132, 134-
    136, 138, 145, 156, 161, 164,
    168, 169, 171, 173, 177, 179,
    180, 190-192, 203, 205
Nous 52, 55, 68, 77, 78

O

On Certainty (Wittgenstein) 32,
    123
oneness of G-d 13, 15, 59, 153
ontological argument 52, 56, 76

orderliness 12, 13, 37-39, 41-45,
    47, 50, 51, 56, 75, 110
Otherworld Journeys (Zaleski) 149
out-of-body experience 137, 139,
    141, 162, 174
overwhelming evidence 18
"Ozymandias" (Shelley) 114

P

Paley, William 40
pantheism 54
Parmenides 79
Peirce, Charles Sanders 44, 45
Philo 41
Plato 12, 57, 73, 77, 86, 101, 104,
    109
positivists 31
practical action 20
practical point of view 28
Prime Mover 54, 55, 58, 68, 73
Principia Ethica 97
principle of induction 27, 30-32,
    34, 87, 91
principle of sufficient reason 33,
    34, 43, 87, 92
pro-choice 96, 97
pro-life 96
probability 19, 20, 38, 135
probability calculation 38
proof 19, 29, 32-34, 36, 83, 101,
    110, 121, 131, 133, 197
prophesy 25
Protagoras 101, 108
prudence 93, 97-99, 108
prudent 97, 99
purpose 12, 13, 19, 38, 40, 45, 69,
    72, 78, 83, 85, 88, 109, 110,
    114, 119, 120, 122, 125, 126,
    142, 154, 159, 171, 182, 183,

184, 191, 193, 195, 197, 199, 201
purpose of the world 193

Q

Queen Jezebel 14

R

Rabbi Judah the Prince 196
Rabbi Schneur Zalman 197, 201, 202
Rabbi Yerachmiel Benjaminson 78
racial discrimination 95
rationality, what is 12
    rational belief 17, 19, 25, 86, 88, 121
    rational intuition(s) 34, 45, 50, 61, 66
Rawls, John 101
reasonable doubt 18, 19
    reasonable or rational 19, 83
Recollections of Death (Sabom) 149
relations of ideas 30
Rembrandt (van Rijn) 115
remorse 87, 95
repentance 196
responsibility 90, 93, 95, 107-109, 146, 171, 193
return against their will 142
review of his life 156
righteous indignation 102, 108
Ring, Kenneth 149, 151, 152
rules of thought 27

S

Sabom, Michael B. 149, 152
Sanders, Steven, and Cheney, David 115, 117, 120, 121, 126
Sartre, Jean-Paul 113, 119, 125

Satan 192
Saved by the Light (Brinkley) 141, 155, 191
second NDE 154, 162
secular world 90
Sefat, 200
semantics 58, 97
sense-perception 97
sense of compassion 102, 106, 107, 172
sense of justice 101, 104, 105, 108
sentient observers 46
separability 52
Septuagint 73
Shakespeare, William 115, 127
Sharp, Kimberly Clark 137-139, 185-187, 189
Shoe on the Ledge, The 137
simplest explanation 62, 63, 64, 66, 70
simplicity 62, 65-67, 71, 177
    simplicity and unity 71
Sisyphus 113, 115
skeptic 32
    skeptical argument, the 121
small acts of kindness 195
societies 101
Sodom and Gomorrah 105
Southampton General Hospital 152
speed of light 132, 133
Spinoza, Baruch 52, 53, 69, 71, 72, 77
spiritual eyes 203
spiritual realms 191, 194, 196, 197
Stanley Cup 151
substance 52, 69, 71, 157, 164
suicide 88, 89, 92, 98, 118
supernal goodness 105

T

Tanya 180, 181, 191, 197, 201
Taylor, Richard 45
Tel Aviv 154, 167
teleological argument 35, 37, 38,
    40-43, 45, 46, 48, 50, 51, 71,
    75
telepathy 144, 156
Temple Mount 195
Theory of Justice, A (Rawls) 101
thirteen Beings (of Light), the 158
Thus Spake Zarathustra (Nietzsche)
    93
tic-tac-toe 38
Timaeus 77
Tolstoy, Leo 114,-115, 125-126,
    195
transcendental 42, 43, 47
    transcendental questions 47
    transcendent being 54
Tzimtzum 182

U

ultimate truth 134, 203
uncaused events 33, 34, 87
uniform experience 131, 135
unintelligible 43, 124, 125
unity of G-d 13, 41, 81, 82, 83,
    127, 128, 183, 204
unity, argument from 35, 71
    unity of all things, the 70
universal mind 42, 45
unmoved mover 53
unsupported natural confidence
    122

V

veridical perceptions 190
verified 14, 36, 47

Vietnam War 156

W

war with Iraq 157
watch 28, 40, 42, 48
water boys and bat girls 198
*Way of Man According to the Teach-
    ings of Hasidism, The* (Buber)
    195
white lie 92, 94
wise 99, 177
Wittgenstein, Ludwig 21, 32, 35,
    88, 97, 123, 125, 212
Wittgenstein Conversations (Bouws-
    ma) 97

Y

Yogi Berra 48, 192
Yom Kippur war 167, 170, 173
Yzerman, Steve 151

Z

Zaleski, Carol 149
Zalman, Rabbi Schneur 197, 201,
    202 Zeus 24, 58, 101, 107,
    108
Zohar 11, 191, 194, 199